the field guide
TO THE NATURE CONSERVANCY

An insider's handbook to places and projects around the world

The Nature Conservancy

SAVING THE LAST GREAT PLACES ON EARTH

the field guide

TO THE ⬤ NATURE CONSERVANCY

An insider's handbook to places and projects around the world

TABLE OF CONTENTS

THE SUM OF OUR PARTS

Welcome to the first *Field Guide to The Nature Conservancy.* Whether you are a staff member, a trustee, a friend or a supporter, I am sure you will find this window on the world of active conservation both interesting and useful.

There was a time when a staff member making a call on a potential donor might have carried along a brochure or two, a handful of press clippings and perhaps some photos of a Conservancy preserve. Today, the Conservancy is so much more than these brief glimpses could even begin to evoke. Today, building on a half century of experience to become even more effective in what we do, we work in every state in the United States and in 26 other countries; we maintain a presence in hundreds of communities and our projects number in the thousands. Conservancy teams assist the Chinese government in developing sound forest and water policies. Chapters from the U.S. Midwest work

with their counterparts in Brazil on the interaction of agriculture and wetlands. Our scientists counsel the Army Corps of Engineers on sound practices for the release of water from Corps-controlled dams. Our financial experts structure innovative and complex deals providing for the long-term conservation of millions of acres of forestland from Maine to Indonesia.

Capturing the entire kaleidoscope of our conservation work in one volume would be a tremendous task. From this representative volume, however, you will sample the full range of our activities. Scores of projects are profiled, each of them a functional landscape of promise across the spectrum of the places where we work. Many of them cross traditional boundaries—political boundaries, geographic boundaries, boundaries of the mind—and reflect the necessity of operating at a scale that can produce tangible and lasting results. There are profiles of the five priority conservation initiatives—Fire, Freshwater, Invasive Species, Marine and Global Climate Change—which are designed to leverage our on-the-ground work. There are maps and data and key points about Conservation by Design, our roadmap for discipline and consistency across the organization.

Each of us who uses this guide will start from a different perspective, such as a familiar place that encapsulates the reason we are conservationists. It is my hope that it also will help us realize that our knowledge of a place local to our daily lives is equally valuable in a similar place perhaps many thousands of miles away, and that we can make contributions to both. Perhaps a donor in New Mexico will discover a place in the Andes, or someone deeply familiar with the myriad inlets of the Chesapeake Bay will find similar fascination in the complexities of the Panama coast or Borneo.

The mission of The Nature Conservancy is to preserve the plants, animals and natural communities that represent the diversity of life on Earth by protecting the lands and waters they need to survive.

That is a daunting task.

In ways both practical and penetrating, this guide will soon become an essential companion for each of us. Take a moment to browse through it and discover the breadth of what we do, and you will quickly see both its utility and its power to inspire. We are an organization made up of many, many parts, and the sum, as this guide demonstrates, is great indeed.

Steven McCormick

Steven J. McCormick
President and Chief Executive Officer

ABOUT THE NATURE CONSERVANCY

San Pedro Riparian Conservation Area, Arizona.

The mission of The Nature Conservancy is to preserve the plants, animals and natural communities that represent the diversity of life on Earth by protecting the lands and waters they need to survive.

Around the world, we identify and protect the Last Great Places—extraordinary natural landscapes that nourish a wealth of plant and animal life, underpin local and national economies and refresh the human spirit.

where we work

- 50 states in the United States, plus two U.S. territories

- 27 countries throughout the Western Hemisphere, Asia, the Pacific and Australia

- Locally, with staff based in hundreds of communities

how we work

We work *collaboratively with partners*—businesses, government agencies, multilateral institutions, communities, individuals and other non-profit organizations.

We pursue *non-confrontational, pragmatic, market-based* solutions to conservation challenges.

We employ the best available *scientific information* and practices to guide our conservation actions.

We tailor our conservation strategies and tools to *local circumstances.*

We work *across landscapes and seascapes* at a scale large enough to conserve ecological processes and to ensure that protected lands and waters retain their ecological integrity.

We work with *willing sellers and donors,* both public and private, to protect ecosystems, plants and wildlife through purchases, gifts, exchanges, conservation easements and management agreements and partnerships.

Outside the United States, we work with government agencies and like-minded partner organizations to provide scientific know-how, infrastructure, community development, professional training and long-term resources.

Conservation planning, China.

how we identify places to protect

Conservation by Design is our strategy for guiding conservation results. It is a systematic, science-based approach to identifying and protecting priority conservation areas.

Through Conservation by Design, we are developing a map of the areas most critical for the long-term protection of ecosystems, plants and wildlife. We follow this Conservation Blueprint when deciding where and how to take action.

The blueprint is composed of portfolios, or groupings, of conservation areas that collectively capture the representative biological diversity of a region.

We plan for conservation within and across ecoregions—distinct divisions in the natural landscape, such as the Sonoran Desert along the U.S.-Mexico border, that follow nature's borders not geopolitical lines.

The Nature Conservancy is
a revolution, an evolution of human beings
in relationship to the land.

—*Terry Tempest Williams*
Environmental author

our values

integrity beyond reproach: We hold paramount the trust
and responsibilities placed in us by our donors, members,
colleagues, partners and the public.

continuity of purpose: We look to our mission to provide
focus and guidance for everything we do.

commitment to people: We respect the needs of local
communities by developing ways to conserve biological
diversity while enabling them to live productively and
sustainably. We value the active involvement of
individuals from diverse backgrounds and beliefs
in conservation efforts.

effective partnerships: We are committed to forging public
and private partnerships that combine diverse strengths,
skills and resources.

innovation and excellence: We are strategically entrepre-
neurial in the pursuit of excellence, encouraging original
thought and its application, and willing to take risks based
on sound business judgment.

One Conservancy: We act as "One Conservancy," with
each program assisting other programs in reaching their
full potential, thereby ensuring the success of the overall
organization.

commitment to the future: We commit ourselves,
individually and collectively, to leaving future generations
a biologically rich world.

Fly fishing guide tying flies, Belize.

Nature guide training, Mexico.

Since 1951, The Nature Conservancy has:

- Protected more than 14.5 million acres in the United States and more than 83.5 million acres outside the United States—an area nearly three times the size of New York State

- Attracted the support of more than 1 million members

- Established more than 1,400 Conservancy preserves

- Opened 400 offices in 27 countries

- Created a network of more than 1,500 volunteer trustees to guide local conservation

- Pioneered innovative land protection tools such as debt-for-nature swaps and conservation easements

- Generated and mobilized hundreds of millions of dollars in public funds to acquire and protect important natural areas

- Helped develop a hemispheric biological inventory to track some 50,000 species and ecological communities

how we rate

In 2001, the Conservancy's programmatic efficiency—the percentage of income dedicated to mission objectives—was 86 percent.

Worth magazine named the Conservancy one of the best 100 charities in America in 2001, and one of eight best environmental charities in 2003.

The Christian Science Monitor listed the Conservancy as the 12th largest U.S. charity, as ranked by total income, in 2002.

ABOUT THE FIELD GUIDE

The Field Guide to The Nature Conservancy is intended to be a useful reference for staff, trustees, donors and others who are interested in learning about where and how The Nature Conservancy works. It is a *representative,* not comprehensive, catalog of our work around the world. Our projects are far too numerous to be covered in any one volume.

initiatives

The field guide features the five initiatives chartered by the Conservancy's Executive Leadership Team in 2002 and highlights several places where the initiatives are at work.

project profiles

The field guide profiles 86 conservation projects. Every state and country program chose one project to feature. A handful of "wild cards"—other timely, far-reaching projects—were selected by regional directors. All are portfolio sites, meaning they were identified during ecoregional planning, or likely will be included in a portfolio once planning is completed.

All of the featured projects are landscapes, and sometimes seascapes—large areas of land and water that can encompass public lands like national parks and forests, marine protected areas, tribal and indigenous lands, towns and communities, and a varied mixture of private lands, including our own preserves. They embrace watersheds, coastlines, rivers, islands, lakes, volcanoes, mountains, grasslands and coral reefs. Many of them are blessed with true wilderness, but all are working landscapes of farms, ranches, commercial fisheries, dammed rivers and timber

production. They are not pristine, but they do offer the promise of functioning over time as healthy, natural ecosystems that support native species.

Project profiles are basic and brief—and by no means comprehensive. They are broad-brush illustrations of places, their histories, ecological challenges and conservation action. The lists of partners and other categories are often, of necessity, abbreviated. Many of our projects are fortunate enough to have dozens of partners involved, but they could not all be listed in this format.

maps

All maps in the field guide (with the exception of the ecoregional maps in the appendices) were created by XNR Productions in Madison, Wisconsin, a small company specializing in custom maps and cartography. Conservancy state and country programs provided detailed location information. Ecoregional maps were created by The Nature Conservancy's Global Priorities Group.

appendices

These include several tools that can be useful in talking and learning about the Conservancy's work.

index

The field guide is cross-indexed to help users locate projects by ecosystem type (e.g., rivers) and recreational opportunities (e.g., hiking), for example. Only those projects profiled in the field guide are indexed. The index does not offer a complete list of all Conservancy restoration projects, for instance, but it does offer a starting point when exploring the universe of our work.

how to find more information

Use the index and contact the staff listed with each initiative and project profile. As a rule of thumb, the information contacts listed with each profile are philanthropy staff. In a few cases, project managers and other staff are listed, and their titles are noted.

key to symbols

The following symbols appear in the project profiles and indicate the types of recreational experiences one can expect at each place.

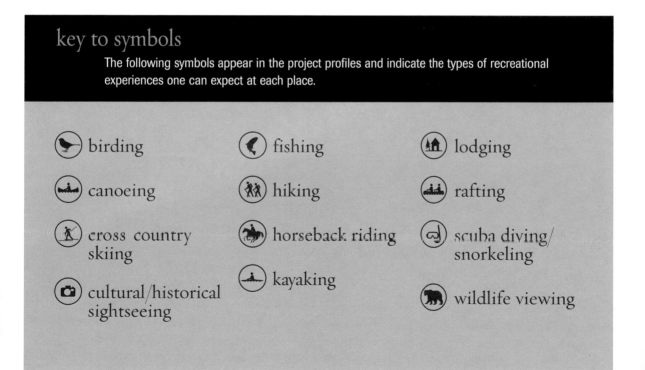

- birding
- canoeing
- cross country skiing
- cultural/historical sightseeing
- fishing
- hiking
- horseback riding
- kayaking
- lodging
- rafting
- scuba diving/ snorkeling
- wildlife viewing

THE NATURE CONSERVANCY'S CONSERVATION INITIATIVES

Our conservation initiatives grew out of the vision of Conservation by Design: to conserve functional conservation areas—places where ecological processes like fire and flood continue to sustain ecosystems and native species.

The initiatives are intended to address pervasive ecological threats across large landscapes and ocean realms. They are cross-boundary in scale and cross-cutting in scope. Through them, we can implement strategies that bring conservation to multiple areas and that address complex issues of public policy and socioeconomic behavior. How do we affect fire policy at national levels so that many forest ecosystems across large geographic areas remain healthy? And how do we work with communities of people in and around those forests who, justifiably concerned about the hazards of catastrophic fire, have long demanded even more fire suppression?

Five conservation initiatives were chartered by The Nature Conservancy's Executive Leadership Team in 2002: Fire, Freshwater, Global Climate Change, Invasive Species and Marine.

fire initiative

freshwater initiative

global climate
change initiative

invasive species
initiative

marine initiative

the FIRE INITIATIVE

fire facts

- Classical Greek philosophers categorized fire as one of the four basic elements that comprise all matter.

- A fire regime is the imprint of fire on an ecosystem, characterized by fire frequency, intensity, duration, size and the season in which it occurs.

- More than 90 percent of the fires that occur around the globe today are thought to be caused by people.

- Each year, worldwide, an area larger than half the size of China burns.

- The fires in Indonesia in 1997 affected the health of 100 million people.

- In 2000, more than $10 billion worth of natural resources and personal property was lost to wildfires in the United States; the government spent more than $2 billion to put out those fires.

information Nicole Basham, (703) 841-4103; nbasham@ tnc.org; nature.org/initiatives

Flames restore a fire-adapted ecosystem in New Mexico.

Fire is an essential force that has shaped ecosystems and life forms around the globe. But in many ecosystems today, the role of fire is severely out of balance, threatening to devastate both human and natural communities.

The Nature Conservancy has identified at least 107 million acres of important conservation areas in the United States alone—more than half of the sites in our Conservation Blueprint—that are threatened by altered fire regimes. The Fire Initiative works to counter these threats that strike at the heart of global conservation efforts.

altered fire regimes

Much of life on Earth evolved with fire. Whether sparked by lightning or set by humans, fire shaped many of the planet's ecosystems and life forms.

Fire-adapted ecosystems are resilient over time to repeated fire. They are places like the pine forests of the American West and Mexico, and the savannas and shrublands of Brazil, Bolivia and Venezuela. Fire helps them thrive.

But fire-sensitive ecosystems evolved without the influence of major fires. They are places like the rain forests of Southeast Asia and the Amazon. Fire can destroy or greatly transform these ecosystems.

In the past century, people have radically changed the role of fire in many ecosystems, both in terms of setting fire and suppressing it. Catastrophic fires like those in recent years in the tropical forests of Central America and Indonesia began with people burning land to clear it for agriculture, but the fires exploded in drought conditions.

Altered fire regimes can have a severe impact on economies, human health and natural resources, from water supplies to forest products.

Controlled burn, Florida.

Conversely, many fire-adapted ecosystems today, like those in the Rocky Mountain West, are fire-starved following decades of fire suppression. One serious result has been the unnatural build-up of fuel—dense stands of flammable trees and thick carpets of dead wood and leaves—that has led to intense and devastating fires like the Los Alamos, New Mexico, fire of 2000.

Such altered fire regimes—too much fire and too little, at the wrong time and in the wrong place—are a sign of ecosystems out of balance. The consequences for both people and nature are serious.

fire initiative: how we work

Building on three decades of experience in ecological fire management and a respected in-house cadre of fire professionals, we have launched the Fire Initiative to address the threat of altered fire regimes on both public and private lands. We pursue five strategies:

Addressing fire-related ecological threats at the places where we work and collaborating with other non-profit organizations and multilateral institutions, such as Conservation International, the United Nations and The World Bank, to set priorities and provide a voice for biodiversity concerns.

Engaging policymakers to address policies, programs and funding sources that either hinder or advance action in fire-altered ecosystems.

Catalyzing fire learning networks by convening land managers, community leaders, landowners, experts, scientists, non-profit partners and policy makers to exchange information and expertise, find solutions to common problems, share best practices and advance fire management. We have established networks in the United States, Mexico, Central America and the Caribbean representing more than 100 million acres of priority conservation areas.

Building partner capacity by working with government agencies and community-based organizations that have the greatest potential to address altered fire regimes at priority conservation areas.

Applying the best available science to the threat of altered fire regimes and supporting best practices for adaptive management and restoration at sites.

Healthy old-growth ponderosa pine forest, Oregon.

restoring fire-adapted ecosystems project

When more than 7.5 million acres of the United States burned in the 2000 fire season, the federal government enacted the National Fire Plan with the aim of fireproofing vulnerable communities and addressing the threat of altered fire regimes. As an extension of the plan, The Nature Conservancy created a partnership with the U.S. Department of Agriculture and the U.S. Department of the Interior, through which we are working with communities to restore fire-adapted ecosystems across 39 million acres of public and private land.

fire initiative: where we work

Loess Hills, Iowa.

Mexico. We are working with Mexican conservation partners to convene fire management forums that bring together government officials, land managers, scientists and fire experts to weigh the ecological costs and benefits of fire in Mexico. A network and mentoring program teams U.S. fire experts with their Mexican counterparts to build ecologically sound and socially acceptable fire management programs.

Upper Deschutes Basin, Oregon. Here in the shadow of the Cascades in central Oregon, a growing human population has created what fire experts call the "wildland-urban interface"—where fire-prone wildlands meet houses and subdivisions. Together with federal and state land management agencies, we are monitoring various approaches to reducing heavy fuel loads in this dangerous zone. To build the most effective models for fire management across the region, we help connect far-flung communities, such as a remote Indian reservation and a subdivision, to share best practices.

Loess Hills, Iowa. With much of the Loess Hills in private ownership, engaging landowners in a sound fire management plan is imperative to ward off wildfires and restore this fire-dependent tallgrass prairie ecosystem. Our workshops to train ranchers and other landowners in prescribed burning have captured the attention of the Iowa Department of Natural Resources and are serving as the springboard for a statewide fire policy (see page 104)

Pine Barrens, New Jersey. Fire is a big issue in the pitch pine forests of the Pine Barrens—only 35 miles from New York City, 25 miles from Philadelphia, and ringed by urban and suburban communities. In this "fireshed," where fire historically occurred but years of fire suppression have created a wildfire hazard, we are employing aerial photography from the early and mid-20th century to help understand what a healthy forest should look like (see page 58).

Gulf Coastal Plain Ecosystem. In the longleaf pine forests and wiregrass systems of northwest Florida and south Alabama, we are working with partners like Eglin Air Force Base and Blackwater State Forest to develop a plan that ranks areas to be treated with prescribed fire based on an analysis of those that are in the greatest need of restoration— thus maximizing limited resources.

the FRESHWATER INITIATIVE

freshwater facts

- Only a fraction of 1 percent of Earth's water is fresh and accessible in rivers, lakes, wetlands and shallow aquifers.

- The economic value of all services provided by freshwater ecosystems has been estimated to exceed $6.6 trillion annually.

- At least 12 percent of the world's known animal species inhabit freshwater environments.

- In the past century, 123 species of fish, mollusks, crayfish and amphibians have gone extinct in North America alone.

- Too much water siphoned out of rivers like the Colorado, Rio Grande and China's Yellow is causing them to dry up before they reach the sea.

- By 2025, the United Nations anticipates that 2.7 billion people will face severe water shortages.

- Nearly half of the rivers in the United States still fail to meet clean water standards.

information Nicole Basham, (703) 841-4103; nbasham@ tnc.org; nature.org/initiatives

Tonging for oysters, a species dependent on freshwater flows, Apalachicola Bay, Florida.

Freshwater ecosystems sustain us all, humans and wildlife alike. Today these ecosystems suffer from the twin assaults of water depletion and water pollution— a degradation whose consequences are vast and severe.

More than half of the places identified in The Nature Conservancy's Conservation Blueprint face serious degradation from these threats. The Freshwater Initiative is tackling both.

troubled waters

Fresh water not only gives life, but it abounds with life. Fish, mussels and shellfish are aquatic creatures that depend on freshwater systems, but so do moose, bears and ducks. Freshwater ecosystems provide drinking water and are used to irrigate crops, process wastes, provide transportation and let us swim, boat and enjoy other forms of recreation.

But in the past century, people have severely strained Earth's freshwater ecosystems with the construction of dams, pollution of waterways and draining of wetlands. Today, altered hydrological regimes and agriculture-related pollution are the two most insidious threats to freshwater ecosystems.

Altered hydrological regimes.
Freshwater ecosystems—rivers, lakes and wetlands—must have sufficient amounts of water to function properly. Without enough water, they suffer, along with aquatic creatures and other animals and plants that depend on these watery worlds. Over time, freshwater ecosystems are shaped by water-flow patterns created by natural events like spring floods and late-summer dry spells. Plants and

Cerrillos Dam, Puerto Rico.

animals that have evolved to hitch their lifecycles to these patterns, such as salmon and sturgeon, can be devastated when flows are disrupted by dams and large water withdrawals, or when too much water is released into the system at the wrong time.

Agriculture-related pollution. Worldwide since 1960, increasingly intensive agricultural practices have engendered a six-fold increase in nitrogen, phosphorus and chemicals flowing into

What oil was to the 20th century, water is shaping up to be for the 21st century: a resource crisis of huge proportions.

freshwater ecosystems. Such pollution can cause unnatural blooms of algae, which consumes oxygen and thus suffocates aquatic life. More, certain agricultural practices flush topsoil and sediment into waterways and wetlands, smothering aquatic organisms like mussels and making clear waters turbid and inhospitable to fish.

freshwater initiative: how we work

Wetlands along the Neversink River, New York.

Green River, Kentucky.

In many rivers, lakes and wetlands around the world, the Freshwater Initiative works to address ecologically incompatible water management and unsustainable agricultural practices. We pursue four basic strategies:

Demonstrating innovative approaches ranging from changing dam operations to securing water rights, from improving agricultural practices to restoring wetlands.

Advancing ecological science by identifying the most important freshwater conservation areas and determining the thresholds of hydrologic alteration and pollution that those ecosystems can tolerate.

Advancing water policy by working with community and government leaders to facilitate the most effective policies that meet human needs for water while sustaining healthy freshwater ecosystems.

Expanding public appreciation of ecosystem services by raising awareness of the value of healthy rivers, lakes and wetlands in our everyday lives.

sustainable rivers project

To help remedy the poor water-flow conditions on many U.S. rivers, we are collaborating with the Army Corps of Engineers to improve dam operations around the country. Through the Sustainable Rivers Project, we are coordinating with the Army Corps on review and modification of operations at 13 dams on nine rivers in nine states; other Corps-operated dams may become part of the project in time. The project is an outgrowth of collaborative work between the two partners on the Green River in Kentucky, now one of the pilot demonstration sites (see page 86).

freshwater initiative: where we work

Neversink River, New York. To restore the Neversink to a more natural state, we are working with the U.S. Army Corps of Engineers and state and local agencies to remove the Cuddebackville Dam, now slated for summer 2003 (see page 60).

Apalachicola River and Bay, Florida. To inform ongoing water compact negotiations that are determining how the river's water will be divided among the states of Georgia, Florida and Alabama, we continue to provide sound scientific information that underscores the link between water flows and ecosystem health (see page 82).

Roanoke River, North Carolina. We are demonstrating to private power companies and the Army Corps of Engineers how their dams can continue producing hydropower and controlling floods while allowing water releases that mimic natural floods to sustain the floodplain forest (see page 92).

Upper Klamath Basin, Oregon/California. In the midst of a much-publicized water conflict between agriculture

Snow geese, Klamath Basin, Oregon/California.

and wildlife interests, we have helped build consensus and worked to ensure enough water for both agriculture and wildlife. We are also helping develop pioneering wetland restoration projects to improve water quality (see page 140).

Maya Mountain Watershed, Belize. We are working to counter the increasing amounts of agriculture- and aquaculture-related pesticides and fertilizers that are flushed into the Monkey River, the sole source of drinking water for local villagers, and that ultimately are contributing

to fish declines on the MesoAmerican Reef (see page 180).

Yunnan Province, China. At the headwaters of four of Asia's major rivers, we have helped local partners conduct comprehensive conservation planning to protect the rivers and the interconnected ecosystems (see page 220).

the GLOBAL CLIMATE CHANGE INITIATIVE

climate change facts

- In the 20th century, the world's average surface temperature rose by approximately .6°C (1°F), a rate greater than in any period over the past thousand years.

- The combustion of fossil fuels and the destruction of the world's forests are the two main factors that have led to higher concentrations of heat-trapping greenhouse gases in the Earth's atmosphere.

- In the past 30 years, sea ice coverage in the Arctic has shrunk by 7 percent and ice thickness has declined by more than 3 feet.

- Deforestation accounts for one-quarter of annual carbon dioxide emissions.

- The protection and restoration of forests may be able to offset up to 20 percent of carbon dioxide emissions over the next 50 years.

information Nicole Basham, (703) 841-4103; nbasham@ tnc.org; nature.org/initiatives

Polar bear in the Arctic, where a changing climate is shrinking sea ice.

The Earth's climate is changing. The build-up of carbon dioxide and other greenhouse gases in the atmosphere has sent temperatures rising and put the cycles of storms and seasons on an uncertain course. Many species and ecosystems, already at risk from other pressures, will be pushed beyond their natural ability to adapt by the pace and severity of threats now posed by climate change.

The Nature Conservancy is committed to confronting this issue head-on through the Global Climate Change Initiative. We are building on our organizational experience in protecting and managing natural areas to help address the causes of climate change and seek solutions that will enable these natural areas to cope.

climate change, changing ecosystems

Since scientists first began writing of a climatic warming trend in the middle of the 19th century, they have been forecasting that the planet's climate—in concert with increases in industrialization—is headed for upheaval. They warned also of the larger phenomenon of climate change: Ice would melt, seas would rise, storms would intensify and seasons would shift. These warnings, once reserved for the distant future, are quickly becoming the reality of the here and now.

The Intergovernmental Panel on Climate Change, an international body of leading scientists, has confirmed the cause-and-effect relationship among the actions of people, the increase in temperatures and alterations in the climate. The panel pointed to the combustion of fossil fuels and the destruction of the world's forests as the factors that have led to higher and higher concentrations of heat-trapping greenhouse gases in the Earth's atmosphere. Climate models now predict that these higher concentrations will lead, by the end of this century, to an increase of 1.4-5.8°C (3-10°F) in the average surface temperature of the

Earth, and to a more chaotic climate.

As temperatures climb and climatic conditions change, many species will not be able to stay in step with their surroundings. In mountainous

Golden snub-nosed monkeys, Yunnan Province, China.

With the pace and severity of climate change, plants and animals must struggle even harder to survive and adapt.

regions, tree lines are already moving higher. In low-lying arid zones, springs and pools are drying up. Some birds and flying insects have been pushed beyond the limits of their traditional ranges. As oceans warm, coral reefs are bleaching and mangroves and swamplands are being engulfed by rising waters.

A warmer world with a more chaotic climate may do its greatest damage as an accomplice to already established ecological troublemakers.

Invasive species, pollution and disease, for example, are threats that might escalate from painful to lethal when given a boost from bad weather. With the pace and severity of climate change, plants and animals must struggle even harder to survive and adapt, and many will not make it on their own.

global climate change initiative: how we work

The Nature Conservancy is joining with many others who share an interest in ensuring that our planet's ecosystems continue to maintain plant and animal diversity, sustain agricultural and forest production, and decrease the risk of catastrophic loss from extreme weather events.

Through the Global Climate Change Initiative, we are identifying and implementing strategies that will help mitigate greenhouse gas emissions while searching for ways to make natural areas more adaptable to climate change. We focus on the nexus between environmental conservation and climate change through three principal approaches:

Protecting and restoring native forests and grasslands. When forests are destroyed, so ends their ability to store carbon dioxide through the process of photosynthesis, and the gas is released back into the atmosphere. At present, deforestation accounts for one-quarter of annual carbon dioxide emissions, while the protection and restoration of forests

may be able to offset up to 20 percent of carbon dioxide emissions over the next 50 years.

Adapting to the change. We are examining the effects of climate change on our ability to conserve important natural areas over the long term. From North Carolina to China, we are adaptively managing sites to adjust for environmental changes such as sea-level rise.

Creating a policy framework. Policies developed to address climate change must account for the role played by forests and other natural systems. We work to make the conservation and restoration of natural areas a

more widely known and broadly applied method for reducing the amount of carbon dioxide in the atmosphere while protecting critical plant and animal habitats.

Macaws, Bolivia.

noel kempff mercado national park, bolivia

When 1.5 million acres of tropical forest adjacent to this national park in northeastern Bolivia were threatened with timber harvesting, The Nature Conservancy turned the threat into an opportunity to offset carbon dioxide emissions. By facilitating a unique partnership among the Bolivian government, our local partner Fundación Amigos de la Naturaleza and three energy companies, we helped terminate the logging rights and the land was incorporated into the national park. This climate action project doubled the protected habitat for wide-ranging species such as jaguar and averted soil runoff into the region's many rivers while reducing net global carbon dioxide emissions. We are also using tools such as satellite imagery to monitor climate-related changes in the park's tropical forests and savannas.

global climate change initiative: where we work

Atlantic Forest, Brazil.

Arctic Coast of Alaska. We are studying the susceptibility of caribou and other target species to climatic changes, identifying areas that may offer them refuge and using that information when setting conservation priorities for the surrounding ecoregion.

Albemarle Sound, North Carolina. If some predictions of global warming hold true, the lower Roanoke River, which empties into Albemarle Sound, could end up a saltwater estuary in 50 to 100 years. We are taking action now to preserve the composition of existing natural areas and are protecting places along the Roanoke that will enable species and their surrounding systems to migrate inland and upstream (see page 92).

Yunnan Province, China. In the Himalayan foothills, we are paying particular attention to the ways in which climate change may impede our ability to measure the success of programs designed to protect and restore native ecosystems (see page 220).

Atlantic Forest, Brazil. Reforestation work here is part of a climate action project—rebuilding and protecting forest, which absorbs carbon dioxide from the atmosphere, as a means to offset greenhouse gas emissions. We have developed climate action projects in Belize, Bolivia and the United States as well. All told, these 1.7 million acres of standing forest, over 40 years, provide a climate benefit equal to keeping 8 million cars off the road for one year (see page 200).

the INVASIVE SPECIES INITIATIVE

invasive species facts

- More than 4,500 foreign species have gained a permanent foothold or taken root in the United States during the past century.

- Invasive species contribute to the decline of 46 percent of the imperiled or endangered species in the United States. Only habitat loss is a greater threat.

- Invasive species cost an estimated $137 billion annually in losses to forestry, agriculture, fisheries and the maintenance of open waterways in the United States.

- New Zealand has the toughest laws in the world against non-native species.

- It's perilously easy to spread invasives. For instance, the seeds of invasive plants can be spread when hikers fail to clean their boots between visits to different areas.

information Nicole Basham, (703) 841-4103; nbasham@ tnc.org; nature.org/initiatives

Purple loosestrife, a European species, invades a North American wetland.

On their home turf, plant and animal populations are kept in check by natural controls, like predators and food supply. But, when a species is introduced into a new landscape, one not adapted to its presence, the consequences can be devastating for native species. "Invading" plants and animals sometimes spread unchecked, disrupting natural cycles, crowding out native communities and costing billions in property damage and lost economic productivity.

Invasive species are one of the top threats across all The Nature Conservancy's priority conservation areas. In response, we created the Invasive Species Initiative.

alien invasions

A primary rule of nature is interdependence: Species evolve to fit perfectly into the dance of life that defines a place. This delicate balance yields the tremendous diversity of nature but also leaves species vulnerable to sudden change. Non-native

Brown tree snake, an alien to Hawaii.

species invasions are one of the most devastating changes.

Invasive species are plants, animals or organisms that are introduced to a new area and, free from their natural competitors, become environmental bullies. Invasive plants outgrow natives, hoarding much-needed light, water and nutrients, sometimes even altering soil chemistry. Invasive animals like the flathead catfish, introduced by anglers and game managers to rivers beyond its range, devour endangered native fish.

Invasions are occurring worldwide at an unprecedented rate and scale. Only habitat loss poses a greater threat to endangered plants and animals. Some foreign species, such as purple loosestrife and water hyacinth, are cultivated intentionally. Others take hold accidentally. For instance, a Caspian Sea tanker dumped the Asian zebra mussel into the Great Lakes along with its ballast water more than a decade ago. Today the zebra mussel threatens to smother 140 mussel species and has cost millions in damage.

Such aquatic and estuarine invasions are especially difficult to contain and reverse, but invasions have exacted heavy losses in nearly all types of ecosystems. Leafy spurge costs ranchers in the Great Plains more

Invasive plants and animals disrupt natural cycles, crowd out native communities and cost billions in property damage and lost economic productivity.

than $144 million a year in losses. All told, invasive species are estimated to cost $137 billion annually in losses to agriculture, forestry, fisheries and the maintenance of open waterways in the United States alone.

invasive species initiative: how we work

Building on years of experience managing invasive species, we created the Invasive Species Initiative, whose specialists work with public and private partners worldwide to pursue the following strategies:

Preventing invasions of alien species offers the greatest benefit for the least cost. We are supporting enhanced port inspections and voluntary efforts to eliminate intentional introductions.

Promoting early detection and rapid response by training teams of volunteers to check for and help eliminate invasives.

Restoring landscapes by collaborating with hundreds of local organizations throughout the Americas, Asia and the Pacific to remove and prevent the spread of invasives.

Undertaking research with leading academic institutions, like the University of California and the

Boy scouts battle invasives, Florida Keys.

Kudzu, a familiar invasive species in the Southeast.

University of Florida, to generate new insights into the management and control of invasives.

Reaching out to key audiences through policies and materials that promote invasive species awareness, management and prevention. We conduct this work in concert with government agencies and international organizations.

eastern invasives management network

To pioneer management techniques and share lessons learned, we created the Eastern Invasives Management Network, which includes more than 25 landscape-scale sites throughout the United States. The network implements key management strategies at four high-priority landscapes, and then shares the experiences and best practices with the other participating sites. The work has produced a variety of management tools and approaches that can be used in other landscapes facing similar invasive species challenges.

invasive species initiative: where we work

The Florida Keys. Working as part of the Florida Keys Invasive Exotic Task Force, the Conservancy directly removed 99 percent of the non-native tree species found on the once heavily invested West Summerland Key. The coalition also launched a public education campaign to encourage the use of native species in landscaping and raised more than $1 million for invasive plant control on public lands.

Cosumnes River, California. Invasive trees threaten to overtake the best remaining reaches of lowland streamside forests in the Central Valley. We have organized a team of volunteers that is battling invasives through early detection and rapid response. Hundreds of hours of monitoring and control have helped clear invasives from the Cosumnes River (see page 150).

Big bluestem, a native of the tallgrass prairie.

Hells Canyon, Idaho. To combat yellow starthistle and other noxious weeds, we helped implement a weed control strategy that includes protecting healthy plant communities, utilizing insects to control weeds and replanting native grasses. Conservancy scientists are pioneering the use of remote sensing tools like satellite imagery to track progress (see page 134).

Berkshire Taconic Landscape, Massachusetts. The Conservancy is mobilizing and organizing local groups and supplying a range of tools

including scientific information, mapping and practical experience. At Kampoosa Bog, a lake basin fen harboring 21 rare species, local citizens have been hand-cutting and destroying *Phragmites australis* for the past six years. The plant has been eliminated from the bog, and continual monitoring helps keep it at bay.

Flint Hills, Kansas and Oklahoma. To control *sericea lespedeza*—a highly invasive weed in the tallgrass prairie—we are advocating environmentally compatible management practices like spot spraying. We are helping the Tallgrass Legacy Alliance implement a cost assistance program to spot spray the weed in a six-county pilot area in Kansas (see pages 118 and 124).

East Maui, Hawaii. Invasive plants and animals, including goats, deer, wild pigs and the weed miconia, represent the greatest threat to Maui's forests. We are building fences to keep animals out of sensitive areas and are part of a multi-partner effort to control a devastating outbreak of miconia (see page 166).

the MARINE INITIATIVE

marine facts

- Some 71 percent of the Earth is covered in saltwater.

- More than half of the world's population lives within 60 miles of a seacoast.

- Marine systems provide an estimated $21 trillion annually in ecological goods and services—70 percent more than those provided by terrestrial systems.

- Oceans yield 16 percent of all animal protein consumed by people around the world.

- Mexico and Panama have each lost more than 60 percent of their coastal mangrove forests in the past 30 years.

- Fertilizers applied to farm fields in the Midwest eventually end up in the Gulf of Mexico, where this pollution has created a "dead zone"—a vast plume devoid of sea life.

- 70 percent of the world's coral reefs could be destroyed by 2050.

information Nicole Basham, (703) 841-4103; nbasham@ tnc.org; nature.org/initiatives

Healthy coral reef teeming with life, Komodo Island, Indonesia.

Although once considered a limitless and inexhaustible resource, the oceans of the world are increasingly in jeopardy. The cycle of influence between land and sea is delicate, and human activities are taking a heavy toll on the health of all ocean systems, from marshes and mangroves to reefs and the deepest reaches.

In response, The Nature Conservancy launched the Marine Initiative to link land and sea conservation in an effort to protect the rich array of marine plant and animal life and safeguard the tremendous benefits the oceans provide.

our threatened oceans

The oceans are home to the bulk of the planet's biodiversity. There can be as many varieties of fish in two acres of coral reef in Southeast Asia as there are species of birds in all of North America.

Another measure of the bounty of marine systems is the value of their ecological goods and services: an estimated $21 trillion annually. They yield 85 million metric tons of fish and other raw materials. Antiviral medicines are derived from marine sponges, and the battle against cancer employs a variety of marine products. Mangroves shield coastlines from storms; seagrass beds filter pollutants from water and protect against erosion and flooding; reefs and kelp forests act as natural breakwaters for coastlines; all serve as nurseries for fish and shellfish. And out at sea, the powerful forces of wind and ocean currents combine to help regulate the globe's climate.

Vast and mysterious, the oceans were once thought of as inexhaustible. But today, with more than half of the world's population living within 60 miles of the coast, the demand for basics such as housing, food and

Olive ridley sea turtles come ashore to nest.

income is damaging ecosystems and depleting marine resources. Wetlands and mangroves are being lost at record rates. Unsustainable fishing practices, such as poisoning and dynamiting coral reefs, plowing the ocean floor and raiding critical spawning areas, exacerbate the problems of overharvesting. Runoff from dredging, paving, mineral extraction, deforestation and unsustainable agriculture pollutes marine waters.

The wide-reaching impact of global climate change is also taking a toll on the oceans. Coral reefs have already experienced the devastating

Scientists estimate that less than 10 percent of ocean life has even been measured, something once compared to exploring life on land by dragging a butterfly net behind an airplane.

effects of warmer water, which causes corals to bleach and can eventually kill them. A warming planet, coupled with habitat loss, pollution and overfishing, often by destructive means, could lead to the loss of 70 percent of the world 's coral reefs by 2050.

marine initiative: how we work

The Marine Initiative is working to improve the long-term survival and resilience of critical coastal and marine habitats from Indonesia in the heart of Asia's coral triangle, across the Pacific's islands, along the Atlantic's North, Central and South American coasts, and into the Caribbean Sea. We pursue three approaches:

Seas-to-summits conservation. We build on our network of partners and innovative approaches developed at sites around the world to pursue integrated coastal conservation that connects land-based, freshwater and marine conservation efforts. We aim to protect and connect critical habitat for marine species while incorporating the economic needs of local communities.

Marine protected areas. We are applying new knowledge to the creation of resilient polar, temperate and tropical marine protected area networks that will endure in the face of threats such as pollution, unsustainable fishing and global climate change.

Red knots and ruddy turnstones, Delaware Bay, New Jersey.

Policy engagement. We collaborate with non-profit organizations, multilateral institutions and government and elected officials to develop and enhance policies and programs that address issues vital to ocean conservation.

Sea star against gorgonia, Papua New Guinea.

transforming coral reef conservation program

The Nature Conservancy and Conservation International have established a worldwide program to transform the way marine protected areas are established, designed, managed and financed for the benefit of coral reefs and associated habitats, and for the people who depend on them. Joined by partners such as the World Wildlife Fund, this collaborative effort known as the Transforming Coral Reef Conservation Program intends to expand the 1 percent of oceans currently in protected status by helping officials and communities safeguard reef systems that are rich in biodiversity and resilient to large-scale threats linked to climate change.

marine initiative: where we work

MesoAmerican Reef, Belize. Satellite data, a depth sounder and a hand-held Global Positioning System unit have helped Conservancy scientists unravel the mystery of the seasonal rituals of reef fish spawning down to the exact spot, month, day and hour. We are working with the Belizean government to establish marine protected areas around 14 identified spawning sites to prevent overfishing and protect reef fish during a particularly vulnerable period of their lifecycle (see page 180).

Red mangrove on the lagoon side of the MesoAmerican Reef, Belize.

Great South Bay, New York. After acquiring 11,500 acres of submerged land here in October 2002, we are working with government, academic institutions, aquaculture companies, non-profit organizations and the local community to protect and manage these submerged lands—nurseries for scallops and other shellfish—in an ecologically sustainable manner that also sustains the local economy.

Republic of Palau. The reefs of this Pacific island nation, which were bleached lifeless in unusually warm ocean waters in 1998, are a pilot site for the Transforming Coral Reef Conservation Program (see page 226).

Komodo National Park, Indonesia. We are working with the Indonesian government and local communities to reduce destructive fishing practices such as blast fishing, which has destroyed more than half of the park's corals. At our request, the government also recently banned the use of hookah compressors, breathing devices used by cyanide fishermen. Mooring buoys have been installed to prevent dive boats from dragging their anchors near fragile coral reefs.

Delaware Bayshores, Delaware and New Jersey. We are working with the National Oceanic and Atmospheric Administration to develop community partnerships that will restore habitat along the Delaware Bay (see page 48) and in some of America's most valuable coastal ecosystems, such as the Florida Keys, California's Santa Clara River, the Chesapeake Bay and Oregon's Siuslaw estuary.

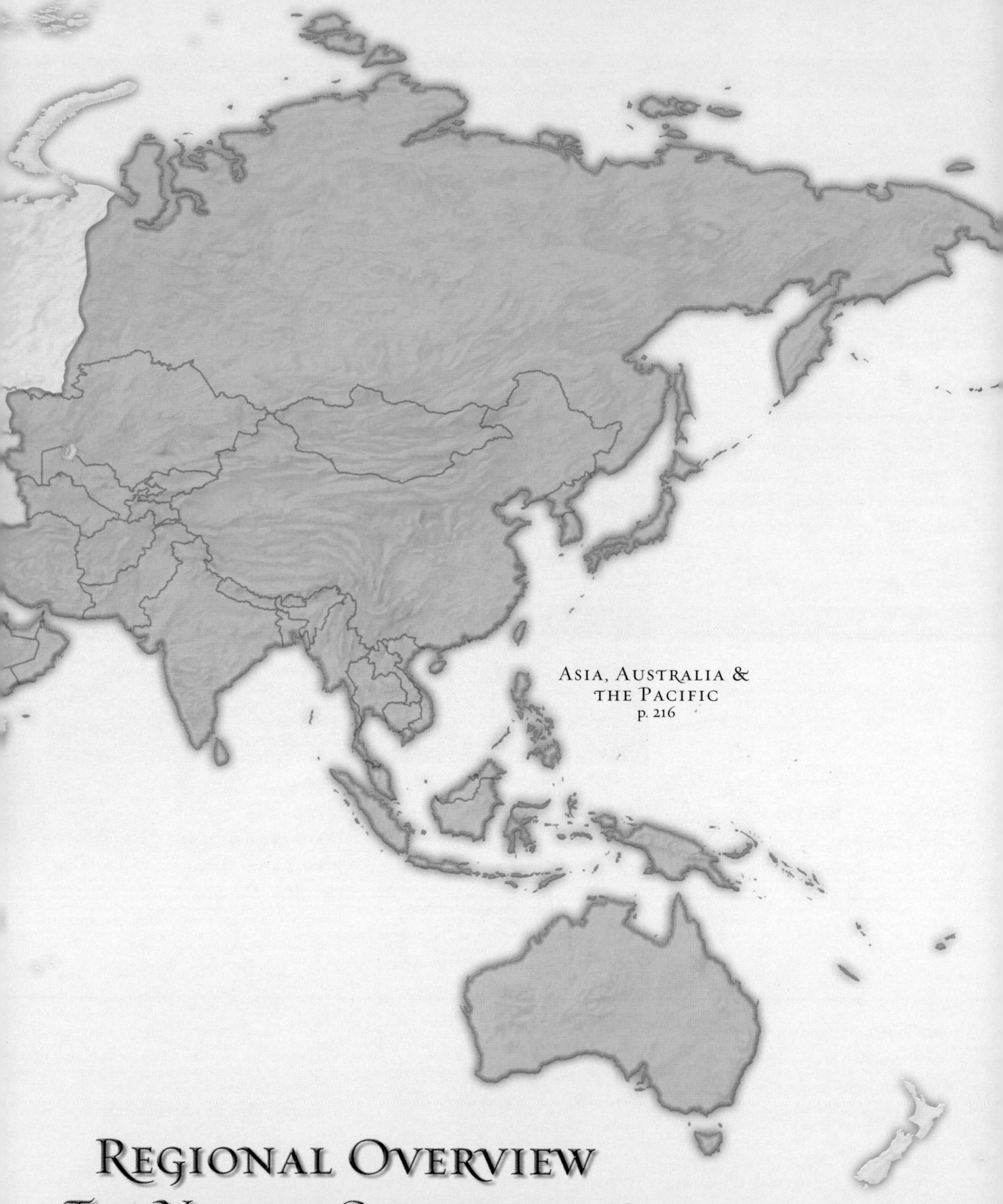

ASIA, AUSTRALIA &
THE PACIFIC
p. 216

REGIONAL OVERVIEW
THE NATURE CONSERVANCY

ALASKA
p. 162

CANADA
p. 36

NORTHWEST/
NORTHERN ROCKIES
p. 132

MIDWEST
p. 98

EAST
p. 44

CENTRAL
p. 116

WEST
p. 146

SOUTH
p. 76

HAWAII
p. 162

MEXICO
p. 36

THE
CARIBBEAN
p. 168

CENTRAL
AMERICA
p. 178

SOUTH
AMERICA
p. 194

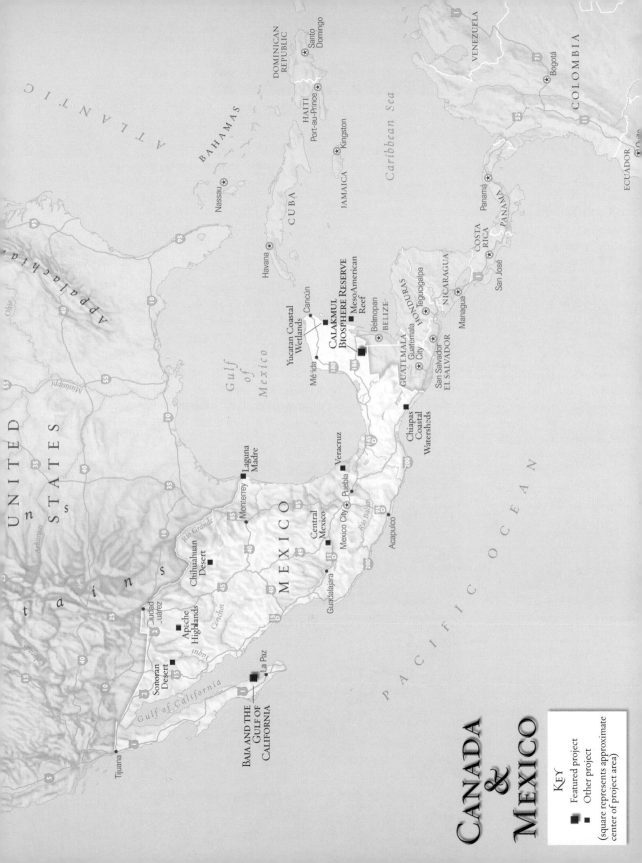

ATLANTIC

UNITED STATES

Appalachia

Ohio
Mississippi
Arkansas

Colorado

Tijuana

Ciudad Juárez

Apache Highlands

Chihuahuan Desert

Sonoran Desert

Río Grande
Conchos
Yaqui

La Paz

BAJA AND THE GULF OF CALIFORNIA

Gulf of California

MEXICO

Monterrey

Guadalajara

Central Mexico

Mexico City

Puebla

Acapulco

Río Balsas

Veracruz

Laguna Madre

Gulf of Mexico

Mérida

Yucatan Coastal Wetlands

Cancún

CALAKMUL BIOSPHERE RESERVE

MesoAmerican Reef

Belmopan
BELIZE

GUATEMALA
Guatemala City

EL SALVADOR
San Salvador

Chiapas Coastal Watersheds

HONDURAS
Tegucigalpa

NICARAGUA
Managua

COSTA RICA
San José

PANAMA
Panamá

Caribbean Sea

CUBA
Havana

BAHAMAS
Nassau

JAMAICA
Kingston

HAITI
Port-au-Prince

DOMINICAN REPUBLIC
Santo Domingo

VENEZUELA

COLOMBIA
Bogotá

ECUADOR

Quito

PACIFIC OCEAN

CANADA & MEXICO

KEY
■ Featured project
■ Other project
(square represents approximate center of project area)

MISSOURI COTEAU
Canada

Conservationists work across an international boundary to protect a unique landscape critical to both agriculture and some of the world's largest concentrations of waterfowl and grassland birds.

location 48 miles west of Regina, Saskatchewan

ecoregion Mixed Grassland

project size 36,000 square miles

preserves John E. Williams and Davis Ranch, in North Dakota; Ordway Prairie, in South Dakota; Thunder Creek, in Saskatchewan (owned by Nature Conservancy of Canada)

public lands Lostwood, Florence Lake, Long Lake, Chase Lake and Lake George national wildlife refuges, in North Dakota

partners Nature Conservancy of Canada, Environment Canada, Saskatchewan Government, Ducks Unlimited Canada, U.S. Fish and Wildlife Service, Saskatchewan Wildlife Federation, Nature Saskatchewan

natural events shorebird migration, late May; migration of the burrowing owl, piping plover, Sprague's pipit and loggerhead shrike, spring and fall

information Amy L. Carlson, (612) 331-0711, acarlson@tnc.org; nature.org/canada

The 36,000-square-mile Missouri Coteau snakes south from Saskatchewan, across the U.S.-Canada border into the Dakotas. Once nomadic tribes followed herds of migrating bison across the landscape's extensive glacial moraine to stay close to their source of food, clothing and tools. Awash with rolling hills and grasslands, saline lakes and wetlands called prairie potholes, the Missouri Coteau is still host to bountiful wildlife.

Usually less than one acre in size, prairie potholes are shallow, freshwater wetlands that were created by retreating

Prairie sunflowers.

glaciers. About 100 potholes can dot a square mile of the Missouri Coteau. Catching snow and rain from surrounding hills, potholes provide perfect habitat for a variety of birds. Nearby forests host ruffed grouse, while grassland birds like Sprague's pipit, long-billed curlew and the burrowing owl roam stands of native shortgrass prairie. The abundance of mallards, gadwalls, northern shovelers and blue-winged teal make this one of the most important areas for waterfowl reproduction in North America.

Since early settlement, this terrain has yielded coal, oil and enough potash—a plant nutrient used in fertilizers and ceramics—to supply the world for a thousand years. The rich tapestry of soils woven from several ice ages drew people who would farm the land. Today much of the native prairie has given way to cultivated grasses of spring wheat, barley and oats. Often prairie potholes have been drained and converted into farmland, or contaminated by nutrients and pesticides applied to crops. These intensive changes are leading to a rapid decline in the diverse birds and prairies that characterize the region.

Founded by The Nature Conservancy and our independent partner Nature Conservancy of Canada, the Canada/U.S. Conservation Partnership is uniting conservationists from both nations to protect threatened natural landscapes that span the international boundary. In the

Burrowing owlets.

Missouri Coteau, the partnership is working to protect at least 10,000 acres over three years through acquisition, easements and innovative partnerships with local government and private landowners.

conservation profile

targets wheatgrass, June grass, wolf willow, snowberry, aspen, Saskatoon, hairy prairie clover, prairie crocus, yellow-bellied racer, burrowing owl, Sprague's pipit, whooping crane, swift fox

stresses unsustainable agriculture, habitat fragmentation, natural resource extraction, invasive non-native weeds

strategies promote ecologically compatible land-use practices, build conservation alliances, undertake scientific research, acquire land, secure conservation easements, protect water quality, combat invasive species

results protected more than 4,000 acres in less than two years through the North American Wetlands Conservation Act grant program

BAJA AND THE GULF OF CALIFORNIA
Mexico

Collaborative management helps alleviate pervasive threats to these warm, sheltered waters, one of the last breeding grounds on Earth for blue whales.

location between the Baja California peninsula and mainland Mexico

ecoregions Cortesian, Magdalena Transition, Mexican Temperate Pacific, Gulf of California Xeric Scrub, California Coastal Sage and Chaparral

project size entire peninsula plus 1.2 million acres of sea (including 900 islands)

preserves San Cosme-Punta Mechudo corridor

public lands Loreto Bay National Park, Islas del Golfo Flora and Fauna Reserve

partners Niparajá, Grupo Ecologista Antares, Comision Nacional de Areas Naturales Protegidas

conservancy initiatives Marine

natural events whales calving and nursing, winter; Gray Whale Festival, San Ignacio, winter

information Steven Walker, (210) 224-8774, ext. 261, swalker@tnc.org; nature.org/mexico

Organ pipe, cholla and other cactus, Isla Cholluda.

Millions of years ago, the Baja California peninsula broke off from the mainland of present-day Mexico. The Pacific Ocean rushed in, creating the Gulf of California, or as it is known in the United States, the Sea of Cortez. Today, rugged coastlines, lagoons, coral reefs and palm oases mark the region where the Baja desert meets the sea.

The gulf's waters teem with unique creatures, from giant manta rays to the world's smallest aquatic mammal, a harbor porpoise found only in these waters. The majestic blue whale, displaced from all but a handful of its breeding grounds worldwide, returns every winter to calve in sheltered lagoons along the peninsula, along with gray, fin and pilot whales. Gentle female gray whales even offer up their young for tourists to pet. On the gulf's islands and beaches, sea lions and five species of sea turtle nest and breed. Only the Red Sea harbors more marine diversity than does the Gulf of California.

Hundreds of prehistoric cave painting sites are scattered throughout the central Baja California peninsula, and recent archeological finds indicate that humans may have discovered the treasures of the gulf more than 20,000 years ago. Giant depictions of humans and animals in red and black, some measuring 40 feet high, these paintings represent the largest trove of ancient rock art in the Americas.

Blue whale fluke.

Pearl diving was once the chief economic activity on the peninsula. The Pericue Indians had been collecting the gems for centuries when the Spaniards arrived. Since the 1970s, commercial fishing fleets have dominated the region, with little regard for local communities. Shrimp trawler nets scoop up manta rays, dolphins, turtles and hundreds of other animals, dooming most to death. By some estimates, nearly 10 pounds of other marine life dies for every pound of shrimp caught. Unregulated tourism development along the coasts and islands also threatens fragile ecosystems and traditional livelihoods.

Since 1998, The Nature Conservancy has worked at two key sites—Loreto National Marine Park and Isla Espiritu Santo—with a broad coalition of partners in both Mexico and the United States through the Parks in Peril program. We have created management plans and strengthened patrolling, thus helping reduce two of the most significant threats: infrastructure development for tourism and overfishing.

conservation profile

targets ringtail cat, barrel cactus; loggerhead, leatherback, hawksbill, green and olive ridley turtles; hammerhead and whale sharks; whipsnake; blue, fin, gray and pilot whales

stresses overfishing, pollution, unregulated tourism development, exotic species

strategies promote ecologically compatible land-use practices, engage community in natural resource management, strengthen local partner organizations, build conservation alliances, promote ecologically sound public policies, acquire land, secure conservation easements

results partnered with local land trust, Niparajá, to protect more than 60 miles of coastline; helped government acquire Isla Espiritu Santo and Isla Partida

CALAKMUL BIOSPHERE RESERVE
Mexico

The dense green embrace of the reincarnated Maya Forest has preserved thousands of temples and stone structures at Calakmul, one of the seats of power of the ancient Maya Empire.

location day's drive from Mérida and Cancún

ecoregions Yucatán Dry Forests, Yucatán Moist Forests, Petén-Véracruz Moist Forests

project size 10 million acres

public lands 48 percent of the reserve is federally owned; the remainder is owned by ejidos, communally owned land collectives

partners Pronatura Peninsula de Yucatán, National Commission for Natural Protected Areas, local landowners, state government of Campeche

conservancy initiatives Global Climate Change

natural events as many as 5 billion birds pass through on their migrations, winter

information Steven Walker, (210) 224-8774, ext. 261, swalker@ tnc.org; nature.org/mexico

Temple, Maya Forest.

The forest of Calakmul sprawls across the southern state of Campeche in the Yucatán Peninsula—once the thriving heart of the Maya Empire. Calakmul was the political rival of nearby Tikal, in Guatemala. At its height, from A.D. 500 through the next 400 years, Calakmul supported a population of as many as 50,000 before the civilization crashed, some believe because of heavy deforestation. Although the Maya culture lives on in its people, the great temples, pyramids and palaces of the past—more than 6,000 structures altogether—have long been engulfed by green jungle, now the protected expanse of the Calakmul Biosphere Reserve.

The reserve anchors the northern end of the humid lowland jungle known as the Maya Forest, which stretches south into Guatemala and Belize. At more than 5.5 million acres, this is the Americas' largest remaining expanse of tropical forest north of the Amazon. It is inhabited by jaguar, puma and howler monkeys. It sustains crested guan, jabiru stork and some 400 other species of birds, including many migratory ones like the indigo bunting and scarlet tanager that winter in the Yucatán.

The same riotous vegetation that has obscured the ruins has also saved them, shielding them from exploitation for decades. Beginning in the early 20th century, people came to harvest *chiclé,* or gum resin, and later mahogany and Spanish cedar. Since the 1970s, another wave of immigrants has come searching for land and opportunity, often escaping political unrest and natural disaster. They bring with them slash-and-burn agriculture and demands for new roads and water supplies.

For the past decade, The Nature Conservancy has worked with Mexican conservation organization Pronatura Peninsula de Yucatán to protect Calakmul. We help communities living within the reserve—collectives of farmers known as *ejidos*—develop alternative approaches to agriculture, such as organic farming, and methods that enhance soils and productivity. In 2002, the Mexican government asked the partners to help purchase and

Mantled howler monkey.

protect nearly 600,000 acres of communally owned, uninhabited lands in and around the reserve.

conservation profile

targets giant anteater, howler and spider monkeys, jaguar, puma, ocelot, jaguarundi, tigrillo, crested guan, great curassow, black-billed cuckoo, king vulture, scarlet macaw

stresses cattle grazing, road building, hunting, intensive agriculture, population growth

strategies strengthen partner organizations, bolster reserve management and infrastructure, promote ecologically compatible farming and forestry practices, secure conservation easements, acquire land and timber rights

results working to protect 600,000 acres at the government's request; developing incentives for private lands protection in a country where none existed before; trained reserve patrol guards and taught methods of fire prevention and control

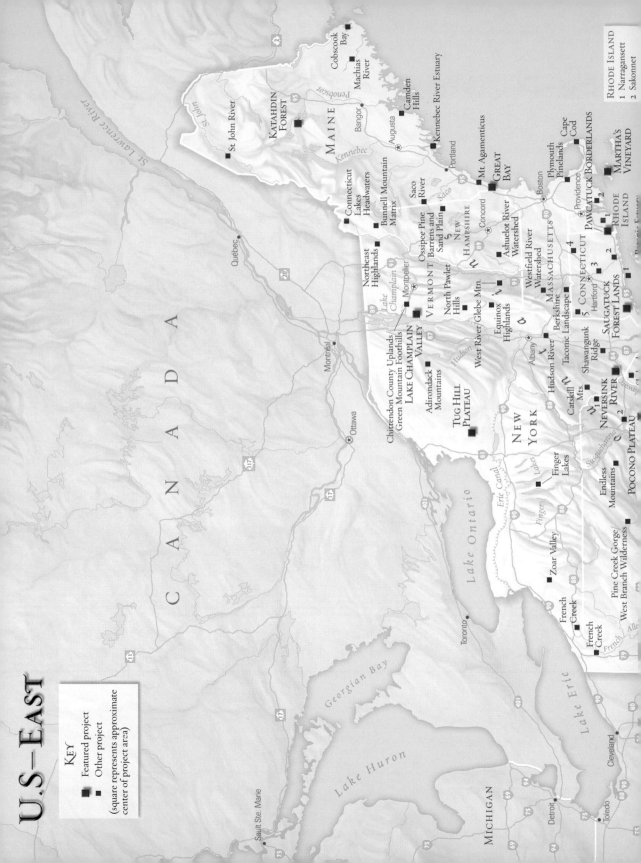

U.S.—EAST

KEY
■ Featured project
■ Other project
(square represents approximate center of project area)

RHODE ISLAND
1 Narragansett
2 Sakonnet

Cobscook Bay
Machias River
Camden Hills
Kennebec River Estuary
St John River
KATAHDIN FOREST
MAINE
Bangor
Augusta
Portland
Mt Agamenticus
GREAT BAY
Plymouth Pinelands
Cape Cod
PAWCATUCK BORDERLANDS
MARTHA'S VINEYARD
Connecticut Lakes Headwaters
Bunnell Mountain Matrix
Saco River
Ossipee Pine Barrens and Sand Plain
NEW HAMPSHIRE
Concord
Ashuelot River Watershed
Boston
Providence
RHODE ISLAND
Northeast Highlands
Montpelier
VERMONT
North Pawlet Hills
West River/Glebe Mtn.
Equinox Highlands
Westfield River Watershed
MASSACHUSETTS
Berkshire
Taconic Landscape
Hartford
CONNECTICUT
SAUGATUCK FOREST LANDS
Chittendon County Uplands/Green Mountain Foothills
LAKE CHAMPLAIN VALLEY
Adirondack Mountains
Albany
Hudson River
Shawangunk Ridge
TUG HILL PLATEAU
NEW YORK
Catskill Mts.
NEVERSINK RIVER
POCONO PLATEAU
Finger Lakes
Endless Mountains
Zoar Valley
Pine Creek Gorge West Branch Wilderness
French Creek
French Creek

St Lawrence River
Québec
Montréal
Ottawa
CANADA
Toronto
Lake Ontario
Erie Canal
Lake Erie
Cleveland
Toledo
Detroit
MICHIGAN
Sault Ste. Marie
Lake Huron
Georgian Bay
Penobscot
Kennebec
Saco
Lake Champlain
Hudson
Susquehanna
Finger Lakes
Allegheny

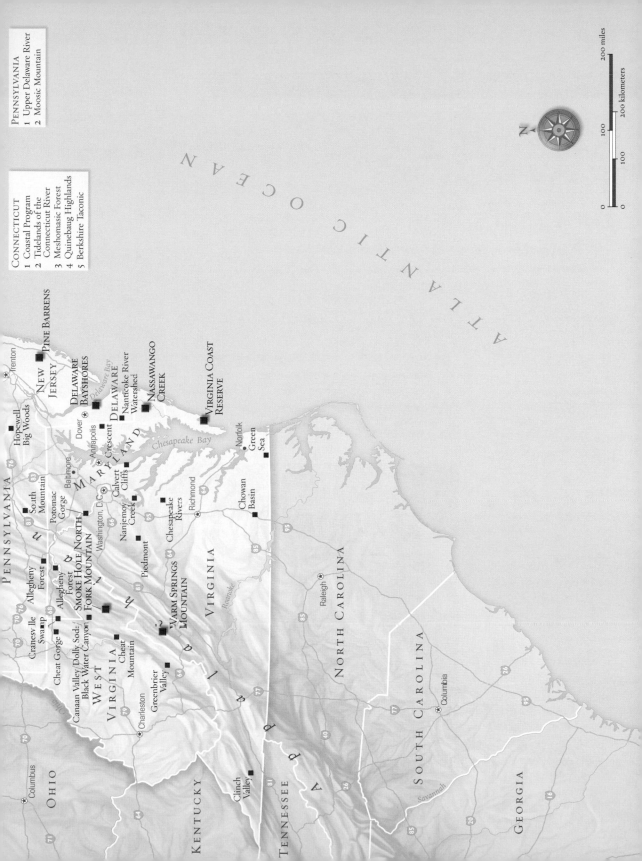

PENNSYLVANIA
1 Upper Delaware River
2 Moosic Mountain

CONNECTICUT
1 Coastal Program
2 Tidelands of the
  Connecticut River
3 Meshomasic Forest
4 Quinebaug Highlands
5 Berkshire Taconic

ATLANTIC OCEAN

PENNSYLVANIA

OHIO

Columbus

Trenton

NEW
JERSEY

PINE BARRENS

Hopewell
Big Woods

DELAWARE
BAYSHORES

Delaware Bay

DELAWARE

Dover

Nanticoke River
Watershed

NASSAWANGO
CREEK

Crescent

Annapolis

MARYLAND

Baltimore

Chesapeake Bay

VIRGINIA COAST
RESERVE

Norfolk

Green
Sea

South
Mountain

Potomac
Gorge

Washington, D.C.

Calvert
Cliffs

Nanjemoy
Creek

Chesapeake
Rivers

Richmond

Chowan
Basin

Allegheny
Forest

Allegheny
Forest

SMOKE HOLE/NORTH
FORK MOUNTAIN

Piedmont

VIRGINIA

Cranesville
Swamp

Cheat Gorge

Canaan Valley/Dolly Sods/
Black Water Canyon

WARM SPRINGS
MOUNTAIN

WEST
VIRGINIA

Cheat
Mountain

Greenbrier
Valley

Charleston

Raleigh

NORTH CAROLINA

Roanoke

Clinch
Valley

KENTUCKY

TENNESSEE

SOUTH CAROLINA

Columbia

GEORGIA

Savannah

N

200 miles

200 kilometers

100

100

100

0

0

SAUGATUCK FOREST LANDS

Connecticut

A native-forest cloister in the densely populated suburbs of southwestern Connecticut, the Saugatuck Forest Lands survive as one of only a few remnants of the great coastal forests that once covered the eastern seaboard.

location five miles northwest of Bridgeport

ecoregion Lower New England

project size 72 square miles

preserves Lucius Pond Ordway/Devil's Den, Katharine Ordway, numerous small land trust preserves

public lands Wooster Mountain State Forest, Collis P. Huntington State Park, Putnam Memorial State Park, numerous municipal conservation reserves

partners Connecticut Department of Environmental Protection, Kelda Group plc, towns of Redding and Weston, Aspetuck Land Trust, Redding Land Trust

conservancy initiatives Freshwater, Invasive Species

natural events woodland wildflowers bloom, spring; migratory songbirds arrive, spring; spectacular fall color; hawk migration, fall

information Priscilla Squiers, (203) 226-4991, ext. 204; psquiers@tnc.org; nature.org/connecticut

Just 50 miles from Manhattan, tucked away in Connecticut's populous southwest corner, the Saugatuck Forest Lands comprise a sanctuary of wooded glens, free-flowing streams and vernal pools.

Native Americans helped create the open, parklike landscape by routinely setting fires to diminish undergrowth, increase visibility for hunting and attract wildlife. Before suburban development could claim it, the

Saugatuck Reservoir from Devil's Den Preserve.

forest was purchased by a water company to protect the watershed. With its mix of more than 500 types of trees, shrubs and wildflowers, it retains its historic character and continues to provide habitat for mink, bobcat, red fox, coyote and as many as 140 bird species.

One of only a few remnants of the coastal forests that once spread along the eastern seaboard from northern Virginia to central Maine, the Saugatuck Forest Lands offer a rare glimpse of the mature mixed hardwood forest native to the region. Small lakes and wetlands lined with maple, hemlock and ferns support frogs, salamanders and wood ducks. Worm-eating warblers dart among dense thickets of mountain laurel as pileated woodpeckers drum their busy rhythm in the broadleaf canopy above. Pink lady's slipper, cardinal flower and Indian pipe color the forest floor.

The Saugatuck and Aspetuck watersheds run through the Saugatuck Forest Lands. In these streams, young author and artist James Prosek, the "Audubon of the Fishing World," cast his first fly rod and developed a passion for trout. Here the legendary Nature Conservancy philanthropist Katharine Ordway made the first of what would become her many donations of land for conservation.

Northeastern coastal forests were the first to suffer when Europeans began to colonize New England more than 300 years ago. What

Cardinal flower.

fragments endure today must compete with the growth of cities and suburbs in one of the most densely populated regions of the United States. The Nature Conservancy joined with the Connecticut Department of Environmental Protection to acquire 15,000 acres of forestland from a private water company.

We will continue to work with these and other conservation partners to protect additional land essential to the integrity of the forest and the Saugatuck River watershed.

DELAWARE BAYSHORES
Delaware and New Jersey

A concerted effort is under way in the two states that ring Delaware Bay to protect an ancient species that roamed the seas before the age of dinosaurs.

location 60 miles south of Philadelphia

ecoregions North Atlantic Coast, Chesapeake Bay Lowlands

project size 1 million acres

preserves Milford Neck, Port Mahon, Great Marsh, McCabe, Manumuskin River, Cape May Bird Refuge, Hand's Landing, Lizard Tail Swamp, Eldora Nature

public lands national wildlife refuges, state wildlife management areas, Delaware National Estuarine Research Reserve, Bellepark State Forest

partners state governments, National Oceanic and Atmospheric Administration, EPA, U.S. Fish and Wildlife Service, Delaware WildLands, Sussex County Land Trust, New Jersey Conservation Foundation, South Jersey Land Trust, farmers

conservancy initiatives Freshwater, Invasive Species, Marine

natural events horseshoe crab spawning and shorebird migration, spring

information Jennifer Burns, (302) 654-4707, ext. 125, jburns@tnc.org; nature.org/delaware

The Delaware Bayshores—with 1,500 square miles of beaches, bays, dunes, wetlands and forest straddling the border between Delaware and southern New Jersey—is a rare find in an extensively developed Northeast corridor. Even more remarkable than this intact natural landscape are its prehistoric inhabitants. The Delaware Bay is home to the country's largest population of American horseshoe crab, one of the oldest living species on Earth.

A closer relative of spiders and scorpions than crustaceans, the horseshoe crab's

Spawning horseshoe crabs.

solid shell, tolerance of extreme temperatures and salinity, and ability to survive several months without food have enabled it to endure for more than 250 million years. Native Americans used their shells to bail water out of canoes, and farmers crushed them to fertilize crops. Today scientists study the horseshoe crab to better understand the human eye and collect their blue blood to test new medicines for harmful bacteria before distribution to the public. Fishermen also covet the crabs as bait for eel and conch.

These ancient creatures are perhaps most valued by the millions of migrating shorebirds like red knots and ruddy turnstones that feast on horseshoe crab eggs. When spring arrives and the moon grows full, horseshoe crabs travel toward the shore from their deep-water winter habitat along the continental shelf to lay their eggs on the beach during high tide. In concert with this extraordinary event is the arrival of shorebirds from South America. Here at the Delaware Bayshores, the birds will double their weight before completing their 10,000-mile journey to the Canadian Arctic.

In recent years fewer shorebirds have returned to the bay, their numbers linked to the decline of spawning horseshoe crabs. From replenishing the beach with suitable sand to counting crabs, The Nature Conservancy is working with partners across state

Cape May National Wildlife Refuge.

boundaries to revive the horseshoe crab population and the shorebirds that depend on these creatures that outlived the dinosaurs.

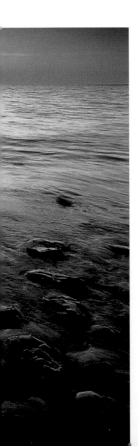

conservation profile

targets migrating shorebirds, neotropical songbirds, bald eagle, piping plover, least tern, horseshoe crab, pink tickseed, Atlantic white cedar, swamp pink, sensitive joint-vetch

stresses incompatible development, unsustainable agriculture, climate change, altered hydrological regime, clearing of coastal forests, oil and hazardous material spills, invasive species

strategies acquire land, secure conservation easements, influence land-use planning, build conservation alliances, undertake scientific research, promote ecotourism and compatible development

results 5,000 acres of beach and marsh protected

KATAHDIN FOREST
Maine

At the foot of Mt. Katahdin, scattered throughout Acadian forest that has not been logged for generations, dozens of wilderness lakes are the crown jewels of Maine's North Woods.

location near Baxter State Park; 2 hours from Bangor

ecoregion Northern Appalachian-Boreal Forest

project size 240,000 acres

preserves Trout Mountain, 40,000-acre core preserve

public lands Baxter State Park, Nahmakanta Public Lands Unit, Allagash Wilderness Waterway, Seboeis Public Lands Unit, lands held under Pingree Partnership easement

partners Great Northern Paper, John Hancock Financial Services, State of Maine, The Wilderness Society, Sierra Club, Northern Forest Alliance

natural events foliage peak, late September–early October; blueberries, blackberries and raspberries fruit, summer

information Kathy Sylvester, (888) 729-5181, ksylvester@tnc.org, nature.org/maine

Near the end of their 2,100-mile journey from Georgia to Maine, "end-to-end" hikers on the Appalachian Trail thread their way among dozens of lakes approaching Mt. Katahdin, their holy grail. These wilderness lakes, deep-blue and fringed in gnarled spruce and fir, are considered some of the most beautiful in the lake-filled state. Native Americans long ago created a network of portage sites here as they carried their birchbark canoes between lakes and across waterfalls and rapids, and the Debsconeag Lakes still bear their ancient name for "carrying place."

Bull moose, Baxter State Park.

Some 12,000 years ago, the glacial ice sheet that covered Mt. Katahdin and the Debsconeag Lakes began to melt northward. For the next thousand years, tundra of scrub and lichens prevailed around the newly carved lakes. But as the climate warmed, trees took root and the forest grew steadily, shifting from boreal forest to Acadian forest of red spruce, balsam fir, birch, maples, white pine and hemlock. Left behind in the wake of the retreating glaciers were landlocked arctic char, a relict of the far north. Native salmon, blueback trout and native brook trout are abundant in the 80-odd lakes and ponds of Debsconeag—the most remote and pristine waters in the North Woods.

Much of this landscape has not been logged for more than 70 years—highly unusual in timber-producing Maine—and the resulting mature forests provide some of the best wildlife habitat in New England. But with current changes in the forest products industry, many corporate forestlands have come up for sale (16 percent of the state changed hands in less than eight months in 1999), making forests like this one at the foot of Mt. Katahdin vulnerable.

Three years later, in 2002, The Nature Conservancy protected more than 240,000 acres of Maine's North Woods, including the Debsconeag Lakes wilderness, through fee acquisition and easements. The project binds together Baxter State Park, the Allagash Wilderness Waterway and other lands into a 400-square-mile wilderness block of protected reserves and sustainably harvested working forests.

conservation profile

targets native salmon, arctic char, blueback trout, native brook trout, bald eagle, golden eagle, moose, black bear, bobcat, rare plants like purple clematis and northern woodsia, lakes, ponds

stresses corporate forestlands for sale because of downturn in paper industry, development pressures

strategies acquire land, secure conservation easements, promote ecologically compatible forestry practices, encourage conservation management of private and public land

results 240,000 acres in conservation management, connecting to six existing conservation lands

NASSAWANGO CREEK
Maryland

Nassawango Creek is a hidden treasure tucked away on the Eastern Shore of Maryland, a state working with its mid-Atlantic neighbors to control burgeoning growth and protect the Chesapeake Bay watershed.

location 150 miles from Baltimore and Washington, D.C.

ecoregion Chesapeake Bay Lowlands

project size 44,000 acres

preserves Nassawango Creek

public lands Pocomoke River State Forest

partners Maryland Department of Natural Resources, Furnace Town Living History Museum

natural events purple martin and Baltimore oriole migration, spring; butterflies congregate, summer

information Martha Roesler, (301) 897-8570, mroesler@tnc.org; nature.org/maryland

A piece of the tropics is tucked away in the heart of Maryland's Eastern Shore, where Nassawango Creek winds its 18-mile course south to the Pocomoke River. A sanctuary within the crowded mid-Atlantic, the creek resembles a Latin American forest of giant trees and the brilliant flash of songbirds. Neotropical migrants such as the prothonotory warbler and the indigo bunting nest and raise their young among the planet's northernmost stands of massive bald cypress, whose emergent knees rise above the swampy waters.

During his pioneering voyages in 1608, Captain John Smith observed single cypress trees at the headwaters of the Nassawango

Bald cypress line Nassawango Creek.

large enough to be fashioned by the Indians into canoes that held 40 men. This and other elaborate descriptions of the area's abundance attracted European settlers. In the early 19th century, the Nassawango Iron Furnace harnessed both the creek's flow and natural resources like charcoal and oyster shells to produce "pig iron."

Captain John Smith would have trouble today recognizing the Chesapeake watershed, transformed as it is by sprawling development and streams clouded by agricultural runoff. But he would find familiar territory along Nassawango Creek. Much of the shoreline mirrors what Smith saw almost 400 years ago. It is a rare place that maintains the delicate yet dynamic rhythms of nature.

To preserve the heart of the Nassawango, The Nature Conservancy recently purchased 3,520 acres along the creek as part of a larger collaborative effort in Maryland and Virginia to address the environmental threats to the Chesapeake Bay watershed. This purchase makes the Nassawango the largest private nature preserve in Maryland, and contributes to the goal identified in the Chesapeake Bay 2000 Compact of having 20 percent of the watershed under conservation management by 2010. The compact, agreed to by the primary bay watershed states, recognizes the participation of land trusts in helping to restore and protect the bay.

Indigo bunting.

targets bald cypress, Atlantic white cedar, prothonotory warbler, wild lupine, Delmarva fox squirrel, seaside alder, black-banded sunfish

stresses nutrient runoff and sedimentation from agriculture, wetland destruction from increased residential development

strategies acquire land, secure conservation easements, promote compatible development, influence land-use planning, restore ecosystems, create conservation corridors

results 3,520 acres purchased in May 2002; all told, one-quarter of 44,000-acre watershed in conservation management

MARTHA'S VINEYARD
Massachusetts

With development rampant on the island and open space at a premium, the south shore's signature coastal sandplain is rapidly becoming one of the world's rarest landscapes.

location 70 miles southeast of Boston

ecoregion North Atlantic Coast

project size 9,000 acres

preserves David H. Smith Fire Trail, Hoft Farm

public lands Manual F. Correllus State Forest, Joseph A. Sylvia State Beach, Edgartown South Beach

partners state government, Martha's Vineyard and Nantucket land banks, Nantucket Conservation Foundation, Nantucket Land Council, Polly Hill Arboretum, Sheriff's Meadow Foundation, The Trustees of Reservations, Tuckernuck Land Trust, Vineyard Conservation Society, Woods Hole Marine Biological Laboratories

conservancy initiatives Invasive Species

natural events migrating warbler and raptor viewing, Gay Head Cliffs, fall and spring

information Kathryn Matthew, (617) 227-7017, ext. 310, kmatthew@tnc.org; nature.org/massachusetts

Martha's Vineyard offers a glimpse back to a bucolic New England countryside of fields and woodlands dotted with gray-shingled farmhouses, bisected by mossy stone walls and set against the dramatic backdrop of the Atlantic. Abundant harvests from land and sea sustained both early English settlers and the island's native Wampanoag tribe.

Gay Head Beach.

On the island's south shore are small patches of coastal sandplain, a seaside prairie of green and yellow grasses, wildflowers and low-lying shrubs. Coastal sandplain was once a signature landscape of Martha's Vineyard and, to a lesser degree, of her cousin to the east, Nantucket. Today only 1 percent of this threatened ecosystem remains, jeopardizing the survival of the short-eared owl, grasshopper sparrow and other species uniquely adapted to the sandplains.

In the past, Native Americans ignited wildfires that maintained the coastal sandplain's openness and allowed its unique mix of treeless vegetation to thrive. But encroaching development and tourism have halted such wildfires, resulting in the spread of oaks and pines among the prairies.

Conducting prescribed burns to restore the vanishing coastal sandplain is a challenge on an island where unbroken open space is as rare as the endangered ecosystem. Land is at a premium in both availability and price. It is being developed at twice the rate at which it is being protected. By 2005, the 9,000 unprotected acres remaining on the island may be fully developed.

In the race to preserve as much prime island real estate as possible, The Nature Conservancy in 2001 purchased Herring Creek Farm, a 300-year-old working farm. At 215 acres, Herring Creek represents one of the largest unbroken tracts of land on Martha's Vineyard. The purchase prevented the development of a 53-lot subdivision and will enable us to burn 62 acres to restore the coastal sandplain.

Northeastern beach tiger beetle larva.

The remaining acreage will be held by the Conservancy or sold to other conservation-minded buyers with legal restrictions limiting development.

conservation profile

targets coastal sandplain grassland, northern harrier, short-eared owl, Nantucket shadbush, bushy rockrose

stresses residential development, road construction, wildfire suppression

strategies acquire land, secure conservation easements, restore ecosystems through fire management, combat invasive species, strengthen local partner organizations, engage community, promote compatible development

results more than 2,000 acres protected since 1993; native plant nursery established to aid in restoration of coastal sandplain

GREAT BAY ESTUARY
New Hampshire

With one-quarter of New Hampshire draining into the estuary, Great Bay's protection depends on both local and distant caretakers.

location 5 miles west of Portsmouth, 40 miles north of Boston

ecoregion North Atlantic Coast

project size 200 square miles

preserves Lubberland Creek

public lands Great Bay National Wildlife Refuge, Great Bay National Estuarine Research Reserve

partners Great Bay Resource Protection Partnership, 17 towns/cities, University of New Hampshire, Jackson Laboratory, local planning boards and land trusts

conservancy initiatives Invasive Species, Marine

natural events waterfowl/shorebird migration, mid-April–June; fish runs and Alewife Festival, May

information Tabitha Deans Riley, (603) 224-5853, ext. 12, triley@tnc.org; nature.org/newhampshire

Great Bay is a delicacy of nature, one that can only result from a 5,000-year-old recipe mixing fresh water from seven rivers and numerous creeks with saltwater from the Atlantic Ocean and the Gulf of Maine. Added in are salt marshes, rocky shores, scattered ponds, rich forests and eelgrass beds. Wedged between Maine and Massachusetts, Great Bay is visible proof of why estuaries are celebrated as one of the most productive environments on Earth.

Great Bay's bountiful resources have been tapped for centuries. Tall white pines

Tidal salt marsh near Moody Point

invited early New England settlers to fashion the world's finest masts and spars for the British Navy. Sawmills and shipbuilders consumed first-growth trees such as oak and red maple. Great Bay's blue clay mudflats were transformed into bricks for the best Boston homes, transported there by the flat-bottomed Gundalow boats that could navigate changing tides and shallow waters before railroads quickened the pace.

But in the natural bounty of Great Bay lay the seeds of its degradation. Much of the estuary was once covered by inches of sawdust from the mills lining its shores. Industry, oil depots and power plants still tax the ecosystem, yet nature's resilience and a strong local conservation ethic have made the estuary healthier today than it has been in 250 years.

Crommett Creek.

The nine-member Great Bay Resource Protection Partnership leads the way in the bay's protection. This collaboration of state and federal government agencies and non-profit organizations such as The Nature Conservancy, Audubon Society and Ducks Unlimited, has acquired more than 3,700 acres of critical habitat including salt marsh, eelgrass beds and mud flats that support mussels, lobster and an abundance of marine life. The partnership continues to work with surrounding towns to identify additional conservation priorities.

conservation profile

targets osprey, eagles, great blue heron, alewife, terns, glossy ibis, Atlantic white cedar, green-winged teal, hooded and common mergansers, black ducks

stresses pollution, residential development, oil spills, development of dock piers and moorings

strategies build conservation alliances, acquire land, secure conservation easements, remove dams, influence land-use planning, combat invasive species, restore ecosystems, improve oil spill prevention measures

results 3,700 acres protected; National Estuarine Research Reserve System grant secured

PINE BARRENS
New Jersey

Cultivating the Garden State's backyard of forests, farms and valuable groundwater requires a strong plan for land use and the commitment of its residents.

location 25 miles southeast of Philadelphia

ecoregion North Atlantic Coast

project size 1.1 million acres

preserves Hirst Ponds, Forked River Mountain, East Plains, Oswego River Lowlands

public lands Pinelands National Reserve includes Cape May and Forsythe national wildlife refuges; Brendan Byrne, Belleplain, Bass River and Penn state forests; Greenwood, Stafford Forge and Forked River Mountain wildlife management areas; and Double Trouble State Park

partners New Jersey Department of Environmental Protection, New Jersey State Department of Agriculture, farmers and the farming community, Pinelands Commission, Pinelands Preservation Alliance

conservancy initiatives Fire, Freshwater

natural events cranberry harvest and flowering of pine barren gentian, fall; Pinelands Month, October; pine barrens treefrog chorus, spring

information Kamala Brush, (908) 879-7262, kbrush@tnc.org; nature.org/newjersey

S preading across the most densely populated state in the country, the New Jersey Pine Barrens remains a dynamic patchwork of open space and rural living. Cranberry and blueberry farms

thrive in the sandy soils once deemed useless by 17th- and 18th-century settlers. The Pine Barrens landscape covers 1 million acres of forest, wetlands and quaint hamlets and represents nearly a quarter of the

Wading River.

state—the most extensive undeveloped area on the eastern seaboard between Boston and Richmond.

This distinctive terrain was shaped by the elements. Ancient seas deposited waves of gravel that, with time, became the sandy soil. Fire swept the land, and it remains a friend to the vast expanses of pitch pine and shrub oak forests that dominate the barrens. Many of the species found here, including the pygmy pines that range from 4 to 10 feet high, depend on regular intervals of intense heat to pop open their cones, releasing seeds and spurring new growth.

Beneath the Pine Barrens lies a vast underground lake known as the Kirkwood Cohansey formation. The porous soils of the barrens led to the creation of this freshwater aquifer that maintains the ecological balance of surface streams, bogs, swamps and estuaries, supports agriculture and provides drinking water for hundreds of thousands of people. Estimated at 17 trillion gallons, the aquifer equates to an amount that would cover the entire state of New Jersey with 6 feet of water.

The Nature Conservancy is committed to protecting this mosaic of undeveloped land and water for which fire is an essential element. To restore fire to key areas where it no longer naturally occurs, we are convening public and private land managers and residents to

Batsto Lake.

talk about the benefits of and barriers to ecological fire management in the region. Conservancy-owned land will be used to demonstrate prescribed fire as an ecological restoration tool. We hope that these efforts will introduce the use of ecological fire to tracts of land that characterize the Pine Barrens.

conservation profile

targets pitch pine barrens, pygmy pine forest, pine barrens treefrog, sand-myrtle, Pickering's morning glory, bearberry, pyxie moss, bog asphodel, blackjack oak

stresses residential and commercial development, agricultural runoff, sand mining, altered natural fire regimes

strategies engage community, acquire land, secure conservation easements, build conservation alliances, promote compatible development, restore ecosystems through fire management

results created two preserves with the purchase of 1,752 acres; influenced the revision of rules for valuing farmland, leading to participation of 85 farms in New Jersey's agricultural development rights program and the protection of thousands of acres

NEVERSINK RIVER
New York

The river where American fly fishing was born is today the scene of maverick approaches to managing freshwater ecosystems for both human and ecological needs.

location 80 miles northwest of New York City

ecoregion High Allegheny Plateau

project size 435 square miles

preserves Neversink, Bashakill (co-managed with Orange County Land Trust)

public lands Neversink Unique Area, Catskill Park, Bashakill Wildlife Management Area, Sullivan State Forest

partners Army Corps of Engineers, U.S. Geological Survey, Bashakill Area Association, Trout Unlimited, towns of Thompson and Deerpark, Delaware River Basin Commission, N.Y. Department of Environmental Conservation, U.S. Fish & Wildlife Service, Orange County Land Trust, Orange County, U.S. Department of Agriculture, Sullivan County

conservancy initiatives Freshwater, Fire

natural events shad run, May/June; one of the largest concentrations of wood ducks on East Coast, fall

information David Ports, (914) 244-3271, dports@tnc.org; nature.org/new york

River birch, Neversink River.

Beginning high in the Catskill Mountains, the Neversink River—black, cold and clean—courses southward over glacial cobbles and gravelly mussel shoals. Long and narrow, with fewer curves and eddies than other Catskill rivers, it cuts a straight course through forests and the marshy haunts of osprey and dragonflies toward its union with the Delaware River.

The fast, bouldery waters of the Neversink presented a seminal challenge in the late 19th century to American fly fishers like Theodore Gordon, who were applying a British sport to New World waters. Gordon, an upstate New York native, realized the dry flies he tried to use in the Neversink's waters imitated English, not American, insects. They also were designed for the smooth currents of English chalk streams, not the swift currents of this wild river. The flies Gordon invented here and the methods he pioneered led to a uniquely American school, and today the Neversink is hailed as the birthplace of American fly fishing.

Although the river's gurgling waters are still a mecca for fly fishers from all over the world, many of the pools where Gordon fished were drowned in the 1950s behind the Neversink Reservoir Dam. Nearly 40 years later, aquatic biologists discovered that this dam and another—the Cuddebackville Dam—were leading to declines in populations of fish like American shad, which could not reach much of their historic spawning grounds. They and other creatures like the dwarf wedgemussel, found nowhere else on Earth, needed natural river flows to survive.

After more than a decade of working on the Neversink, The Nature Conservancy has reached an agreement with the U.S. Army Corps of Engineers and state and local agencies to remove the Cuddebackville Dam in summer 2003, opening up nearly 30 miles of

fish spawning habitat. With more than 80 percent of the river's flow pumped to New York City (it is considered the metropolis' purest source of drinking water), we are now working to develop a model for ecologically sustainable water management throughout the Delaware River Basin, one that balances human needs with those of freshwater ecosystems.

Swollen mussels and dwarf wedgemussels.

targets American shad, American eel, dragonflies, Bashakill bottomland swamp, brook trout, blue spotted sunfish, freshwater mussels, forests of sycamore, river birch and red maple

stresses disruption of water flow patterns, invasive species, pollution, aquatic and terrestrial habitat fragmentation from incompatible development, forestry, mining, dams

strategies remove dams and other riverine barriers, restore ecosystems, promote ecologically compatible development and land use, acquire land, secure conservation easements

results Cuddebackville Dam scheduled to be removed in summer 2003; water management project launched with four states, New York City and a federal commission

TUG HILL PLATEAU
New York

Tug Hill marks the westernmost edge of the Great Northern Forest, 26 million acres of mountainous woodland extending from Lake Ontario to eastern Maine.

location 30 miles north of Syracuse

ecoregion Northern Appalachian–Boreal Forest

project size 720,000 acres

preserves Tug Hill Conservation Area

public lands Tug Hill Wildlife Management Area, Winona State Forest, Whetstone Gulf State Park, Littlejohn Wildlife Management Area

partners New York State Department of Environmental Conservation, Tug Hill Commission, East Branch of Fish Creek Working Group, Tug Hill Tomorrow Land Trust, GMO Renewable Resources

natural events bird migrations, May; wildflower blooms, May; fall foliage, September

information Judith Lemoncelli, (585) 546-8030, jlemoncelli@tnc.org; nature.org/newyork

Atop the Tug Hill Plateau stretch 150,000 acres of unbroken northern hardwood forest, its bounds encompassing the headwaters of four major rivers and thousands of acres of streams and wetlands. River gorges cut chasms of layered stone 300 feet deep. This forested plateau sandwiched between Lake Ontario and the Adirondacks is home to numerous birds and mammals needing extensive intact forest to forage and breed.

Beaver pond, Tug Hill Plateau.

Water shapes the Tug Hill landscape, and the plateau's extensive waterways are fed by its extreme climate. Each year, winds sweeping eastward off Lake Ontario unload an average of 55 inches of precipitation on the plateau, more than a third falling as snow. The region receives the highest snowfall east of the Rockies— more than 20 feet per year.

To date, Tug Hill's heavy precipitation coupled with poor soils have kept its upper reaches undeveloped and free of roads. Europeans arriving at the plateau via Lake Ontario in the early 1800s were greeted by towering red spruce rising above a lower canopy of maple, yellow birch and beech. Trees soon became, and continue to be, the foundation of the region's economy. As a result of intensive softwood harvesting in the late 1800s, hardwoods overtook the plateau. Local mills now process birch, maple and black cherry into lumber for export or sale to other local businesses that fashion products ranging from bowling pins to fine furniture.

In our largest-ever New York acquisition, The Nature Conservancy in 2002 brokered a deal with the state and a private timber company to protect 45,000 acres in the heart of Tug Hill Plateau— one-third of its core forest and critical habitat for forest birds and wide-ranging animals like

Bog copper butterfly.

fisher and bobcat. Under this agreement, much of the forest will be logged sustainably and compatible public recreation will be permitted. The most sensitive ecological areas, like those near watercourses and wetlands, will be preserved and restored.

conservation profile

targets spruce northern hardwood forest, interior-forest nesting birds like blackburnian warbler, fisher, bobcat, three-toed woodpecker, eastern pearlshell mussel

stresses forest fragmentation from roads and development, sedimentation of streams from unsustainable forest management and all-terrain vehicle trails

strategies acquire land, secure conservation easements, build conservation alliances, encourage sustainable management of private timberland, restore ecosystems

results 45,000 acres in conservation management

POCONO PLATEAU
Pennsylvania

Time will tell if this primordial pocket of nature in northeastern Pennsylvania—shaped by ice-age glacial expansion—can survive modern-day urban growth.

location 90 miles west of New York City

ecoregion High Allegheny Plateau

project size 24,000 acres

preserves Tannersville Bog, Long Pond, Thomas Darling, Moosic Mountain, Cherry Valley

public lands Hickory Run State Park, Pennsylvania State Game Lands, Delaware State Forest, Delaware Water Gap National Recreation Area

partners state, county and municipal government; U.S. Army Corps of Engineers, Wildlands Conservancy, Pocono Heritage Land Trust

conservancy initiatives Invasive Species

natural events flowering of the Rhodora heaths of Long Pond, May; nesting songbirds and raptors, May–July; fall foliage, October

information Molly Anderson, (610) 834-1323, manderson@tnc.org; nature.org/pennsylvania

Ski slopes and lakeside resorts have drawn vacationers to the Poconos for decades, but the quiet beauty of these mountains is the real allure. This Pennsylvania plateau was glaciated at least three different times within the past million years. An ancient world of relict northern climes, the Pocono Plateau is still being sculpted by ice and water.

At first glance this slice of wilderness resembles the Canadian backcountry, with its remnant populations of boreal plants, animals, lakes and bogs. Prominent among the natural wonders here is the glacially influenced Hickory Run Park Boulder Field, unchanged after 20,000 years.

The Pocono Plateau boasts black bear populations containing the largest and most prolific individuals in the country. Abundant native river otters are a source for the species' reintroduction in other places where they have become scarce. It is also the only place on Earth with heath lands dominated by Rhodora, a beautiful wild azalea that attracts photographers from around the world and received a poetic tribute from Ralph Waldo Emerson. In early May when the rest of the plateau still wears its winter cloak, Rhodora's pink blossoms spread their carpet—a striking sight to behold.

Today the Rhodora heaths and other primitive remnants of the Poconos' past are jeopardized by encroachments of a non-glaciated kind: expansion from nearby metropolitan areas growing at a pace that is 300 times faster than anywhere else in Pennsylvania. In response, The Nature Conservancy participates in numerous municipal and county open-space advisory committees and joins local citizens, organizations and governments in marshalling resources to protect important areas and guide responsible growth.

Rhodora in bloom with pitch pine.

Black bear.

conservation profile

targets black bear, river otter, osprey, snowshoe hare, flypoison bulb-borer moth, pitcher plants, whippoorwill, heath lands, oak barrens

stresses haphazard development, fire suppression, water pollution, invasive plants and animals

strategies acquire land, secure conservation easements, restore ecosystems through fire management, strengthen local partner organizations, engage community, influence land-use planning, encourage conservation management of public and private land

results $25 million bond referendum for land conservation passed; more than 10,000 acres protected as a result

PAWCATUCK BORDERLANDS
Rhode Island

Pristine and flowing with some of the cleanest waters in New England, the Pawcatuck watershed is a rare and quiet breed in an urbanized landscape.

location 20 miles southwest of Providence, 60 miles east of Hartford

ecoregion Lower New England and North Atlantic Coast

project size 136,000 acres

preserves Long Pond/Ell Pond, Canonchet Brook

public lands Pachaug State Forest, Arcadia Management Area

partners state governments, Avalonia Land Trust, Hopkinton Land Trust, West Greenwich Land Conservancy, North Stonington Citizens Land Alliance, Coventry Land Trust, Wood Pawcatuck Watershed Association, Denison-Pequotsepos Nature Center, local landowners

natural events spectacular foliage, fall; alewife runs, spring

information Sheila Hughes, (401) 331-7110, shughes@tnc.org; nature.org/rhodeisland

Embraced by forest, the Pawcatuck River sculpts a natural boundary between Rhode Island and Connecticut. A few textile and sawmills populate its banks. Remnant dairy farms and scattered stone walls frame a picturesque rural setting. After sunset, this undisturbed landscape comprises the only strip of darkness between Washington, D.C., and Boston when viewed from the sky.

Pachaug State Forest.

Thick stands of oak, hickory, maple and pine dominate 85 percent of the Pawcatuck Borderlands, the largest unfragmented forest in the urbanized Northeast corridor. Dry and sandy soils punctuated by wetlands nurture giant rhododendron and Atlantic white cedar, prized by early European settlers for its rot-resistant qualities and harvested for fencing and shingles. Pileated woodpeckers, scarlet tanagers, fisher, black bear and the rare butterfly Hessel's hairstreak thrive in these extensive, unbroken woodlands.

The Pawcatuck Borderlands' forests filter and channel water that drains into some of the cleanest watersheds in New England: the Wood, the Pachaug, the Mossup and the Shunock. These clear rivers, streams, ponds and ground waters support much of Rhode Island's and Connecticut's basic human needs for water while sustaining hearty populations of native brook trout, alewife and herring. The best way of drinking in this beauty is to canoe some of the rivers, observing rare dragonflies, painted turtles and great blue heron up close.

The Nature Conservancy is working across 200 square miles of the Pawcatuck Borderlands to respond to development and tourism pressures that have emerged in this once-quiet corner of New England. We are working with towns and local residents to protect high-quality forest as well as clean water and the watershed's rural character.

Painted turtle.

targets forests, rivers, alewife, blueback herring, Atlantic white cedar swamps, Hessel's hairstreak, banded boghaunter, green adders mouth orchid

stresses residential development, road construction, resort development

strategies acquire land, secure conservation easements, restore ecosystems through fire management, strengthen local partner organizations, promote compatible development

results 10,000 acres protected since 1990; helped two communities pass open-space funding initiatives

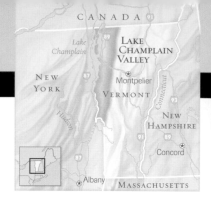

LAKE CHAMPLAIN VALLEY

Vermont

Nestled between New York's Adirondack Mountains to the west and the Green Mountains of Vermont to the east, the Champlain Valley is home to about 190,000 people and 100,000 cattle.

location 20 miles west of Montpelier; 90 miles north of Albany, New York

ecoregion St. Lawrence/ Champlain Valley

project size 1.1 million acres

preserves East Creek, Otter Creek Swamps, H. Lawrence Achilles Natural Area at Shelburne Pond, Helen W. Buckner Memorial Preserve at Bald Mountain

public lands Missisquoi National Wildlife Refuge, Kingsland Bay State Park; Little Otter Creek, Dead Creek and Snake Mountain wildlife management areas

partners Vermont Land Trust, Environmental Protection Agency, Natural Resource Conservation Service, state agencies, farmers

conservancy initiatives Freshwater, Invasive Species

natural events fall foliage, October; animal tracking, winter; maple sugaring, late winter

information Trevor Law, (802) 229-4425, tlaw@tnc.org; nature.org/vermont

Looking west across Lake Champlain, with the Adirondacks in the distance.

Lake Champlain meanders river-like—the largest lake in New England but spanning only 12 miles at its widest point. Fed by several major rivers, the lake is surrounded by a mosaic of bogs, fens and swamps that harbor 21 species of amphibians and tens of thousands of migrating waterfowl each year. Forested floodplain and hillsides buffer the rich aquatic systems from pollutants and sustain forest-dependent birds and mammals. Both lake and valley bear the name of Samuel de Champlain, an early French explorer of North America.

Thousands of years ago, the Champlain basin was at different times inundated with both fresh water and saltwater, which shaped its soils and vegetation. When the Abenaki Indians arrived here 8,000 years ago, they encountered a land almost entirely forested. European settlers, however, brought about dramatic changes to the landscape in a short period of time. Between 1750 and 1850, some 75 percent of the state of Vermont was cleared of forest and sheep grazed almost every hillside. When the settlers departed for the promise of better soils in the Midwest, much of the state reverted to forest.

The Champlain Valley's rolling countryside is today dominated by dairy farms, their ubiquitous black-and-white Holsteins coming to symbolize Vermont. Although a land use preferable to road and housing development, which fragments the landscape, livestock farming has far-reaching consequences for the valley's abundant waterways. Cattle allowed to drink from rivers and streams erode fragile banks, and their waste adds excess nutrients, degrading water quality and choking the life forms that depend on clean water.

To ensure the survival of amphibians, mussels and fish that rely on these waters, The Nature Conservancy is paying farmers to keep their cows out of streams and wetlands. Through the federally funded Partners for Wildlife program, we pay a percentage of the cost of building fences and drilling artesian wells on

Valley dairy farm.

farms. To date we have installed 30 miles of fencing along major rivers to exclude cattle from waterways. We are also planting native trees and shrubs on riverbanks and floodplain lands owned by the Conservancy and farms enrolled in Partners for Wildlife.

conservation profile

targets Lake Champlain, wetlands, claypin forest, northern hardwood forest, wintering raptors, striped chorus frog, Indiana bat, eastern spiny softshell turtle, bobolink

stresses habitat fragmentation from road and associated development, altered hydrological regime, invasive species, incompatible agricultural and forestry practices

strategies acquire land, secure conservation easements, protect water quality, restore ecosystems, influence land-use practices, build conservation alliances, undertake scientific research, engage community

results 100,000 acres in conservation management

VIRGINIA COAST RESERVE
Virginia

Preserving local traditions may be the best solution to protecting the last stretch of coastal wilderness remaining between Maine and Florida.

location 240 miles from Washington, D.C.; 20 miles from Virginia Beach

ecoregion Chesapeake Bay Lowlands

project size 670 square miles

preserves Virginia Coast Reserve

public lands Chincoteague and Fisherman's Island national wildlife refuges, Assateague National Seashore, Kiptopeke State Park

partners U.S. Fish and Wildlife Service, National Oceanic and Atmospheric Administration, National Science Foundation, Center for Conservation Biology, Virginia Marine Resources Commission, Virginia Department of Environmental Quality, Coastal Virginia Avian Partnership, Ducks Unlimited

conservancy initiatives Fire, Freshwater, Global Climate Change, Marine, Invasive Species

natural events Eastern Shore Birding Festival, October; migration of shorebirds, April–June

information Gregory Edwards, (434) 295-6106, gedwards@tnc.org; nature.org/virginia

Across the Chesapeake Bay from Virginia's mainland, the tip of the Delmarva Peninsula forms a narrow finger of farm field and salt marsh laced with tidal creeks, mud flats, shallow bays and ponds. Together with the 18 sandy barrier islands that shift along its margins, this flat

and fragile landscape comprises the longest stretch of coastal wilderness remaining on the Atlantic Coast of the United States.

Here on Virginia's Eastern Shore, 850 miles of shoreline provide varied and ample habitat for 380 species of resident and migratory birds. In autumn, one of the

Winter sunset, Phillips Creek Marsh.

greatest concentrations of Atlantic Flyway neotropical songbirds and raptors converge in mixed-hardwood forests along the shore. Winter brings thousands of ducks and geese to the marshes. And piping plovers make their nests on broken-shell beaches in spring while shorebirds, including 80 percent of the Northern Hemisphere's whimbrel population, arrive in droves to feed and rest on the mudflats.

The barrier islands have been at various times the hunting grounds of Native Americans, a hide-out for pirates and a resort for well-heeled hunters. Some islands hosted short-lived settlements, but frequent storms prevented any long term occupancy. Vestiges of fishing villages now lie beneath the waves. Beginning in 1969, The Nature Conservancy bought 14 of the islands as the core of the Virginia Coast Reserve, to ward off huge development schemes that would have seen marinas, bridges and condos built. Parts of the mainland were later added to the reserve to safeguard coastal marsh lagoons—nurseries for fish and shellfish.

Today lower land prices and the Eastern Shore's rural charm are attracting residential development from nearby Virginia Beach and other cities of Hampton Roads—only 20 miles away via the Chesapeake Bay Bridge-Tunnel. Unplanned development will undermine not only this world-class ecosystem but also its historic farm and fishing communities. The Nature Conservancy works to influence land-use planning and is helping local communities learn about development approaches that preserve local character, history, traditions and, ultimately, the ecosystem itself.

conservation profile

targets Chesapeake Bay estuary, barrier islands, coastal lagoons, salt marsh, Delmarva fox squirrel, piping and Wilson's plovers, American oystercatcher, terns, black skimmer

stresses inappropriate development and agricultural practices, overfishing, incompatible forestry practices, invasive species

strategies acquire land, secure conservation easements, promote ecologically compatible land-use practices, build conservation alliances, protect water quality and supply

results approximately 100,000 acres in conservation management; 14 barrier islands protected; last undeveloped coastal barrier island lagoon system on eastern seaboard protected; local citizens groups established

WARM SPRINGS MOUNTAIN
Virginia

A keystone land acquisition on Warm Springs Mountain knits together thousands of acres of undeveloped land in the central Appalachians.

location Allegheny Mountains, 90 miles west of Charlottesville

ecoregion Central Appalachian Forest

project size 562 square miles

preserves Warm Springs Mountain

public lands George Washington National Forest, Douthat State Park

partners U.S. Forest Service, Cowpasture River Preservation Association, Valley Conservation Council, Virginia Outdoors Foundation, state government, private landowners

conservancy initiatives Invasive Species

natural events spectacular foliage display, fall

information Carol Wise, (434) 295-6106; cwise@tnc.org; nature.org/virginia

The view from Warm Springs Mountain.

The view from Warm Springs Mountain is a rolling sea of mountain and vale clear to the western horizon—an unexpected, unbroken forest in a well-traversed part of America. For the Algonquin people, who were here before all others, the view was similarly infinite. These mountains still bear their word for "endless": Allegheny.

Following bison trails as did the Native Americans before them, colonists in the 1720s discovered the warm springs

that gave the mountain its name. The reputed medicinal properties of their waters drew scores of colonial Americans, notable among them a young George Washington. The springs eventually gave rise to The Homestead, one of the country's grandest resorts, and to the tradition of retreating to these gentle mountains to let nature renew body and spirit. More than a dozen U.S. presidents would later find refreshment and quietude in these highlands, including Thomas Jefferson, who visited the area frequently while planning the University of Virginia.

Another sort of history pervades the mountain and the pristine Cowpasture River cutting along its toe. Ecologically, the area offers a window to the past, when all the eastern mountain ranges were as untrammeled as Warm Springs Mountain is today. Plants like bunchberry and unusual moths, increasingly rare in the central Appalachians, still flourish here. Common hardwood forest gives way to rare montane pine barrens—a drier terrain of stunted pitch pine and other fire-dependent species.

Such biological richness drew the attention of Nature Conservancy scientists, who marked a large tract on Warm Springs Mountain as one of the keystone privately held parcels in the Central Appalachian Forest ecoregion. When the 9,000-acre tract came on the market in March 2002, we acquired it, securing a 13-mile boundary with undeveloped national forestlands and lots of room for migratory birds and black bear to roam. Battling invasive species and reintroducing fire to the landscape are the next challenges.

Flame azalea.

conservation profile

targets montane pine and shale barrens, high-elevation wetlands, black bear, ruffed grouse, flame azalea, lady's slippers, rare moths, dragonflies and damselflies, bunchberry, Fraser's marsh St. John's-wort

stresses incompatible timber harvesting, invasive species, fire exclusion, residential development

strategies combat invasive species, acquire land, secure conservation easements, encourage conservation management of public land, restore ecosystems through fire management

results 360,000 acres in conservation management; last large, privately owned parcel now protected

SMOKE HOLE/NORTH FORK MOUNTAIN

West Virginia

Gaining popularity as a weekend retreat, this rare pocket of isolated Eastern wilderness risks being spoiled by those who come to enjoy it.

location 3 hours west of Washington, D.C.

ecoregion Central Appalachian Forest

project size 120,000 acres

preserves Panther Knob, Pike Knob, Little Creek

public lands Monongahela National Forest

partners U.S. Forest Service, West Virginia Department of Natural Resources, West Virginia University, private landowners

conservancy initiatives Fire, Freshwater, Invasive Species

natural events raptor migration, September–November; maternity colonies of Virginia big-eared bats gather, summer; prairie plants in peak bloom, late May–early July

information Jamie L. Serino, (304) 345-4350, jserino@tnc.org; nature.org/westvirginia

On its northeast course through the rolling mountains and valleys of West Virginia, the South Branch of the Potomac makes an abrupt turn, squeezing between Cave and North Fork mountains and carving a half-mile-deep canyon called Smoke Hole. A misty fog often covers the river, resembling

Moonrise over North Fork Mountain.

smoke leaving a hole as it drifts out of the narrow gorge. Some believe the name may derive from the days when these corrugated hills concealed moonshiner's stills, or when Native Americans made smokehouses of the limestone caves that pockmark the region.

In the hills above the gorge, true prairies, not unlike those found on the high plains, display such towering grasses as little bluestem, Indian grass and side oats gramma. Tundralike summits and other subalpine plant communities include botanical specimens that were described by science only in the past 15 years. And, at the higher elevations where cold winds prevail, rare fire dependent pine barrens survive. Many pine barrens have endured because local residents burned the heaths to stimulate the growth of blueberries.

Beneath the forest floor, a subterranean community of life thrives. One limestone cave alone supports the largest concentration of mammals in the ecoregion, accommodating more than 100,000 hibernating bats every winter. In warm months, throngs of the fluttering furry mammals—including one third of the endangered Virginia big-eared bat population—emerge from the gaping hole into the dusk.

Smoke Hole and North Fork Mountain partially overlap with the Monongahela National Forest and other popular

Peregrine falcon.

wilderness and recreation areas. All are within a day's drive of one-third of the U.S. population and a few hours from Washington, D.C. In response to an alarming increase in vacation-home development, The Nature Conservancy is negotiating voluntary protection agreements with private landowners and establishing preserves at critical locations.

conservation profile

targets pine barrens, prairies, cedar glades, Virginia big-eared bat, bobcat, black bear, peregrine falcon, bald eagle, migrating raptors

stresses incompatible residential development, limestone quarrying, invasive species

strategies acquire land, secure conservation easements, combat invasive species, restore ecosystems through fire management, encourage conservation management of public land, engage community in natural resource management, prevent or minimize impact of limestone quarrying

results initiated first successful private landowner protection program in the state; more than 5,000 acres in conservation management

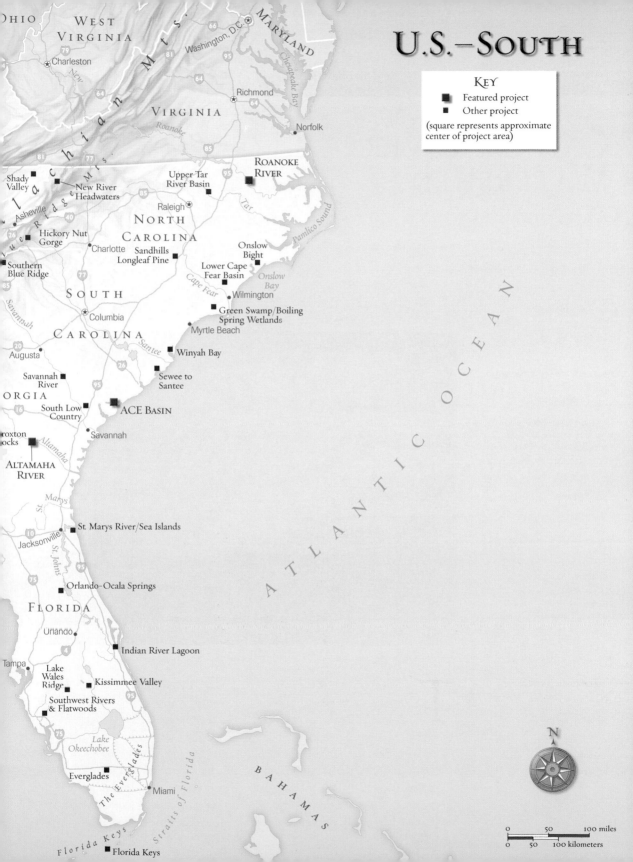

U.S.–SOUTH

KEY
■ Featured project
■ Other project
(square represents approximate center of project area)

OHIO

WEST
VIRGINIA

Charleston
79

New

Washington, D.C.
66
81
95

MARYLAND

Chesapeake Bay

VIRGINIA

64
64

Richmond ⊛

64
81
77

Roanoke
85

Norfolk

Shady
Valley
New River
Headwaters

Asheville

40

Upper Tar
River Basin

Raleigh ⊛

ROANOKE
RIVER

95

Tar

Pamlico Sound

Blue Ridge Mts.

Appalachian Mts.

NORTH
CAROLINA

26

Hickory Nut
Gorge

Charlotte

Sandhills
Longleaf Pine

Onslow
Bight

Southern
Blue Ridge

77

Lower Cape
Fear Basin

Onslow
Bay

85

SOUTH

Cape Fear

Wilmington

Columbia ⊛

Green Swamp/Boiling
Spring Wetlands

Savannah

CAROLINA

20

Santee

Myrtle Beach

Winyah Bay

Augusta

26

Sewee to
Santee

Savannah
River

95

South Low
Country

ACE BASIN

ORGIA

16

roxton
ocks

Savannah

Altamaha

ALTAMAHA
RIVER

Marys

St.

St. Marys River/Sea Islands

10

Jacksonville

St. Johns

95

75

Orlando-Ocala Springs

FLORIDA

Orlando

4

Indian River Lagoon

Tampa

Lake
Wales
Ridge

Kissimmee Valley

Southwest Rivers
& Flatwoods

95

ATLANTIC OCEAN

75

Lake
Okeechobee

The Everglades

BAHAMAS

Straits of Florida

Everglades

Miami

N

Florida Keys

Florida Keys

0   50   100 miles
0   50   100 kilometers

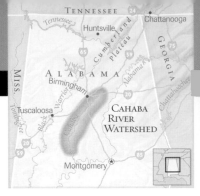

CAHABA RIVER WATERSHED
Alabama

Nearby urban growth is taking a toll on the extraordinary aquatic life of the Cahaba River, which needs clear, free-flowing waters to thrive.

location from Birmingham southward

ecoregions Cumberlands and Southern Ridge and Valley, Upper East Gulf Coastal Plain

project size 1,870 square miles

preserves Barton's Beach, Kathy Stiles Freeland Bibb County Glades, Pratt's Ferry

public lands Cahaba River National Wildlife Refuge, Brierfield Ironworks State Park, Oak Mountain State Park, Talladega National Forest

partners Cahaba River Society, U.S. Fish and Wildlife Service, U.S. Forest Service, U.S. Army Corps of Engineers, Black Warrior-Cahaba Land Trust, Alabama Department of Conservation and Natural Resources, timber companies

conservancy initiatives Invasive Species, Fire, Freshwater

natural events Cahaba lilies flower, May–June

information Mark Driskill, (205) 251-1155, ext. 24, mdriskill@tnc.org; nature.org/alabama

Cahaba lilies in bloom.

The lilies rise out of the swift-flowing waters of the Cahaba, clusters of thousands of delicate white flowers spanning the river for miles. They congregate mid-river, wedging their bulbs into crevices in the sandstone rock. These shallows of Alabama's longest free-flowing river are home to the largest known stands of the Cahaba lily remaining in the world. Two centuries of dam-building on Southeastern rivers have drowned most of their native habitat.

The Cahaba was spared, ironically, more than a century ago by commercial "progress." In the years following the Civil War, government engineers planned to dam the river, thereby flooding the shoals, to improve steamboat navigation. But the emergence of the railroad as the preferred mode of transportation spelled the end of steamboat commerce, and the dams were deemed unnecessary.

In 1992, in a biological discovery whose magnitude has been likened to legendary surveys in the tropics, Georgia botanist Jim Allison discovered eight plant

Canoeing the Cahaba.

the protection and management of large forest blocks along the river. The Nature Conservancy has engaged government at all levels to establish, expand and manage a network of public conservation lands within the watershed. Working with key members of Congress, we helped establish the 3,500-acre Cahaba River National Wildlife Refuge, a political feat that has been lauded by citizens, corporate leaders, the media and local government.

species previously unknown to science in cedar glades along the river. Aquatic diversity is similarly high. Scientists believe the concentration of rare species may be explained by the Ketona dolomite that underlies the glades and other unique geological substrates in the riverbed.

Flowing through Birmingham, the state's largest city, the river is threatened by the effects of development—both direct habitat loss and degradation of water quality caused by runoff and erosion. Key to countering these threats are

conservation profile

targets Cahaba lily, Cahaba shiner, alligator, red-cockaded woodpecker, mountain longleaf pine forest, bald cypress swamps, chalk prairies, Bibb County glades, endemic wildflowers

stresses habitat loss and sedimentation from residential and commercial development, pollution from sewage treatment plants, industry and stormwater runoff, invasive exotic species, excessive water withdrawal

strategies encourage conservation management of public land, acquire land, secure conservation easements, influence land-use planning, restore ecosystems through fire management, promote compatible development

results more than 4,000 acres in conservation management

STRAWBERRY RIVER
Arkansas

Cattle-grazing practices threaten the survival of an unusual treasure trove of aquatic diversity in one of the state's last free-flowing rivers.

location 140 miles northwest of Memphis

ecoregion Ozarks

project size 470 square miles

preserves Strawberry River Preserve and Demonstration Ranch

partners U.S. Fish and Wildlife Service, Natural Resources Conservation Service, Sharp County Soil and Water Commission, Sharp County Conservation Board, Federation of Fly Fishers, Arkansas Game and Fish Commission, private landowners

natural events Strawberry River orangethroat darter spawns, February–May

information Harryette Shue, (501) 614-5072; hshue@tnc.org; nature.org/arkansas

Wending its way through the eastern Ozark Mountains on a 70-mile journey, the Strawberry River meanders through rolling hills of pasture and woodland. Limestone bluffs rise sharply from its banks to heights of 100 feet, and overhanging tree limbs form a cool canopy—relief for canoeists in the summer sun. Although the U.S. Army Corps of Engineers periodically has considered damming the river since 1938, the dam project was recently de-authorized and the Strawberry remains one of the few free-flowing rivers in the state.

Best known to fly fishers for its smallmouth bass, the Strawberry River's waters also harbor 107 other species of fish. Particularly prized is the 2-inch-long

Strawberry River orangethroat darter, found nowhere else in the world. The river's gravel bed and rocky shoals are awash in healthy populations of 39 types of freshwater mussels and at least four species of cray-fish—two of the country's most imperiled species groups.

But current practices on nearby cattle ranches are turning these clear waters murky. Cattle allowed to wade in the Strawberry and its tributaries trample streambank vegetation, causing the banks to erode and fill the river with sediment. Their waste adds excess nutrients, another major threat to water quality in the watershed.

The Nature Conservancy in 2000 purchased more than 1,000 acres here, including a five-mile stretch of the Strawberry River, to establish a nature preserve and demonstration farm to show-case ecologically friendly cattle ranching techniques that also are profitable for ranchers. We are working with local ranchers here and on their own farms to fence cattle out of streams and restore degraded streambanks. Working with the U.S. Fish and Wildlife Service and local agriculture agencies, we are also helping landowners pay the costs of switching to these river-friendly practices.

Smallmouth bass.

conservation profile

targets freshwater fish, mussels and crayfish, Strawberry River orangethroat darter

stresses habitat destruction, water quality decline caused by forest conversion, current agricultural practices, runoff from roads

strategies acquire land, restore ecosystems, promote ecologically compatible land-use practices, engage community in natural resource management

results 1,457 acres and seven miles of stream frontage in conservation management; demonstration farm established to showcase ecologically friendly cattle ranching techniques

Above the Strawberry River.

APALACHICOLA RIVER AND BAY
Florida

Local legend places the Garden of Eden here in the Florida Panhandle, but it might be paradise lost if freshwater flows from river to bay decrease.

location 45 miles west of Tallahassee

ecoregion East Gulf Coastal Plain

project size 1 million acres

preserves Apalachicola Bluffs and Ravines, John S. Phipps, Jeff Lewis Wilderness

public lands Apalachicola National Forest, St. Vincent National Wildlife Refuge, Apalachicola River Water Management Area, Apalachicola National Estuarine Research Reserve, Tate's Hell State Forest

partners Florida Fish & Wildlife Conservation Commission, Northwest Florida Water Management District, Florida Department of Environmental Protection, U.S. Forest Service, U.S. Fish and Wildlife Service, National Oceanic and Atmospheric Administration

conservancy initiatives Freshwater

natural events carnivorous plants flower in the sandhills, spring

information Debbie Keller, (850) 222-0199, dkeller@tnc.org; nature.org/florida

Oyster boats, Apalachicola Bay.

The lands and waters of the Apalachicola—river and bay, swampy forest and white-sand island—are tinged with the primeval. The river spreads out sleepily among dense bottomland hardwood forests of tupelo, cypress, gum and oak before emptying into Apalachicola Bay. In the piney uplands, ravines cut deep gashes in the sandy soil, their depths trickling with spring water and lined with mountain laurel and magnolia. The shapes and ways of the fantastic creatures themselves tell of ancient days: lumbering sea turtles, burrowing gopher tortoises and a fish—the Gulf sturgeon—that has been plying river and sea for more than 30 million years.

The bay is a major nursery for fish, shrimp and blue crabs. The honey-producing tupelo forest is the largest in the world. In the river and floodplain live the highest concentration of amphibian and reptile species north of Mexico. Rare species like the Florida torreya, an evergreen, have helped earn this part of the Florida Panhandle the title as one of six biodiversity "hotspots" in the United States.

But the creature for which the Apalachicola is most known is the humble oyster. The bay accounts for 10 percent of the nation's oyster harvest and 90 percent of Florida's harvest. A fertile stew of leaf litter and just the right amount of fresh water flowing into the bay nurtures the prized oyster beds. Today, however, the Apalachicola oyster and other denizens of river and bay are in jeopardy as upstream agricultural operations and burgeoning cities like Atlanta want to take more of the river's water for their own use.

The Apalachicola River is now at the center of one of the most contested water conflicts in the country. Proposals from Georgia and Alabama for heavier upstream water withdrawals would result in unnaturally low water flows in

Red-cockaded woodpecker.

the Florida reaches. The Nature Conservancy has worked for eight years to inform the tri-state water compact negotiations by providing sound scientific information that demonstrates the link between water flows and ecosystem health.

conservation profile

targets Gulf sturgeon, freshwater flows, oyster beds, sea turtles, fire-back crayfish, Apalachicola dusky salamander, red-cockaded woodpecker, gopher tortoise, steephead ravines

stresses dam and reservoir operations, upstream water management, rapid development, forest destruction, irrigated farming, river dredging, invasive species

strategies acquire land, restore ecosystems, protect water supply, modify dam operations, undertake scientific research, promote ecologically sound public policies

results more than 500,000 acres in conservation management; continue to inform ongoing water compact negotiations

ALTAMAHA RIVER
Georgia

A local coalition of fishermen, farmers and citizens works to balance economic and environmental needs along what is often called "Georgia's mightiest river."

location near Lumber City to Darien; 45 minutes south of Savannah

ecoregion South Atlantic Coastal Plain

project size 1.2 million acres

preserves Carr's Island, Cathead Creek, Moody Forest Natural Area

public lands Moody Forest Natural Area, Hofwyl-Broadfield Plantation State Park; Savannah Ridge, Bullard, Big Hammock, Griffin Ridge, Sansavilla and Paulk's Pasture wildlife management areas

partners Georgia Department of Natural Resources, McIntosh Sustainable Environment and Economic Development Initiative, U.S. Fish and Wildlife Service, U.S. Environmental Protection Agency, International Paper, Plum Creek, Georgia Power Company

conservancy initiatives Freshwater, Invasive Species

natural events swallow-tailed kite migration, late July; Radford dicerandra blooms, fall

information Kara Land, (404) 873-6946, kland@tnc.org; nature.org/georgia

I t would be hard to imagine a more Southern river than the Altamaha, its slow-moving waters creeping through cypress swamps, tidal marshes and abandoned rice fields. Just as it has for more than 20 million years, the Altamaha flows undammed across Georgia to the Atlantic, its watershed covering one-quarter of the state.

Humans first appeared in the basin some 11,000 years ago, and they since have navigated the river in a range of vessels that marks the ages—from dugout cypress canoes, to Spanish galleons in search of gold, to rafts of lumber and tobacco bound for coastal ports. Today fishing boats are more common than cars along some parts of the river, which is crossed only five times by roads

and twice by railroads. Alligators still prowl the muddy waters and bald eagles circle overhead, just as they did centuries ago when the Guale people hunted and fished these shores.

The Altamaha's wild character makes it a haven for some of the world's rarest species. Among the longleaf pine forests that flourish above the floodplain is the Moody Forest, the world's only remaining stand of longleaf pine mixed with blackjack oak. The dry, sandy ridges on the river banks shelter a cinnamon-scented plant called the Radford dicerandra that grows only in two places along the Altamaha, and its waters harbor seven pearly mussel species found nowhere else.

The Nature Conservancy has been working to protect the Altamaha River for more than 30 years, combating threats like development, fire suppression and unsustainable fishing and forestry practices. In 1997, we helped organize a community coalition, now a non-profit organization of its own focused on compatible development issues and encouraging a viable economy in the watershed without jeopardizing the health of the river system. With the Georgia Department of Natural Resources, we will comanage the Moody Forest, conducting prescribed burns and longleaf pine restoration and providing educational and recreational opportunities to the public. The Moody Forest partnership is the first public/private land-management agreement in the state of Georgia.

Spanish moss at the mouth of the Altamaha.

The meandering lower river.

conservation profile

targets red-cockaded woodpecker, gopher tortoise, swallow-tailed kite, eastern indigo snake, longleaf pine wiregrass system

stresses excessive groundwater/surface water withdrawal, incompatible development practices, invasive species, fire suppression, land conversion for agriculture and silviculture

strategies promote ecologically compatible land-use practices, protect water supply, engage community, restore ecosystems through fire management, acquire land, secure conservation easements

results more than 33,000 acres protected; McIntosh Sustainable Environment and Economic Development Initiative created

GREEN RIVER
Kentucky

Two aquatic underworlds—one under ground, the other under water—depend on the natural flows of water borne by the Green River.

location 80 miles south of Louisville

ecoregion Interior Low Plateau

project size 1,500 square miles

public lands Mammoth Cave National Park

partners Kentucky Department of Natural Resources, U.S. Army Corps of Engineers, U.S. Department of Agriculture, local communities

conservancy initiatives Freshwater

natural events colorful darters spawn, April–May

information Logan McCulloch, (502) 589-9224, lmcculloch@tnc.org; nature.org/kentucky

The land of south-central Kentucky rolls and dips, betraying a labyrinth of caves and sink-holes just below the surface. Underneath the dimpled farm fields and woods lies a vast karst system whose Mississippian limestones were laid down more than 300 million years ago by a shallow saltwater sea. Mammoth Cave—national park, World Heritage Site and longest cave system in the world—offers a legendary entrance to this subterranean world of marine fossils and strange aquatic creatures like troglobites and sightless crayfish.

Above the Green River.

The Green River is the lifeblood of the cave ecosystem, its flows bearing food and sediment. Aptly named, the Green meanders between mossy limestone banks and tangles of sycamore, river birch and box elder. Vines of Virginia creeper hang close to the water, further deepening the green hue. Beneath the surface is a colorful world of aquatic diversity. Nearly 150 species of fish—more than in all of Europe—and 70 species of mussels make the Green the fourth-most biologically diverse river in the world.

The life forms that gather on the river's rocky shoals and ply its clear waters have been increasingly threatened since 1969, when the Green River's seasonal floods were tamed behind the concrete wall of the Green River Dam. Today seven species of mussels are federally listed as endangered; fish and crayfish have been hurt as well. Because the dam releases too little water in spring and more water in fall than would have coursed downstream in an undammed river, the Green's natural flows are out of balance and the ecosystem's health has faltered.

In 1999 The Nature Conservancy went to the source of that ecological stress: the U.S. Army Corps of Engineers, the dam's operator. Their discussions led to an agreement by which the Army Corps will modify its water releases from the dam to improve the ecological health of the river. The

Drapery Room, Mammoth Cave National Park.

agreement in turn engendered a similar national-level cooperative partnership between the Conservancy and the Army Corps.

conservation profile

targets river flows, karst systems, mussels like the clubshell and ring pink, fish like the spotted darter and splendid darter, Indiana and gray bats, bottlebrush crayfish

stresses altered hydrological regime, sedimentation from agricultural practices, incompatible rural development

strategies modify dam operations, restore ecosystems, secure conservation easements, encourage conservation management of private land

results agreement with Army Corps of Engineers secures ecologically compatible water releases from the Green River Dam

CYPRESS ISLAND
Louisiana

Life among the bayous and rivers of Acadiana country is intimately connected to floodwaters unleashed by the mighty Mississippi River.

location 60 miles west of Baton Rouge

ecoregion Mississippi River Alluvial Plain

project size 20,000 acres

preserves Cypress Island

partners Louisiana Department of Wildlife and Fisheries, U.S. Army Corps of Engineers, Louisiana Department of Natural Resources, St. Martin Parish, local landowners

natural events arrival of 10,000–30,000 pairs of water birds, spring; alligator mating and nesting, summer

information Cindy Brown, Acadiana program manager, (225) 338-1040, ext. 216, cbrown@tnc.org; nature.org/louisiana

In southern Louisiana's Acadiana country, alligators travel quietly among bayous and swamps, eyes raised just above the water's surface. Beaver and nutria, an exotic animal originally from South America, splash and forage in rivers and streams. The wildlife is viewed best from a pirogue, or "cajun canoe," originally created by the Acadians—explorers from Canada—to navigate the dense forest's

Bald cypress.

watery highways. These flat-bottomed boats are fashioned out of cypress logs from the swampy forests like those of Cypress Island.

Here on the Mississippi River floodplain's western edge, thousands of years of flooding have cultivated a wet forest of oak, bald cypress and tupelo. Shallow waterways, protruding tree roots, Spanish moss and thick vegetation evoke images of the distant Amazon. It is a unique habitat that attracts many warm-water fish, reptiles, amphibians and mammals, and serves as a migratory flyway for 60 percent of all U.S. bird species.

With spring's earliest blooms appear thousands of pairs of wading birds that make Cypress Island one of the largest rookeries in North America. Little blue herons, snowy egrets, white ibis and roseate spoonbills spend the summer building nests and raising their young among cypress branches and button bush. Joining the chorus is the hammering of red-bellied woodpeckers and the legendary hooting of the barred owl. Ruby-throated hummingbirds and red-winged blackbirds move in with the cooler weather, as summer residents migrate farther south.

Over the past 200 years, Louisiana and nearby states have seen their floodplain forests shrink from 24 million unbroken acres to 4.9 million scattered acres, leading to a decline in many of the birds that visit to rest and raise their young. Floods are essential to the forests' survival, as they bear nutrients and trigger tree regeneration. But levee construction, dredging and channelization along the Mississippi have limited the amount of natural flooding these forests

receive. In response, The Nature Conservancy established the Cypress Island Advisory Council to produce a blueprint that will guide land use in the vicinity, including flood-control projects and our own efforts to restore the area's extraordinary wetland forests.

American alligator.

PASCAGOULA WATERSHED
Mississippi

A strong sense of heritage and local activism has allowed the Pascagoula River to remain the only free-flowing waterway of its size in the lower 48.

location 15 miles north of Biloxi

ecoregion East Gulf Coastal Plain

project size 9,600 square miles

preserves Charles M. Deaton, Herman Murrah

public lands Pascagoula River Wildlife Management Area, Ward Bayou Management Area, Mississippi Coastal Preserves, Mississippi Sandhill Crane National Wildlife Refuge, Grand Bay National Wildlife Refuge, DeSoto National Forest

partners Pascagoula River Basin Alliance, Audubon Society, Mississippi Departments of Wildlife and Fisheries, Environmental Quality and Marine Resources, U.S. Fish and Wildlife Service

conservancy initiatives Freshwater

natural events spring and fall bird migrations; Gulf sturgeon discovery field trips, summer

information Alice Perry, (334) 865-5244, aperry@tnc.org; nature.org/mississippi

Those who have fallen under the spell of its poignant history and mossy banks, like many Mississippi natives, call the Pascagoula the "Singing River." According to legend, the peace-loving Pascagoula Indian tribe sang as they walked hand-in-hand into the river to avoid fighting with the invading Biloxi tribe. So the story goes, on a quiet night you can still hear them singing their death chant

Swamp forest of cypress and tupelo gum.

The Pascagoula watershed also rings with the calls of 327 species of birds that breed among the sprawling cypress-tupelo swamps, oxbow lakes and pine ridges. Wading birds croon as they forage throughout the bayous. Graceful swallow-tailed kites search for prey among the extensive bottomland forest. The distinctive clattering bugle of the rare Mississippi sandhill crane is heard as it fashions a home in the pine savanna.

Over the years, discordant intrusions from timber harvesting, shipbuilding, oil and gas production and even tourism have threatened the songbirds and other melodies of the Pascagoula. In 1974, The Nature Conservancy and other dedicated conservationists rallied to bring 35,000 acres of the watershed under public protection. This "grassroots epic," as E.O. Wilson called it, led to a present-day river corridor buffered by almost 70,000 acres of public and private conservation lands.

Today competing demands for water to quench a growing population's thirst and to nourish the river's natural bounty leave the watershed hanging in the balance. The Conservancy continues to play a role in maintaining the grassroots momentum fueled almost 30 years ago, most recently through our role in establishing the Pascagoula River Basin Alliance. Created in 2001, this broad-based coalition promotes the ecological, economic and

Great egret.

cultural health of the watershed through the research, communication and action needed to ensure that the Pascagoula remains one of the nation's best-preserved river systems.

conservation profile

targets Gulf sturgeon, striped bass, swallow-tailed kite, yellow-blotched map turtle, pearl darter, bottomland hardwood forest, longleaf pine upland, tidal marsh, seagrass beds

stresses proposed dams, dredging, water withdrawal, forest conversion, incompatible silviculture, habitat fragmentation, mining

strategies build conservation alliances, strengthen local partner organizations, acquire land, secure conservation easements, restore ecosystems through fire management, promote compatible development and ecotourism, engage community

results 70,000 acres under public and private conservation protection; Pascagoula River Basin Alliance established in 2001

ROANOKE RIVER
North Carolina

Floods are the life force that sustains this bottomland hardwood forest and, in turn, the local economy.

location 100 miles east of Raleigh

ecoregion Mid-Atlantic Coastal Plain

project size 150,000 acres

preserves Camassia Slopes, Devil's Gut, Larkspur Ridge

public lands Roanoke River National Wildlife Refuge, Roanoke River Game Lands

partners U.S. Fish and Wildlife Service, North Carolina Wildlife Resources Commission, North Carolina Department of Environment and Natural Resources, Roanoke River Partners, Roanoke River Basin Association

conservancy initiatives Freshwater, Global Climate Change, Marine

natural events neotropical songbird migration, spring; blossoming trees and wildflowers, late March–early April

information Scott Belan, (919) 403-8558, ext. 1013, sbelan@tnc.org; nature.org/northcarolina

Near the end of its 400-mile journey from the Blue Ridge Mountains to Albemarle Sound, the Roanoke River winds a lazy course through North Carolina's coastal plain, spreading wide among moss-draped tupelos and the knees of ancient bald cypress. Muddy channels and blackwater tributaries conceal the largest and most diverse collection of migratory fish in the

Canoeing the Roanoke.

mid-Atlantic. In 2000 the endangered short-nosed sturgeon was discovered at the mouth of the Roanoke, possibly signifying the existence of a small breeding population of the rare fish.

Roanoke is a Native American word meaning "river of death," a reference to the dramatic floods that have often taken human lives over the centuries. But the Roanoke is also a river of life, for these same floods supply valuable nutrients to sustain the loamy bottomland hardwood forest supporting North Carolina's healthiest black bear population, as well as river otter, bobcat and myriad amphibian, reptile and insect species. This swampy sanctuary also serves as a natural aviary for as many as 214 bird species. Barred owls and bald eagles patrol treetop perches, while long-legged egret and heron tiptoe through the muddy shallows below. The Roanoke beckons 88 breeding birds, including 44 neotropical migratory songbirds that visit every spring.

In the late 1990s a paddling trail was designed to give access to this vast, watery landscape and demonstrate the value of protecting ecosystems to generate ecotourism dollars. Secluded camping platforms and more than 200 miles of rivers and creeks create a unique wilderness experience that is gaining international attention.

But this wilderness could be in jeopardy if the natural water flows of the river are not restored. A series of upstream dams flattens out high and low flows and threatens to degrade the rich ecosystem. By preserving the flow requirements of a naturally functioning river, The Nature Conservancy is demonstrating to private power companies and the U.S. Army Corps of Engineers how their dams can continue producing hydropower and controlling floods while allowing water releases that mimic natural floods.

Wood duck.

conservation profile

targets old-growth water tupelo, old-growth bald cypress, short-nosed sturgeon, black bear, cerulean warbler, wood duck, bald eagle

stresses dams that interfere with natural floods, habitat fragmentation, overharvesting of timber

strategies restore ecosystems, modify dam operations, acquire land, secure conservation easements, promote ecotourism

results 60,000 acres in conservation management; working with U.S. Army Corps of Engineers to improve dam operations; Roanoke River Paddle Trail established

ACE BASIN
South Carolina

Private landowners continue a tradition of land and water stewardship at this large, pristine estuary, known fondly as "the Pearl of the Low Country."

location 30 miles south of Charleston

ecoregion South Atlantic Coastal Plain

project size 350,000 acres

preserves Bailey Island

public lands ACE Basin National Estuarine Research Reserve, ACE Basin National Wildlife Refuge, Bear Island Wildlife Management Area, Donnelley Wildlife Management Area, Edisto Beach State Park, Hunting Island State Park

partners private landowners, Ducks Unlimited, U.S. Fish and Wildlife Service, S.C. Department of Natural Resources, Lowcountry Open Land Trust, Nemours Wildlife Foundation, Mead Westvaco Corporation

natural events loggerhead turtle nesting, late spring and early summer; wood storks arrive in March, peak numbers in spring and summer

information Gina Whelchel, (803) 254-9049, gwhelchel@tnc.org nature.org/southcarolina

With its meandering blackwater rivers, dense cypress swamps and teeming estuary, the ACE Basin recalls a fertile Southern coast that, well over a century ago, fueled dreams of glory for ambitious rice plantation owners. Men like Nathanial Heyward, who owned 17 plantations in the basin, led a rice boom that fed much of the nation from 1850 to 1860. When the boom ended, wealthy individuals purchased the decaying estates, restored the rice fields and water

Moonrise, Edisto River.

management systems to attract waterfowl, and created private hunting retreats.

The ACE Basin remains one of the largest undeveloped estuaries on the East Coast Formed by the confluence of three undammed and free-flowing rivers—the Ashepoo, Combahee and Edisto, thus the name "ACE"—the basin encompasses a remarkable web of ecosystems, from upland pine forests to bottomland hardwoods, from barrier beaches to freshwater marshes.

A wealth of wildlife abounds: alligators, endangered loggerhead turtles, bobcat and mink. During the early 1980s, the ACE Basin played a critical role in the recovery of the southern bald eagle and the wood stork. With the help of biologists, their populations rebounded from just a handful of nests to more than 100.

Private landowners have led the effort to conserve this special place. Voluntary conservation easements have protected some 64,000 acres of private property. The Nature Conservancy holds 20 percent of these easements. We also helped charter the ACE Basin Task Force, a coalition of businesses, landowners and private organizations taking the lead to promote traditional land uses like farming and forestry while protecting the estuary and the shoreline from strong development pressure.

Wood storks on nest.

conservation profile

targets migratory waterfowl, wood stork, southern bald eagle, loggerhead turtle; maritime, longleaf pine and bottomland hardwood forests

stresses incompatible residential and commercial development

strategies acquire land, secure conservation easements, promote compatible development, build conservation alliances

results 150,000 acres in conservation management; ACE Basin Task Force launched

CUMBERLAND PLATEAU
Tennessee

A once-remote wilderness is now attracting increased recreational use and second-home development, placing new pressures on the world's longest hardwood-forested plateau.

location between Nashville and Knoxville

ecoregion Cumberlands Southern Ridge and Valley

project size 3.5 million acres

preserves Tally Wilderness, Jim Creek, Obed River, David Carter Tract, Keel Mountain

public lands Big South Fork National River and Recreation Area, Frozen Head State Park and Natural Area, Catoosa Wildlife Management Area, Pickett State Park and Forest, Obed Wild and Scenic River, Fern Cave National Wildlife Refuge, Skyline Wildlife Management Area, Monte Sano State Park, Franklin State Forest, Carter Caves State Natural Area

partners National Park Service, U.S. Forest Service, U.S. Fish and Wildlife Service, Tennessee Wildlife Resources Agency, land trusts

conservancy initiatives Freshwater

natural events bats emerge from caves, late spring and summer

information Gina Hancock, (615) 383-9909, ghancock@tnc.org; nature.org/tennessee

Frozen Head State Park and Natural Area.

Stretching across eastern Tennessee from Alabama north into Kentucky, the Cumberland Plateau rises more than 1,000 feet above the Tennessee River Valley to a vast tableland of sandstone and shale dating as far back as 500 million years. Carved over time by flowing water, the plateau today is a labyrinth of rocky ridges and verdant ravines dropping steeply into gorges laced with waterfalls and caves, ferns and rhododendrons.

The Cumberland Plateau's rivers and streams sustain some of the country's greatest variety of fish and mollusk species, and ravines and deep hollows are among the richest wildflower areas in southern Appalachia. John Muir was one of the first naturalists to document the natural bounty of this, the world's longest expanse of hardwood-forested plateau. He memorialized his crossing of the Cumberland Plateau in the book, *A Thousand Mile Walk to the Gulf.*

For thousands of years, the Cumberland Plateau remained a remote and rugged paradise. Infertile soil and rough terrain discouraged early settlement. Artifacts found in caves and rock shelters suggest Mississippian and later Cherokee hunters camped here but never established permanent dwellings. English, Scotch-Irish and German settlers staked their claims mostly in the valleys and ventured to the plateau only sporadically to mine coal and harvest timber. Today, however, the plateau is not so remote. Increased recreational use, especially by all-terrain vehicles, and a growing demand for idyllic retirement locales have placed new pressures on it.

Significant tracts on the Cumberland Plateau have already been set aside in state parks and wildlife management areas. But only a few virgin remnants of the region's once-dense hardwood forests stand in isolated hollows. The remaining second- and third-growth trees comprise the largest unprotected forest in the Southeast. At the same time, residential development continues to infiltrate previously untouched areas, threatening habitat and water quality. The Nature Conservancy has responded by forming partnerships with

Obed Wild and Scenic River.

local land trusts and resource agencies to protect more land and promote compatible land-use practices.

conservation profile

targets cerulean warbler, white fringeless orchid, temperate hardwood forests, black bear, more than 20 species of mollusk, Cumberland rosemary

stresses incompatible residential development and forestry practices

strategies acquire land, secure conservation easements, promote ecologically compatible land use practices, build conservation alliances, protect water quality, restore ecosystems, encourage conservation management of public lands

results more than 3,000 acres in conservation management; Pickett State Forest protected from development and bisection

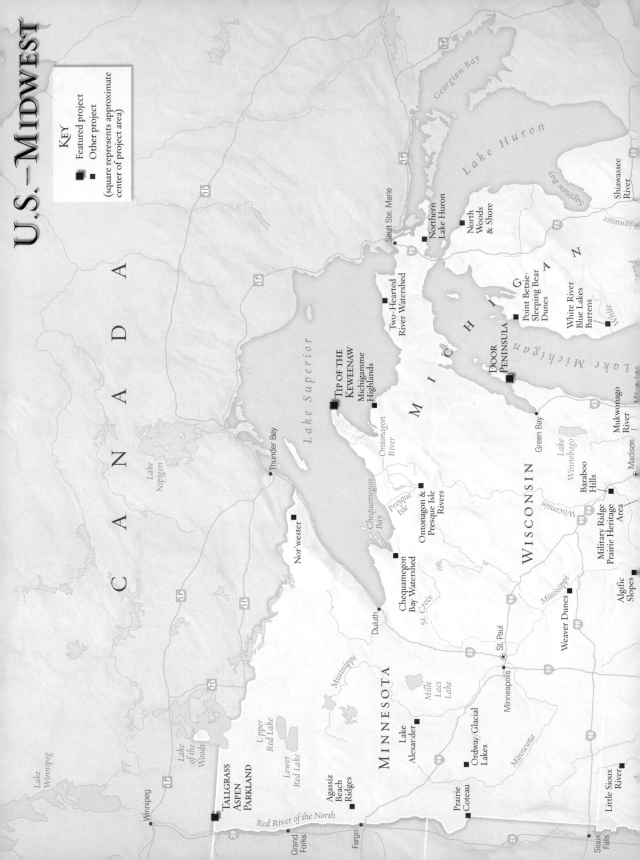

U.S.–MIDWEST

KEY

■ Featured project
■ Other project

(square represents approximate center of project area)

CANADA

Winnipeg

Lake Winnipeg

Lake of the Woods

Lake Nipigon

Thunder Bay

Nor'wester

Duluth

Lake Superior

Chequamegon Bay

Presque Isle

Ontonagon River

Sault Ste. Marie

Georgian Bay

Lake Huron

Saginaw Bay

Shiawassee River

Northern Lake Huron

North Woods & Shore

MICHIGAN

Two-Hearted River Watershed

TIP OF THE KEWEENAW
Michigamme Highlands

Point Betsie-Sleeping Bear Dunes

White River Blue Lakes Barrens

White

Lake Michigan

DOOR PENINSULA

Green Bay

Lake Winnebago

Mukwonago River

Madison

Baraboo Hills

Wisconsin

WISCONSIN

Military Ridge Prairie Heritage Area

Algific Slopes

Ontonagon & Presque Isle Rivers

Chequamegon Bay Watershed

St. Croix

Mississippi

MINNESOTA

Lake Alexander

Mille Lacs Lake

Ordway/Glacial Lakes

Minnesota

Weaver Dunes

St. Paul

Minneapolis

TALLGRASS ASPEN PARKLAND

Upper Red Lake

Lower Red Lake

Agassiz Beach Ridges

Prairie Coteau

Red River of the North

Little Sioux River

Grand Forks

Fargo

Sioux Falls

Winnipeg

ILLINOIS RIVER
Illinois

Imitating natural processes from more than a century ago is the remedy to restoring a river too long regulated by man-made structures.

location 50 miles southwest of Chicago to confluence with the Mississippi

ecoregion Central Tallgrass Prairie

project size 273 river miles; more than 250,000 acres

preserves Spunky Bottoms, Emiquon, Lake Senachwine, Chinquapin Bluffs

public lands Meredosia, Emiquon and Chautauqua national wildlife refuges; state fish and wildlife areas including Anderson Lake, Banner Marsh, Rice Lake

partners U.S. Army Corps of Engineers, U.S. Fish and Wildlife Service, Natural Resources Conservation Service, Illinois Department of Natural Resources, The Wetlands Initiative

conservancy initiatives Freshwater

natural events migrations of songbirds, waterfowl and white pelicans, spring and fall; Havana Eagle Days, February

information Rebecca Girvin-Argon, (312) 580-2153, rgirvin-argon@tnc.org; nature.org/illinois

Spunky Bottoms.

The seasonal rise and retreat of water—a river's pulse—was once the natural rhythm of large-floodplain rivers like the Nile, Amazon, Mississippi and Illinois before they were dammed, diked and otherwise tamed. When a river's pulse disappears, the surrounding ecosystem suffers. This is what happened a little more than a century ago on the Illinois River, cutting east to west across north-central Illinois. Prior to that, much of its 273-mile-long floodplain was undeveloped, and the river could spread unhindered during floods.

For centuries the natural rhythms of the Illinois nourished generations of

Native Americans with abundant waterfowl, fish, mussels, deer and rich soils. Early American explorers encountered a profusion of paddlefish, gar and sturgeon—ancient fishes that predate the dinosaurs. Migrating ducks visited by the

millions. It supported more freshwater mussels per mile than any river on the continent.

Today 90 percent of the state's population lives within an Illinois River basin that has lost 85 percent of its wetlands. Despite the ecological damage wrought by dams and levees, the National Research Council identified the Illinois as one of three large-floodplain river systems in the lower 48 with the potential to be restored to some semblance of their outstanding biological past.

To reverse the effects of more than a century of diverted flow and stifled rhythms, The Nature Conservancy is working to restore four Illinois River sites that will collectively offer a model of how mimicking natural ecological processes can resuscitate large-floodplain river systems. One of those sites is Emiquon. Once draped by canopy forest and carpeted with prairie and marsh, levees have created a floodplain of row crops here.

With The Nature Conservancy's purchase of 7,600 acres spanning five river miles, Emiquon became the largest wetland restoration project in the country, outside of Florida. Our conservation plan aims to re-establish

American white pelicans.

natural ecological processes on the Illinois in the hope that lessons can be applied to the restoration and management of other large-floodplain river systems around the world.

conservation profile

targets ancient fish like paddlefish and sturgeon, freshwater mussels, floodplain plants like decurrent false aster, red-shouldered hawk, river otter

stresses habitat loss and degradation, altered hydrological regime, poor water quality

strategies restore ecosystems, modify dam operations, engage community in natural resource management, protect water quality, acquire land, secure conservation easements, build conservation alliances, promote ecotourism

results more than 7,750 acres acquired for restoration

KANKAKEE SANDS
Indiana

Although the splendor of the prairies that once covered parts of Indiana and Illinois is relegated to history books, the promise of a new chapter has emerged.

location 70 miles south of Chicago

ecoregion Central Tallgrass Prairie

project size 25,000 acres

preserves Efroymson Restoration at Kankakee Sands, Conrad Station Savanna, Rix Wildlife Sanctuary

public lands Willow Slough Fish and Wildlife Area, Bill Barnes, Conrad Savanna and Beaver Lake state nature preserves, Iroquois County State Wildlife Area

partners Indiana Departments of Natural Resources and Environmental Management, Natural Resource Conservation Service, North American Waterfowl Management Plan, National Fish and Wildlife Foundation, universities and colleges in Indiana and Illinois, Indiana Heritage Trust, Lilly Endowment, Waterfowl USA

conservancy initiatives Global Climate Change

natural events migration of arctic shorebirds, spring

information Betsy Smith, (317) 951-8818, betsy_smith@tnc.org; nature.org/indiana

In the 1800s, horizon-to-horizon expanses of prairie carpeted northwestern Indiana and the sandy soil surrounding Beaver Lake, once the largest freshwater lake in Indiana. Thimble weed, wool grass, coneflower and saddle-high seas of waving big bluestem concealed a world that included grasshopper sparrows and leopard frogs. Tundra swans, meadowlarks and Canada geese rested in marshes of switchgrass on their migrations. This thick maze of grass and wildflowers was also famous for hiding horse thieves and counterfeiters.

Today the landscape known as Kankakee Sands would be unrecognizable to the

Kankakee savanna in bloom.

outlaws who hid out among the tall grasses. By 1900, Beaver Lake was drained to plant corn, beans and wheat; surrounding marsh, native grasses, wildflowers and other prairie plants were also plowed under to be replaced by agricultural fields. Only scattered remnants of prairie remain—specifically, a thousand acres of the 2 million acres of prairie that once rolled across this part of Indiana. But these small, isolated leftovers lack the sheer mass of open prairie needed to sustain birds, reptiles, amphibians and the ecosystem itself.

To reverse the decline and heal this signature landscape, The Nature Conservancy is participating in the only sand prairie restoration effort east of the Mississippi River. Conservation work began in 1997 with the purchase of 7,200 acres of land that had been farmed for 100 years. Although full restoration will take years to achieve, it will be worth the wait to recapture a small portion of what was witnessed in 1835.

The greatest challenge in the restoration effort is collecting, drying and separating enough seed—often finer than talcum powder—to plant up to 500 acres per year with native vegetation. We are using historical accounts to identify native species and have established a nursery capable of producing the necessary amount of seed. Satellite imaging and research have helped determine where and when to reintroduce these native plants. And equipment usually used to spread fertilizer has been employed to meet the grand scale of the project.

Walking sticks in prairie grasses.

conservation profile

targets native grassland prairie and savanna, plains pocket gopher, bobolink, regal fritillary butterfly, prairie fame flower, grassland birds like upland sandpipers, grasshopper sparrow, Henslow's sparrow, northern harrier

stresses agricultural conversion, hydrologic alteration, habitat loss

strategies restore ecosystems, secure conservation easements, engage community

results 9,000 acres protected surrounding the 7,200-acre restoration project; native seed nursery established; 1,600 acres restored

LOESS HILLS
Iowa

Wind and silt shaped this loess topography—considered the best in North America—but native prairies of the Loess Hills may soon be lost without fire to restore and sustain them.

location 10 minutes from Omaha, Nebraska

ecoregion Central Tallgrass Prairie

project size 100,000 acres

preserves Broken Kettle Grasslands, Folsom Point, Sioux City Prairie, McCormack Natural Area

public lands Five-Ridge Prairie, Hitchcock Nature Area, West Oak Preserve, Loess Hills State Forest, Stone State Park, Waubonsie State Park, Brickyard Hill Natural Area, Star School Hill

partners Natural Resources Conservation Service, U.S. Fish and Wildlife Service, National Park Service, Missouri Department of Conservation, Iowa Department of Natural Resources, county conservation boards, Loess Hills Alliance

conservancy initiatives Fire, Invasive Species

natural events migrating raptors, fall and spring; cut-your-own cedar Christmas tree and holiday event, early December; Loess Hills Prairie Seminar, May/June

information Ann Robinson, (515) 244-5044; arobinson@tnc.org; nature.org/iowa

Rising up 200 feet from the floodplain, the Loess Hills form a 200-mile-long wrinkled-bluff border along the Missouri River. Dry, grass-covered ridges fall off steeply into shady, moist ravines where leafy plants and mosses thrive. Loess—a soft, wind-blown silt—covers most of Iowa and is the reason for its fertile soil. But only in China and along the Rhine River do loess deposits rival the depth of Iowa's Loess Hills.

Once covered entirely in prairie grasses, the Loess Hills were described by Lewis and Clark as "bald pated" during

Atop a Loess Hills ridge.

their expedition in 1804, as they traveled upriver beneath the bluffs in their keelboats. Fifty years later, the Mormon Trail passed through these same ridges. The dugouts cut into the bluffs by west-bound Mormons as shelter from wind and weather are still evident today.

The Loess Hills' rugged topography and mix of dry soil, exposed slopes and wet hollows enable western species like yucca, cowboy's delight and skeleton weed to flourish alongside plants native to eastern states. Rare species like the ornate box turtle, bobcat and Great Plains skink make their home here. In 1984 a previously unde-scribed fern, the prairie moonwort, was discovered in these hills. The varied landscape also attracts as many as 19 species of raptors, which follow the ridgelines on their annual migrations, getting lift from the updrafts of wind rising from the slopes.

Regal fritillary on butterfly milkweed.

we will also reintroduce these ungulates as an important component of native prairie restoration.

More than a century of agricultural cultivation and accompanying fire suppression has allowed eastern red cedar, elm and dogwoods to take hold on slopes where native tallgrass prairie once grew. To return fire to the landscape and thus eliminate these invasive species, The Nature Conservancy is working with federal resource agencies and local conservation and agricultural interests to initiate a controlled burning program. Recognizing that grazing bison once helped shape the prairie, in time

conservation profile

targets butterflies like the regal fritillary, upland sandpiper, ornate box turtle, bobcat, plains pocket mouse, Great Plains skink, yucca, skeleton weed, prairie moonwort

stresses fire suppression, residential develop-ment, invasive species, inappropriate grazing, fill dirt mining

strategies acquire land, secure conservation easements, restore ecosystems through fire management, engage community in natural resource management, encourage conservation management of public land, promote ecologi-cally compatible land-use practices

results nearly 27,000 acres in conservation management; collaborative fire program launched

TIP OF THE KEWEENAW
Michigan

At the northernmost point of the Upper Peninsula, shoreline development threatens to degrade the world's largest freshwater lake and a rich forest ecosystem.

location 216 miles from Duluth, Minnesota

ecoregion Great Lakes

project size 25,000 acres

preserves Mary Macdonald Preserve at Horseshoe Harbor, East Shore Bluffs

public lands Fort Wilkins State Park, Copper Country State Forest

partners Michigan Department of Natural Resources, International Paper, Keweenaw Land Trust, Eagle Harbor Township, Grant Township

natural events Northern Lights, most visible fall and winter; thousands of migrating raptors, songbirds and shorebirds, spring and fall

information Jean Morgan, (517) 316-0300, jmorgan@tnc.org; nature.org/michigan

The tip of the Keweenaw Peninsula juts 60 miles into Lake Superior, its fingerlike extension discernible from the moon. This zenith of Michigan's Upper Peninsula is a product of volcanic activity, formed at least 1 billion years ago. Now, wave-eroded rock defines the rugged shoreline where only the hardiest vegetation withstands constant exposure to the Great Lakes' ferocious winds.

Traveling the Great Lakes Flyway, thousands of raptors gather each spring and fall on the Keweenaw's shores, among

Bette Grise Bay and Mount Houghton, Lac La Belle.

them bald eagle and peregrine falcon. Inland, waterfalls and glacial lakes punctuate forest of balsam fir, white cedar, spruce and birch. More than 900 species of plants blanket the peninsula, providing food and shelter for animals as large as black bear and moose and as small as the tawny crescent, a rare butterfly.

Known as "copper country," the Keweenaw was a booming mining hub at the turn of the century—once the largest single source of the metal in the Western Hemisphere. Copper was transported from the peninsula entirely by ship. The Keweenaw is today primarily working forestland and a summer tourist destination. Tourism-related development, especially new homes proliferating along the forested shoreline, threatens to fragment forest habitat and degrade the lake's clear waters.

White-tailed deer.

Seizing a rare opportunity to protect more than five miles of pristine shoreline and significant inland habitat, The Nature Conservancy in 2002 brokered a land transaction between International Paper and the Michigan Department of Natural Resources. Through the agreement, the state will pay $12.5 million to permanently safeguard the property. The land, previously planned for subdivision, will be open to the public for recreation and will link a Conservancy preserve with another protected area, creating a vast contiguous corridor for wildlife.

conservation profile

targets boreal forest, peatlands, alpine bistwort and pale Indian paintbrush, rayless mountain ragwort, black bear, peregrine falcon, tawny crescent

stresses incompatible shoreline development, incompatible forestry practices

strategies acquire land, encourage conservation management of public and private forest, secure public funding, engage community in natural resource management

results more than 10,000 acres in conservation management, including five miles of lake shoreline

TALLGRASS ASPEN PARKLAND

Minnesota

Large contiguous blocks of parkland are needed to maintain the delicate balance of woodland and prairie in this dynamic system.

location 85 miles north of Grand Forks, North Dakota

ecoregion Northern Tallgrass Prairie

project size 700 square miles

preserves Norway Dunes, Wallace C. Dayton Conservation and Wildlife Area

public lands four wildlife management areas (Caribou, Beaches Lake, Skull Lake and Roseau River); Gardenton Community Pasture, Canada

partners Minnesota Department of Natural Resources, U.S. Fish and Wildlife Service, Manitoba Department of Natural Resources, Nature Conservancy of Canada

conservancy initiatives Fire

natural events sandhill crane migration and nesting, May–October; large breeding colony of Franklin's gulls, summer; flowering of western prairie fringed orchid, first two weeks in July

information Beth Hayden, (612) 331-0702, bhayden@tnc.org; nature.org/minnesota

Aspen on the prairie parkland.

Islands of trembling aspen and balsam poplar dot the sweeping expanse of the Tallgrass Aspen Parkland, a vast patchwork of trees, brush, prairie and wetlands extending from northwest Minnesota into Manitoba, Canada. This woodland-prairie mosaic remains much unchanged since 1857, when explorer Henry Hind

wrote about "hummocks of aspen and willow" on ancient lake ridges. Here the prairie of America's heartland transitions to the conifer forests of the north.

Some 10,000 years ago, a mile-high sheet of ice shaped this land. Its successor, Glacial Lake Agassiz, leveled the land, its shoreline leaving behind sand and gravel beach ridges that rise 25 feet above the plains, winding northward. The Sioux and Chippewa Indians used these ridges in their journeys. The most prominent of the ridge trails became the Pembina Trail, a major 19th-century fur trading route between Winnipeg and Minneapolis-St. Paul.

The arrival of railroad service to northwestern Minnesota rendered the trail obsolete. In 1879 the U.S. government granted a checkerboard of square-mile tracts to a railroad company to finance the construction of the rail. Though much of this prairie was purchased and converted to cropland, vast blocks of aspen parkland were deemed poorly suited to agriculture and were later protected by state wildlife officials and The Nature Conservancy.

Today these assembled remnants of parkland are large enough—thousands of acres in some places—to allow for the dynamic interplay of drought, flooding, fire and natural recovery that shaped the ecosystem. Here the Conservancy and our partners, both in the United States and in Canada, focus on ecosystem restoration, primarily a careful prescription of fire that prevents forests from taking root while maintaining characteristic shrubs and woodland patches among the tallgrass prairie.

Prairie blazing star.

conservation profile

targets northern tallgrass prairie, peatlands, aspen/oak savanna, floodplain forests, timber wolf, moose, elk, black bear, great gray owl, yellow rail, LeConte's sparrow, sandhill crane, western prairie fringed orchid

stresses invasive plants, reduced frequency of fire, drainage of wetlands and channelization of rivers, habitat conversion to agriculture, grazing practices, road construction

strategies acquire land, secure conservation easements, restore ecosystems through fire, grazing, water and forest management, encourage conservation management of public land

results 350,000 acres in conservation management; cross-border prescribed burns conducted

LOWER OZARKS
Missouri

Whether in streams, springs or rivers, water is the lifeblood of the Lower Ozarks, creating a watershed rich in unique but imperiled communities.

location south-central Missouri; three hours from St. Louis

ecoregion Ozarks

project size 2.1 million acres

preserves Chilton Creek, Thorny Mountain, Shut-in Mountain Fens, Grasshopper Hollow, Bat Cave

public lands Mark Twain National Forest, Ozark National Scenic Riverways

partners Missouri Department of Conservation, Missouri Department of Natural Resources, National Park Service, U.S. Forest Service, University of Missouri, Bat Conservation International, National Wild Turkey Federation, New York Botanical Gardens

conservancy initiatives Fire, Freshwater

natural events cold-water canoeing in summer; displays of fall foliage, October

information Fred Fox, project manager, (573) 323-8790; ffox@tnc.org; nature.org/missouri

Beneath the ancient hills of the Lower Ozarks, water is plentiful, but often unpredictable. Streams sink into their own beds or squeeze into narrow rocky gorges. Springs burst up suddenly from underground torrents, issuing

hundreds of millions of gallons of water a day. Frequent rapids make the Eleven Point and Current rivers a mecca for canoeists from around the world.

The riot of water aboveground reflects similar activity below. A complicated natural

Big Spring, Ozark National Scenic Riverways.

plumbing system carries cool, clear groundwater for miles, recharging streams and springs. The underground flow also creates unique fen communities—wet, stony ground of grasses and sedges, knee-deep in water, that harbors rare salamanders, wood frogs and dragonflies. Sprawling hardwood forests—the largest solid expanse of woodland in the Midwest—thrive here as well, providing critical habitat for several species of migratory and nesting birds.

Despite this richness, two of the region's native communities—canebrakes and shortleaf pines—are all but gone today. Canebrakes, a form of bamboo that grows along the Current River, were decimated by open-range grazing practices, now illegal, and fire suppression. Most of the shortleaf pines were gone by 1920, felled by a lumber boom in the late 19th century that fueled what was once the world's largest sawmill. Fire suppression and logging remain threats to the Lower Ozarks' diversity, along with land conversion for pasture and development.

The Nature Conservancy has joined forces with federal agencies and many partners to restore these two habitats and protect the region's natural systems. With the Mark Twain National Forest, we identified a handful of sites that still harbor shortleaf pine and have the potential to be restored. We began work at the first site in

Fire pink and phlox.

2002 by removing hardwoods and conducting prescribed burns, and eventually plan to reintroduce the red-cockaded woodpecker and brownheaded nuthatch, two native birds that long ago left these woods. Along the Current River, we are working with the National Park Service to restore three large cane stands, providing crucial nesting habitat for the Swainson's warbler.

conservation profile

targets canebrakes, shortleaf pine, Swainson's warbler, fen complexes, Hine's emerald dragonfly, four-toed salamander, wood frog, gray bat, igneous glade complex, Ozark hellbender, Current River orangethroat darter

stresses fire suppression, land conversion to pasture and homes, clear-cut logging

strategies acquire land, promote ecologically compatible land-use practices, protect water quality, restore ecosystems, engage community, restore ecosystems through fire management

results more than 80,000 acres of upland timber protected; fire reintroduced at Thorny Mountain, opening corridors for collared lizards to migrate from Stegall Mountain

EDGE OF APPALACHIA
Ohio

In the age-old forests of southern Ohio, an innovative conservation tool aims to restore a slice of Appalachia and reduce the threat of global warming.

location 90 miles east of Cincinnati, 120 miles south of Columbus

ecoregions Interior Low Plateau, Western Allegheny Plateau

project size 130,000 acres

preserves Strait Creek, Blue Jay Barrens

public lands Shawnee State Park and Forest, Ohio State Natural Areas and Preserves, Adams Lake Prairie, Chaparral Prairie, Davis Memorial, Indigo Barrent and Whipple Preserve

partners Cincinnati Museum Center at Union Terminal, Planning Adams County's Tomorrow, Ohio Department of Forestry, Appalachian Ohio Regional Investment Coalition, Farm Fresh Growers Association, Ohio State University Extension, U.S. Department of Agriculture

conservancy initiatives Global Climate Change

natural events prairie blooms, late summer; Prairie Daze festival, August

information Lucy Miller, (937) 544-1022, lmiller@tnc.org; nature.org/ohio

Turkey Creek Lake, Shawnee State Park and Forest.

On the periphery of the Appalachian escarpment in southern Ohio, the Edge of Appalachia embraces unbroken stands of oak, tulip, American beech, yellow buckeye and sugar maple that echo with the wild turkey's clangorous call. Brilliant wildflowers, including great white trillium and rare nodding mandarin, carpet the understory.

Reliant on these dense, deciduous forests are 60 species of birds that winter in the tropical forests of Belize, returning to this collection of 11 preserves each spring. Wood thrushes, summer tanagers, hooded warblers, orchard orioles and ruby-throated hummingbirds journey here to nest and raise their young.

The 13,000-acre Richard and Lucile Durrell Edge of Appalachia Preserve System was inspired by the ecologist E. Lucy Braun and named for two of her dedicated students. Their passion for the pastoral but rugged landscape of rolling meadows, giant promontories, waterfalls, streams and remnant patches of prairie persisting on cliffs and narrow ridges led to early protection efforts in this region. In 1959, The Nature Conservancy and the Cincinnati Museum of Natural History and Science established this preserve system informally known as "The Edge."

Today the Conservancy's work at The Edge is innovative and far-reaching. Together with Cinergy Corp. and neighboring Indiana, we are reforesting 925 acres of degraded habitat in Ohio and Indiana with 300,000 trees. This climate action project, an approach pioneered by the Conservancy, establishes more forest to absorb carbon dioxide—a greenhouse gas—released from Cinergy's power plants. The result will be 54,496 metric tons of carbon stored in the forests of The Edge and Indiana. Another key conservation partnership is with the Programme for Belize's Rio Bravo Conservation and Management Area in Belize, aimed at protecting the birds, both migratory and resident, of two forests half a hemisphere apart.

North American wild turkey.

conservation profile

targets unfragmented forest, exposed dolomite cliffs and promontories, remnant prairie, tall larkspur, ear-leaf foxglove, green salamander, Allegheny woodrat

stresses incompatible logging, woody plant invasion, erosion, second home development

strategies restore ecosystems through reforestation and fire management, promote compatible development and ecotourism, engage community, acquire land, secure conservation easements

results 250 acres reforested along the eroding stream bank of Ohio Brush Creek

DOOR PENINSULA
Wisconsin

Jutting north into Lake Michigan, the Door Peninsula's rugged coastline and thick forests beckoned early sailors and continue to draw thousands of visitors each year.

location 50 miles northeast of Green Bay

ecoregion Great Lakes

project size 190,000 acres

preserves Bay Shore Blufflands, Mink River Estuary, Kangaroo Lake, Meridian Park, North Bay, Shivering Sands

public lands five state parks; multiple federal lands including Green Bay Islands Wildlife Refuge and Plum, Pilot and Cana islands; Toft Point and Central Peninsula owned by the University of Wisconsin

partners Door County Land Trust, The Ridges Sanctuary, Ducks Unlimited, Wisconsin Department of Natural Resources, U.S. Fish and Wildlife Service, University of Wisconsin at Green Bay, Illinois Natural History Survey, the Green Fund

natural events neotropical migratory songbirds arrive to feed, mid-May; stunning orchid display, early June; salmon, trout and bass fishing, summer

information Mary Donahue, (608) 251-8140, mdonahue@tnc.org; nature.org/wisconsin

It is easy to imagine the Door Peninsula, with its 100-foot bluffs and rocky headlands, inspiring a mixture of awe, relief and terror in early sailors on the Great Lakes. To arrive safely, captains had to navigate the dangerous currents between the tip of the peninsula and Washington Island. So many perished that the French called the channel *Portes des Mortes*—"Death's Door"—thus giving both

Rocky shoreline, Lake Michigan.

peninsula and county their current names. More light-houses line the complex shoreline of Door County than any other county in the United States.

Once on land, however, sailors were met with a rich abundance. In spring and summer dozens of different native orchids burst into bloom. Ancient dwarf white cedars grow slowly out from the rocky face of the western bluffs, never getting large and heavy enough to collapse. Conifer forests fringe wetlands that harbor unique species like the Hine's emerald dragonfly, believed to be extinct for 40 years before its stronghold here was rediscovered.

Hine's emerald dragonfly.

This rich diversity attracts increasing numbers of tourists and new residents to the peninsula each year. With this influx of people, however, have come rural development and pollution, both of which threaten fragile wetlands and the plants and animals that depend on them. Exotic species invasions are a pervasive threat as well.

The Nature Conservancy has been working to protect the Door Peninsula since the early 1960s, when we helped The Ridges Sanctuary, a National Natural Landmark, acquire critical acreage. Land acquisition and conservation easements have remained a key element of our strategy here, and we have acquired seven preserves totaling more than 3,000 acres. We manage these

properties with the help of a cadre of dedicated volunteers. We also work with local landowners to promote ecologically compatible land management techniques.

conservation profile

targets native orchids like yellow lady's slipper and ram's-head lady's slipper, dwarf lake iris, Hine's emerald dragonfly, sand ridge and swale wetlands, marl fens, lowland white cedar swamps

stresses rural residential development, exotic species, improper forest management, agricultural runoff

strategies acquire land and easements, promote ecologically sound public policies, raise public funding for conservation, engage community in natural resource management, combat invasive species

results protected 3,000 acres; helped found the Green Fund to raise money for land protection

U.S.—CENTRAL

CANADA

KEY
- ■ Featured project
- ▪ Other project

(square represents approximate center of project area)

CANADA

Lake Superior

MINNESOTA

Duluth

St. Croix

St. Paul
Minneapolis

WISCONSIN

Madison

Mississippi

ILLINOIS

Springfield

St. Louis

Des Moines

IOWA

Council Bluffs

Mississippi

MISSOURI

Jefferson City

Kansas City

Marais des Cygnes

Missouri

Red River of the North

Grand Forks

Grand Forks Prairie

Fargo

SHEYENNE DELTA

Sheyenne

Prairie Coteau

James

Sioux Falls

Missouri

Omaha

Lincoln

Eastern Saline Wetlands

Rulo Bluffs/ Loess Hills

Topeka

FLINT HILLS

Kansas

NORTH DAKOTA

Missouri Coteau

Missouri River

Lake Sakakawea

Killdeer Mountains Little Missouri Badlands

Bismarck

Ordway

Lake Oahe

Pierre

SOUTH DAKOTA

Cheyenne

Moreau River

Moreau

Northern Hills Spring Creeks

Rapid City

Wind Cave/ Custer Prairie

CHEYENNE RIVER CANYONS

Badlands National Park Complex

Pine Escarpment

Niobrara

Middle Niobrara River Valley

Sandhills

Western Saline Wetlands

NEBRASKA

Grand Island

PLATTE RIVER

Platte

Rainwater Basin

Republican

Sandsage Prairie

N. Platte

KANSAS

Central Kansas

Smoky Hills

Smoky Hill

Chalk Breaks

Arkansas River Sandsage

G r e a t

P l a i n s

MONTANA

Little Missouri

Belle Fourche

WYOMING

Cheyenne

N. Platte

COLORADO

Denver

Arkansas

S. Platte

R o c k y   M o u

Missouri

FLINT HILLS
Kansas

The same forces that shaped the North American tallgrass prairie for millennia—
fire and grazing—are the key to its survival.

location north of Tulsa to the
Kansas-Nebraska border

ecoregion Osage Plains/Flint
Hills Prairie

project size 4.9 million acres

preserves Konza Prairie, Flint
Hills Tallgrass Prairie, Sunset
Prairie, Tallgrass Prairie

public lands Tallgrass Prairie
National Preserve, Fort Riley
Military Reservation

partners ranchers, Kansas
Livestock Association, Tallgrass
Legacy Alliance

conservancy initiatives
Invasive Species

natural events greater prairie
chicken courtship dances, spring,
peaking in April; wildflowers
bloom, spring and summer

information Ruth Palmer,
(785) 233-4400;
rpalmer@tnc.org;
nature.org/kansas

Stretching in a narrow band across east Kansas and dipping into northeast Oklahoma, the tallgrass prairie rolls in gentle waves over the Flint Hills. Waist-high grasses blanket the plains, studded with spring and summer wildflowers and sheltering nests of grassland birds such as the greater prairie chicken.

In 1806, during his western explorations, Lieutenant Zebulon Pike named the

Tallgrass prairie.

region for the flinty rock underlying the grasslands. From 1821 until 1870, people traveled through the Flint Hills on the Santa Fe Trail, the major trade and migration route from the East to the Southwest. In places, the trail's granite markers and wagon wheel ruts are still evident.

The tallgrass prairie evolved under the influence of herds of elk and bison, whose selective grazing and hooves "tilled" the plains and made way for diverse grasses. Fire burned the plains, ignited by lightning and the Kansa and Osage tribes, and fire-tolerant grasses thrived in its wake.

Greater prairie chicken displaying.

More than a century ago, when it once blanketed much of Kansas, the tallgrass was Willa Cather's muse.

Today across North America less than 10 percent remains of the original extent of tallgrass prairie, and the Flint Hills is by far its largest, most intact landscape. The hills' rocky terrain favored grazing over farming, an agricultural reality that left large swaths of prairie unplowed. Today invasive plants and residential and commercial development assault the last stand of the tallgrass.

Local ranchers and The Nature Conservancy are exploring approaches to conserve the Flint Hills while sustaining an ecologically compatible business. In one such effort, the Kansas Live-stock Association, in

collaboration with the Conservancy, seeks to establish a land trust to hold conservation easements on ranches in the Flint Hills.

conservation profile

targets native tallgrass prairie, oak/native bluestem grass community, streams, grassland nesting birds such as the greater prairie chicken

stresses habitat loss to industrial and residential development, invasive species, altered fire and grazing regimes, damming of streams

strategies secure conservation easements, combat invasive species, restore ecosystems through fire management and grazing, engage community

results 10,788 acres protected in two Conservancy preserves; program established to control invasive plants

PLATTE RIVER
Nebraska

Conservationists mimic the essential role of seasonal flooding in the Platte River ecosystem as part of an effort to restore sandhill crane habitat.

location 90 miles west of Lincoln

ecoregion Central Mixed Grass Prairie

project size 358,000 acres

preserves Anderson, Brown, Cavney, Derr/Dahms, McCormick, Studnicka

partners Prairie Plains Resource Institute, Platte River Whooping Crane Trust, Nebraska Game and Parks Commission, National Audubon Society, Rowe Sanctuary, Nebraska Environmental Trust Fund, ConAgra Foundation, Peter Kiewit Foundation, Kellogg Foundation, U.S. Fish and Wildlife Service, Natural Resource Conservation Service, Environmental Protection Agency

conservancy initiatives Freshwater

natural events sandhill crane migration, March; whooping crane and waterfowl migration, February and March

information Brent Lathrop, project director, (402) 694-4191, blathrop@tnc.org; nature.org/nebraska

Sandhill cranes roosting on river sandbars at dawn.

From high in the Rockies, melting snow descends onto the plains, amassing into what becomes the Platte River. The river weaves its way across Nebraska like a pushed rope, bending in numerous shallow braided channels. Sandy islands emerge among the plaits, with wet meadows and scattered trees lining the banks. For millennia, spring floods scoured the sandbars, creating ideal tree-less roosting habitat for migrating birds. Milder summer flows then exposed the sandbars, offering ample space for nesting and feeding.

Half a million sandhill cranes—90 percent of their entire population—visit the Platte each spring to rest and feed on corn, snails, earthworms and insects before migrating north. Joined by millions of ducks, geese and other birds, even endangered whooping cranes, the sandhills congregate along Big Bend

Reach in south-central Nebraska. This 80-mile curving stretch of the river is the "pinch in the hourglass" of the Great Plains Flyway, which funnels birds between Canada and Texas. When they gather at dusk to roost, their calls are likened to a crowded football stadium. Cranes have been stopping at the Platte for thousands, perhaps tens of thousands of years, based on clues contained in prehistoric fossils.

Yet, today, less than half of the Platte's open, braided river habitat remains. Dams and water diversions in Wyoming, Colorado and western Nebraska have reduced water flows and floods, and in their absence, willow, eastern red cedar and cottonwood forests have taken root on sandbars. Not only has this unique bird habitat been lost, but reduced flows have also lowered groundwater levels beneath the wet meadows, drying out other essential habitat for migratory birds.

To ensure that the sandhills and other avian visitors have a place to return to, The Nature Conservancy and our partners are working to restore critical habitat along the Platte. Employing a combination of prescribed burning and manual tree removal, we are mimicking the tree-clearing process once triggered by seasonal floods in the hopes that wet meadows and prairie will re-emerge and continue to host this annual migratory phenomenon for generations to come.

conservation profile

targets Platte River, migratory waterbirds like the sandhill crane, whooping crane, interior least tern, piping plover, ducks, geese; grassland species like the bobolink and sedge wren

stresses hydrologic alteration, land conversion, invasive species, fire suppression, sand and gravel extraction, residential development

strategies restore ecosystems, employ fire management, engage community in natural resource management, influence land-use planning, secure conservation easements, promote compatible development

results 3,000 acres protected within Big Bend Reach

SHEYENNE DELTA
North Dakota

Fire and improved grazing practices are essential to restore and keep alive a rare expanse of sandy Dakota prairie sculpted eons ago by wind and water.

location 55 miles southwest of Fargo

ecoregion Northern Tallgrass Prairie

project size 236,000 acres

preserves Brown Ranch, Pigeon Point

public lands Sheyenne National Grasslands

partners U.S. Forest Service, Coordinated Resource Management Group, ranchers

conservancy initiatives Fire, Invasive Species

natural events prairie wildflowers bloom, late May–early August; prairie fringed orchid blooms, late June–mid-July; shorebirds, waterfowl, prairie birds migrate, spring

information Gerry Reichert, field representative, (701) 222-8464, greichert@tnc.org; nature.org/northdakota

Bounded to the north by the Sheyenne River, the prairies of the Sheyenne Delta emerge from riverine forests and fens to spread a polychromatic green carpet that rises and falls in gentle hummocks. Its dunelike uplands are tinged with a shifting palette of purple, white, red and yellow blooms for much of the year, while water-loving grasses, shrubs and hardwoods cluster artfully in swales and the narrow channels of spring-fed streams.

The Sheyenne Delta exhibits an uncommon carpet of tallgrass prairie—some of the largest expanses remaining anywhere—woven in a tapestry of mixed-grass prairie, sedge meadows, fens and oak savanna. In summer, prairie flowers attract

Black tern in prairie slough.

22 species of butterflies, among them the imperiled Dakota skipper. Grasses shelter one of North Dakota's few remaining populations of greater prairie chicken and also support a dazzling array of sparrows. Wetlands come alive in spring with the flapping wings and harsh chatter of migrating ducks.

Known as the "sandhills," the Sheyenne Delta was formed more than 10,000 years ago when the silty remnants of a glacial lake were wind-blown into hillocks and mounds. The sandy soil may be the reason why some prairies in the area were spared the plow when European immigrants settled the plains. But as many as 70,000 acres in the Sheyenne Delta were heavily cultivated and grazed. During the Dust Bowl days of the 1930s, this agricultural land received federal relief, and in 1960 it was restored and became the Sheyenne National Grasslands, which today is leased for cattle grazing.

In the national grasslands and other vestiges of native prairie, heavy grazing regimes and the lack of fire have disrupted the natural processes that maintain native prairie. On our preserves, The Nature Conservancy is demonstrating prairie restoration through the use of prescribed fire. We are also working with ranchers and government agencies to improve grazing practices on grasslands across the Sheyenne Delta.

Western prairie fringed orchid.

FLINT HILLS
Oklahoma

Only in the Flint Hills can one still experience horizon-to-horizon vistas of native tallgrass prairie, once one of the continent's most extensive natural systems.

location north of Tulsa to the Kansas-Nebraska border

ecoregion Osage Plains/Flint Hills Prairie

project size 4.9 million acres

preserves Tallgrass Prairie, Konza Prairie, Flint Hills Tallgrass Prairie, Sunset Prairie

public lands Tallgrass Prairie National Preserve, Fort Riley Military Reservation, Western Wall Wildlife Management Area

partners ranchers, U.S. Department of Agriculture, U.S. Fish and Wildlife Service, Oklahoma Department of Wildlife Conservation, Oklahoma State University, Tulsa University, University of Oklahoma, Kansas State University

natural events greater prairie chicken courtship dances, spring; bison calve, April–June; prescribed prairie fires, April; peak wildflower blooms, mid-May–mid-June, August–September

information Deirdre McArdle, (918) 293-2912, dmcardle@tnc.org; nature.org/oklahoma

Tallgrass Prairie Preserve.

To early explorers and pioneers, the undulating hills of northern Oklahoma were an endless sea of grass blanketing the land in all directions. The grasses—big bluestem, Indian grass and switchgrass—grew to more than 10 feet, high enough to brush saddle horns and require settlers to stand in the saddle to locate their grazing cattle. The tallgrass prairie harbored abundant wildlife like the greater prairie chicken, coyotes and bobcats—but the bison that roamed in massive herds most symbolize its grandeur.

For millennia, the tallgrass prairie defined the Great Plains, stretching from Texas to Canada and covering 142

million acres of America's heartland. The landscape was shaped and sustained by the natural forces of climate, fire and grazing interacting over time and across wide-open spaces. Today, less than 10 percent of the tallgrass prairie remains in isolated fragments. The largest tracts are in the Flint Hills of Kansas and Oklahoma.

Most tallgrass prairie disappeared when the pioneers pushed westward, planting corn and transforming the plains into the breadbasket of a growing nation. With their rocky terrain making them untillable, the Flint Hills became an enclave of ranches and cowboys amidst the Great Plains' crops and farmers. But without the grazing patterns of native ungulates like bison and the regular sweep of wildfire, the tallgrass prairie has suffered.

The Nature Conservancy in 1989 seized a rare opportunity to restore a functioning tallgrass prairie ecosystem to presettlement condition. We purchased the Barnard Ranch, a 29,000-acre grass-land in Osage County, Oklahoma, anchoring the southern end of the greatest stretch of tallgrass prairie remaining in North America. Here at what became the Tallgrass Prairie Preserve we have reintroduced fire and, in 1993, we released a herd of 300 bison to roam freely on the preserve. Since then their numbers have grown to some 2,000. In reuniting these two native elements of the

Prescribed burn, Tallgrass Prairie Preserve.

tallgrass—fire and bison—we are restoring a piece of North America's natural heritage.

conservation profile

targets native tallgrass prairie, bison, greater prairie chicken, big bluestem

stresses habitat loss to industrial and residential development, invasive species, altered fire and grazing regimes

strategies secure conservation easements, develop techniques to combat invasive species, restore ecosystems through fire management and grazing

results 32,800-acre preserve created; bison herd established; preserve hosts 20,000 visitors per year

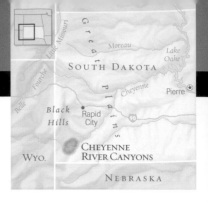

CHEYENNE RIVER CANYONS
South Dakota

Private ranchland is key to protecting this diverse canyon, river and prairie system in the Black Hills, where terrain of the West meets forest of the East.

location 65 miles southwest of Rapid City

ecoregion Black Hills

project size 73,000 acres

preserves Nathaniel and Mary Whitney Preserve at Cascade Creek

public lands Black Hills National Forest, Bureau of Land Management lands

partners U.S. Forest Service, National Park Service, private landowners

conservancy initiatives Fire

natural events orchids bloom, second half of June; tulip gentians bloom, second half of July; Townsend's big-eared bats welp pups, mid-summer; elks bugle, mid-September; Custer State Buffalo Roundup, September–October

information Bob Paulson, (605) 342-4040, bpaulson@tnc.org; nature.org/wyoming

Thirteen deep parallel canyons cut through the Black Hills of western South Dakota, their springs and seeps gathering and ultimately draining into the Cheyenne River. Ponderosa pines dot the canyons' flat-topped ridges above a sea of prairie grasses where bison, elk and wild horses roam. Once the homeland of

Roughlock Falls, Black Hills National Forest.

the Sioux, the Black Hills—with their abundant wildlife and water—remain sacred ground to many Native Americans.

A mixture of Rocky Mountain terrain, Midwestern prairie and Eastern deciduous forest, this ecological crossroads brings together wildlife and vegetation that coexist nowhere else on Earth. Birds of both eastern and western North America flock here. Cascade Creek, a tributary of the Cheyenne River, is a warm-water system that remains ice-free throughout the year—an important water source for local wildlife in winter and habitat for four plant species normally found only in the southern Great Plains. The

American bison, Black Hills National Forest.

craggy walls of the canyons are home to raptors and mountain lions; bighorn sheep have recently returned to the region.

This part of the Black Hills was spared from early development when the town of Cascade, founded in 1892, was abandoned two years later as the path of the railroad was diverted. Today Cheyenne River Canyons is a patchwork of public, private and tribal ownership. Although the landscape remains remarkably intact, residential development from the growing town of Hot Springs threatens to fragment this unique canyon system.

The Nature Conservancy seeks to avert subdivision within the entire project area, particularly in the largest undeveloped landscape in the Black Hills—42,000 acres

with only one cabin. We are working with private landowners in this core landscape to protect their land through both outright acquisition and conservation easements. In 2000, we helped the U.S. Forest Service acquire critical private inholdings in the Black Hills National Forest in exchange for surplus federal lands.

conservation profile

targets warm-water spring and riparian system, bighorn sheep, elk, mountain lion, Townsend's big-eared bat, four rare plants (tulip gentian, stream orchid, southern maidenhair fern and beaked spikerush) reliant on warm-water riparian habitat

stresses habitat fragmentation from subdivision, reduced frequency of fire

strategies acquire land, secure conservation easements, promote land exchanges, encourage conservation management of public land, restore ecosystems through fire management

results 33,000 acres in conservation management; fire management agreement signed with National Park Service

DAVIS MOUNTAINS
Texas

In Texas, where more than 97 percent of the state is privately owned, working with private landowners like those in the Davis Mountains to protect their land is essential to meet conservation goals.

location 3.5 hours from El Paso

ecoregion Chihuahuan Desert

project size 90,000 acres

preserves Madera Canyon, Davis Mountains

public lands Davis Mountains State Park, Fort Davis National Historic Site

partners ranchers and other private landowners, Buffalo Trail Boy Scout Council, Davis Mountains Education Center, University of Texas McDonald Observatory

natural events hummingbird migration and festival, near Labor Day; monsoon rains bring forth wildflowers, June–early October

information Karen Cornelius, (713) 524-6459; kcornelius@tnc.org; nature.org/texas

The mountains rise like a purple mirage out of the mesquite flats of West Texas. This is what Texans call the Trans-Pecos—beyond the Pecos River, the rainfall meridian, west of which marks desert. But the Davis Mountains, climbing skyward to 8,300 feet, are cool and forested—an anomaly in an arid land.

An isolated mountain range surrounded by desert and grasslands, the Davis Mountains are a "sky island." Scattered

Puertacitas Mountains.

across the Southwest, sky island ranges receive more precipitation than do the plains below, creating a true island of life for many plants and animals uniquely adapted to the cooler climate and higher terrain.

Once the domain of the Mescalero Apache, the range was named for Jefferson Davis, who, in 1854, as U.S. Secretary of War, ordered a fort built in the rugged mountains to protect stage coaches and emigrants traveling westward. From the ancient pictographs that color canyon walls, to ranch gates with colorful names like U Up U Down burned into wood, the long and fabled history of the people of the Davis Mountains is evident.

Klein cholla.

The night skies over this remote part of wild West Texas are the darkest in the nation—so dark that astronomers count the University of Texas McDonald Observatory, near Fort Davis, as one of the best places for deep-space gazing in the world. But those night skies risk being lit up with an influx of new residents, many of whom come to build vacation homes in the mountains. Development also taxes water resources and fragments habitat. The Nature Conservancy encourages private landowners to place conservation easements on their land to prevent future subdivision and, in many cases, has found conservation-minded individuals to buy properties for sale.

conservation profile

targets creeks, springs, evergreen forests, aspen groves, Montezuma quail, Mexican spotted owl, Rio Grande chub, mountain short-horned lizard, Mexican black bear, Livermore paintbrush, Big Bend blackheaded snake

stresses habitat fragmentation from sub-division, overuse of water resources from a growing population, overgrazing, lack of a natural fire regime

strategies acquire land, secure conservation easements, restore ecosystems, encourage conservation management of private land

results more than 90,000 acres in conservation management, including some 70,000 acres protected through donated conservation easements

LAGUNA MADRE
Texas

Collaboration and restoration are helping protect the "mother lagoon," named for her ability to nurture life in many forms, from tiny fish to migrating birds to prowling wildcats.

location from Corpus Christi Bay south to Rio Soto la Marina in Tamaulipas, Mexico

ecoregion Gulf Coast Prairies and Marshes

project size 5.15 million acres

preserves South Padre Island, Southmost, Redhead Pond

public lands Padre Island National Seashore, Laguna Atascosa National Wildlife Refuge, Lower Rio Grande Valley National Wildlife Refuge

partners U.S. Fish and Wildlife Service, National Park Service, Texas Parks and Wildlife Department, Valley Land Fund, Ducks Unlimited, Texas A&M, University of Texas, Pronatura Noreste, Mexican park service, private landowners

conservancy initiatives Invasive Species, Global Climate Change, Marine

natural events peregrine falcons migrate, South Padre Island, September–October

information Karen Cornelius, (713) 524-6459, kcornelius@tnc.org; nature.org/texas

Shallow, salty and teeming with life, the Laguna Madre holds a near-spiritual allure for naturalists. Just five miles across at its widest point, the "mother lagoon" stretches more than 200 miles from southern Texas into northern Mexico, sheltered by a system of barrier islands and mainland beaches. Ranching empires have been built on these shores, and the careful stewardship of families, sometimes for more than a century, has helped preserve these extraordinarily rich wetlands.

Meadows of seagrass thrive in the lagoon's briny waters—one of the five saltiest bodies of water on Earth—providing a nurturing home for fragile young finfish, shrimp and shellfish.

Redfish and spotted sea trout glint beneath the waters, and a host of birds, from redhead ducks to migrating peregrine falcons, depend on the undisturbed wetlands for survival. Endangered sea turtles share the beaches and coastal mainland with two magnificent wildcats: ocelot and jaguarundi.

Like many of its wild inhabitants, this ecosystem is being pushed to its limits by haphazard development, pollution and rapid growth. All-important seagrass beds are declining, threatening not only the lagoon's rich diversity, but also Texas' shrimp industry and its commercial and recreational fishing economies. The loss could be significant, as angling and other leisure activities in and around the lagoon contribute more than $500 million annually to the Texas economy.

The Nature Conservancy has worked here for more than 15 years, helping protect critical lands through acquisition, easements and collaboration with other conservation organizations. In March 2000, we acquired nearly 25,000 acres on South Padre Island and will eventually convey most of the land to the Laguna Atascosa National Wildlife Refuge. We are also working closely with Mexican partner Pronatura Noreste to establish a Mexican protected area in the region and to provide conservation assistance to private Mexican landowners.

Padre Island National Seashore.

Reddish egret.

conservation profile

targets Kemp's ridley sea turtle, neotropical migratory songbirds, wintering redhead ducks, seagrass beds, brown pelican, piping plover, peregrine falcon, ocelot

stresses incompatible commercial and agricultural development, polluted runoff, overfishing in Mexico, habitat fragmentation in Texas

strategies acquire land, restore ecosystems, build conservation alliances, encourage conservation management of public land, promote private land conservation in Mexico

results protected nearly 30,000 acres, including 24,500 acres at South Padre Island; collaborated with Pronatura Noreste to secure protection of 1.5 million acres in the Mexican portion of Laguna Madre

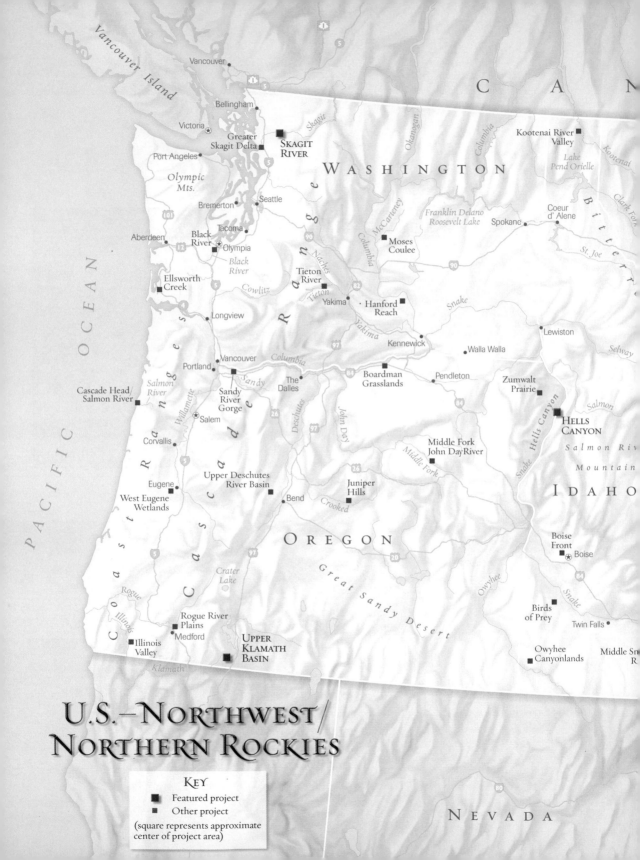

Vancouver Island

Vancouver

Bellingham

Victoria

Greater
Skagit Delta

SKAGIT
RIVER

Skagit

WASHINGTON

Kootenai River
Valley

Port Angeles

Olympic
Mts.

Bremerton

Seattle

Okanogan

Columbia

Lake
Pend Orielle

Kootenai

Aberdeen

Black
River

Tacoma

Olympia

Black
River

Cowlitz

McCartney

Franklin Delano
Roosevelt Lake

Spokane

Coeur
d' Alene

Bitterre

Clark Fork

St. Joe

Ellsworth
Creek

Tieton
River

Tieton

Columbia

Yakima

Hanford
Reach

Snake

Lewiston

Selway

Longview

Naches

Yakima

Kennewick

Walla Walla

Cascade Head/
Salmon River

Portland

Vancouver

Sandy

The Dalles

Columbia

Boardman
Grasslands

Pendleton

Zumwalt
Prairie

Salmon

Salmon River

Mountain

IDAHO

Salmon
River

Sandy River
Gorge

Salem

Willamette

Deschutes

John Day

Middle Fork

Middle Fork
John DayRiver

Hells Canyon

HELLS
CANYON

Corvallis

Eugene

West Eugene
Wetlands

Upper Deschutes
River Basin

Bend

Crooked

Juniper
Hills

OREGON

Boise
Front

Boise

Crater
Lake

Great Sandy Desert

Owyhee

Snake

Rogue River
Plains

Medford

Rogue

Illinois

Illinois
Valley

UPPER
KLAMATH
BASIN

Klamath

Birds
of Prey

Twin Falls

Owyhee
Canyonlands

Middle Sn
R

PACIFIC OCEAN

C A N

Range

Coast Range

Cascade Range

U.S.–NORTHWEST/
NORTHERN ROCKIES

NEVADA

KEY

■ Featured project

■ Other project

(square represents approximate
center of project area)

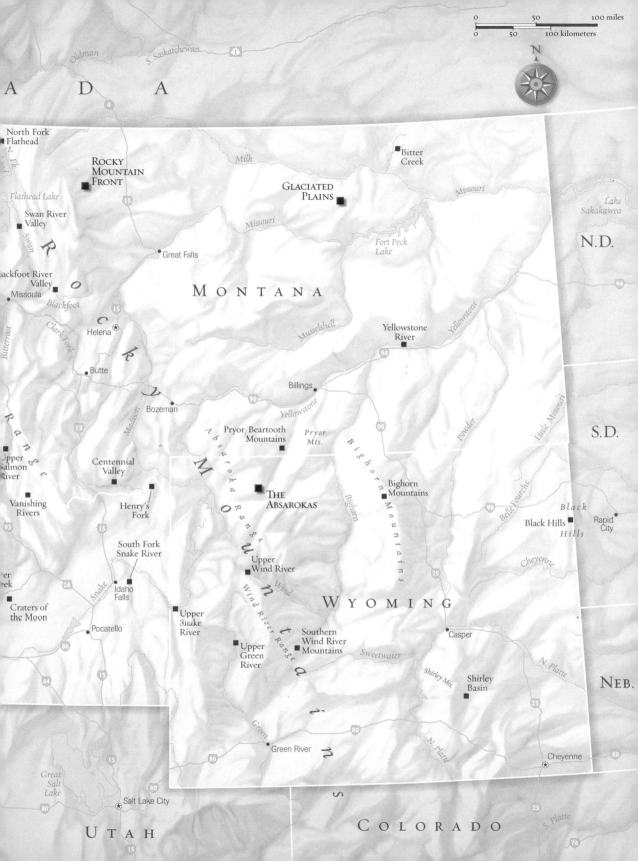

0   50   100 miles

0   50   100 kilometers

N

CANADA

Oldman

S. Saskatchewan

1

4

North Fork
Flathead

ROCKY
MOUNTAIN
FRONT

Milk

Bitter
Creek

GLACIATED
PLAINS

Missouri

Missouri

Fort Peck
Lake

Lake
Sakakawea

N.D.

Flathead Lake

Swan River
Valley

Swan

15

Great Falls

MONTANA

ackfoot River
Valley

Missoula

Blackfoot

15

Musselshell

Yellowstone
River

Yellowstone

94

ROCKY

Helena

Clark Fork

Bitterroot

Butte

90

Billings

Yellowstone

90

Powder

Little Missouri

S.D.

Madison

Bozeman

15

Pryor Beartooth
Mountains

Pryor
Mts.

Absaroka Range

Bighorn Mountains

Belle Fourche

96

Black
Hills

Cheyenne

Black Hills
Hills

Rapid
City

Range

Upper
Salmon
River

Centennial
Valley

THE
ABSAROKAS

Bighorn
Mountains

Bighorn

Vanishing
Rivers

93

Henry's
Fork

South Fork
Snake River

15

M o u n t a i n s

Upper
Wind River

Wind

WYOMING

25

Wind River Range

r
eek

26

Snake

Idaho
Falls

Craters of
the Moon

Pocatello

Upper
Snake
River

Upper
Green
River

Southern
Wind River
Mountains

Sweetwater

Casper

N. Platte

NEB.

Shirley Mts.

Shirley
Basin

86

44

15

Green

Green River

80

N. Platte

25

Cheyenne

80

Great
Salt
Lake

80

15

Salt Lake City

UTAH

COLORADO

25

S. Platte

76

HELLS CANYON
Idaho

Hard work and high-tech tools are eradicating invasive weeds in North America's deepest river gorge.

location Hells Canyon Dam is 120 miles northwest of Boise

ecoregion Middle Rockies-Blue Mountains

project size 1.15 million acres

preserves Garden Creek Ranch

public lands Nez Perce and Wallowa national forests, Cottonwood BLM district, Craig Mountain Wildlife Management Area, Nez Perce tribal lands

partners Bureau of Land Management, U.S. Forest Service, Idaho Fish and Game, Nez Perce Tribe, Rocky Mountain Elk Foundation

conservancy initiatives Invasive Species, Fire

natural events steelhead and salmon migration, spring; raptor and waterfowl migration, fall; winter range for elk and bighorn sheep, spring; wildflower blooms in the Palouse prairie and bluebunch grasslands, spring

information Gretchen Grindle, (208) 726-3007, ext. 12; ggrindle@tnc.org; nature.org/idaho

Looking into Hells Canyon.

Two centuries ago, Lewis and Clark decided it would be easier going to cross the Bitteroot Mountains rather than this Snake River canyon running along Idaho's western border. In 1895, *McCurdy's Marine History of the Pacific Northwest* described an astonishing canyon in which "the river winds like a serpent and the rocks tower to such a height that they almost shut out the sun."

Settlers veered their wagons south to avoid the canyon on their way west.

Hells Canyon survives much as it did then—an untrammeled wilderness where bighorn sheep still spar

on the rocks above whitewater rapids laden during migration season with salmon, steelhead and sturgeon. It is the deepest river gorge in North America—more than 1.5 miles deep and 10 miles wide—exceeding the Grand Canyon in depth by 100 feet.

Nine rare plants cling to life on steep canyon walls, and sweeping grasslands glow green in spring and turn rich browns and oranges by fall. In recent years, however, another color—yellow—has washed over entire mountain slopes and benches at an alarming rate.

Hells Canyon faces an invasion of yellow starthistle and other noxious weeds. Starthistle alone has spread from about 200 acres in the canyon to more than 10,000 acres in the past decade, and it continues to advance, particularly on steep southerly slopes. To counter this threat, The Nature Conservancy has enlisted the help of local partners and volunteers to implement a weed control strategy that includes protecting healthy plant communities, utilizing insects to control weeds and replanting native grasses. Conservancy

New lodgepole pines, Wallowa National Forest.

scientists are pioneering the use of remote sensing tools like satellite imagery to track progress in controlling weed invasions.

conservation profile

targets bighorn sheep, mule deer, elk, golden eagle, bald eagle, mountain lion, black bear, bluebunch wheatgrass communities, Spalding's silene, western ladies tress, stalk-leafed monkey flower

stresses invasive species, altered flows on the Snake River, water pollution, large wildfires

strategies combat invasive species, encourage conservation management of private land, engage community in management of natural resources, protect water quality, restore ecosystems

results 14,000 acres protected; extensive field surveys and mapping of rare plant occurrences and weed infestations completed

GLACIATED PLAINS
Montana

Big-sky ranches of native prairie are central to the survival of grassland birds, whose populations are declining faster than any other group of species in North America.

location 200 miles northeast of Great Falls; 89 miles northeast of Lewistown

ecoregion Northern Great Plains Steppe

project size 2.5 million acres

preserves Matador Ranch

public lands Charles M. Russell National Wildlife Refuge, Fort Belknap Indian Reservation, Bureau of Land Management and Montana State trust lands

partners U.S. Fish and Wildlife Service, Montana Fish, Wildlife and Parks, Bureau of Land Management, ranching community, Fort Belknap Indian Reservation

natural events grassland birds breed, June; Fort Belknap Indian Reservation Pow Wow, summer; Lewis and Clark bicentennial events celebrated along the Missouri River, beginning 2004

information Betsy Baur, (406) 443-0303, bbaur@tnc.org; nature.org/montana

The wedge of Great Plains between the Milk and Missouri rivers rolls tan and treeless beneath the dome of blue sky. Winters roar down from Canada bitter cold and dry, plunging temperatures to -40° F but sending little snow. With only 12 inches of precipitation a year, the windswept grasses are short, a burnt-tawny stubble spreading across the plains of north-central Montana. These plains are glaciated, having been scraped bare some 18,000 years ago by an ice sheet that halted its southward slide at the present-day Missouri River.

Missouri River, Charles M. Russell National Wildlife Refuge.

Down in the Missouri Breaks, where the plains drop off into weathered badlands, Lewis and Clark campsites are scattered along the river banks. This wilderness section of river is the least-changed landscape along the Corps of Discovery's entire route. In 1877, Chief Joseph and the Nez Perce crossed the river and fled north toward Canada and their only hope for independence. Days later, on the plains, these last free members of the tribe that had helped Lewis and Clark survive surrendered to pursuing federal troops and were sent to live on reservations. From this land spring stories of defiance and lawlessness, of cattle rustlers and Kidd Curry and the Hole-in-the-Wall Gang.

The country remains somehow untamed and unbowed, perhaps because it is also unpeopled. Like much of the Great Plains, this part of Montana has seen an exodus of human residents since the 1920s. Even though bison and grizzly bears disappeared long ago, wild nature remains. The glaciated plains are the epicenter of grassland bird diversity, with excellent native prairie remaining for long-billed curlews and their brethren—birds that have experienced the steepest population declines of any group of North American species.

The legacy of cattle barons, big ranches offer the best hope of protecting Montana's grasslands. But hard times are forcing some ranchers to sell, allowing mechanized agriculture to move in and plow native prairie. As a primary conservation strategy, The Nature Conservancy works with local ranchers. In 2000, we purchased the 60,000-acre Matador Ranch and are pioneering cooperative grazing management agreements in which ranchers share the

Matador's grassland forage in exchange for wildlife protection on other grazing lands. We have also brought together ranchers, federal agencies and conservation organizations to restore populations of prairie dogs, which are the central prey of black-footed ferrets, the most endangered mammal in North America.

Black-footed ferret.

conservation profile

targets black-footed ferret, black-tailed prairie dog, mixed-grass prairie, grassland birds including ferruginous hawk, long-billed curlew

stresses invasive species, plowing of prairie grasslands, incompatible grazing practices, mass poisoning of black-tailed prairie dogs

strategies promote ecologically compatible grazing practices, encourage conservation management of public land, build conservation alliances, combat invasive species

results 60,000-acre Matador Ranch acquired; local advisory committee convened; 42 black-footed ferrets reintroduced, with two young born in the wild

ROCKY MOUNTAIN FRONT
Montana

Where high plains meet mountain wilderness, private lands are the thread that could unravel a wild tapestry of grizzlies and their wide-open expanses.

location 125 miles northwest of Helena

ecoregions Canadian Rockies, Northern Great Plains Steppe

project size 5 million acres

preserves Pine Butte Swamp, Crown Butte

public lands Lewis and Clark National Forest, Bob Marshall Wilderness Complex, Glacier National Park, Waterton National Park, Canadian Crown lands

partners U.S. Forest Service, U.S. Fish and Wildlife Service, Blackfeet Indian Land Conservation Trust, Boone and Crockett Club, landowners and ranching community, Montana Fish, Wildlife, and Parks, Southern Alberta Land Trust, Nature Conservancy of Canada

conservancy initiatives Invasive Species

natural events grizzly bears move from mountains to plains to forage, early summer

information Betsy Baur, (406) 443-0303; bbaur@tnc.org; nature.org/montana

Rising from the Great Plains as far as the eye can see, the mountainous wall of the Rocky Mountain Front looms jagged and brooding. Along this natural divide Native Americans traveled north and south for thousands of years, their ancient journeys etching the Old North Trail into the hard earth.

For the Blackfeet people the mountains are the *miistakis*—the backbone of the world.

The Rocky Mountain Front, running from Alberta south through Montana, marks the easternmost edge of a functioning wilderness. This is the only place in the world where you can still see grizzly bears in their native plains habitat just as Lewis

Grizzly bear and mountain goats.

and Clark encountered them. In summer, the bears descend onto the plains to feed on chokecherries and serviceberries growing thick along streams. To the west the bears thrive in the Bob Marshall Wilderness Complex and other wild strongholds of public land. With the exception of bison—the former lifeblood and currency of the Blackfeet and other plains tribes—all of the native mammals that inhabited this land when Lewis and Clark passed through survive here.

The grizzlies' timeless migrations are today at risk as their routes of passage are cut by fences, roads and other developments that threaten to overtake the private lands along the Rocky Mountain Front. More people moving in means more encounters with bears—encounters that can be more fatal for bears than for people. In general, ranchers have tolerated bears on their rangelands. But if and when those ranches are sold and vacation-home "ranchettes" sprout in their place, the big territories needed by bears will be further divided—a shrinking habitat for a wide-ranging animal.

It is in these private lands that The Nature Conservancy works to protect prime bear habitat along the front. We have facilitated conservation easements on working ranches, a mutually beneficial arrangement that gives tax breaks to cash-strapped ranchers. On the Blackfeet Reservation, we assisted in the creation of a

Ear Mountain.

tribal land trust to secure easements. These efforts are just a few of many designed to give the bears the freedom to roam.

conservation profile

targets grizzly bear, native prairie, streams and wetlands, fens, grassland birds like long-billed curlew, rough fescue grasslands

stresses invasive weeds, habitat fragmentation from development, altered fire regime

strategies secure conservation easements, combat invasive species, restore ecosystems through fire management, encourage conservation management of public and private land

results 46,000 acres in conservation management; Blackfeet Indian Land Conservation Trust launched; cooperative fire and weed management projects in place

UPPER KLAMATH BASIN

Oregon

Despite widely divergent interests, local people are coming together to ensure adequate water resources for human and natural communities in the Klamath Basin.

location from Crater Lake to Mount Shasta

ecoregion East Cascades and Modoc Plateau

project size 500,000 acres

preserves Sycan Marsh, Williamson River Delta

public lands Winema National Forest; Klamath Marsh, Upper Klamath Lake, Tule Lake and Lower Klamath Lake national wildlife refuges

partners National Fish and Wildlife Foundation, U.S. Fish and Wildlife Service, U.S. Bureau of Reclamation, Natural Resources Conservation Service, Klamath tribes, PacifiCorp, ZX Ranch, Upper Klamath Basin Working Group

conservancy initiatives Freshwater, Invasive Species

natural events spring and fall bird migrations among the most spectacular in North America

information Carrie Walkiewicz, (503) 230-1221, cwalkiewicz@tnc.org, nature.org/oregon

Snow geese.

Although dammed and diked for agriculture, the Upper Klamath Basin is still the heart of a great wetland system. A birder's paradise, this stopover on the Pacific Flyway hosts the largest congregation of wintering bald eagles outside Alaska, and millions of ducks, geese and swans pass through on their fall migrations. Its shallow waters and rivers, springs and marshlands harbor at least 25 species of fish, freshwater mollusks and land snails found nowhere else on Earth.

The unusual aquatic diversity of the Upper Klamath Basin has ancient beginnings. Most of the Pacific Northwest was repeatedly engulfed by glaciers and lava flows that, each time, wiped the ecological slate clean—but not the Klamath Basin. Instead, aquatic creatures and their habitats persisted and evolved through radical climate changes, shifting river courses and, 7,000 years ago, the explosion of Mt. Mazama. That traumatic event built Crater Lake—one of the world's deepest lakes—and blanketed the land with volcanic ash and dust.

When droughts in the mid-1990s constricted the amount of water reaching Klamath Basin farms, major divisions emerged between residents and conservationists. To help alleviate this conflict, The Nature Conservancy works to build consensus and to provide enough water for both agriculture and wildlife. For instance, in 2002 the Conservancy waived its right to withdraw water from Upper Klamath Lake, leaving more water in the lake for fish and farmers. (The water rights came with our purchase of a farm in the basin.) In exchange, we asked the federal government to increase its support for wetland restoration. We collaborate with wildlife authorities, the Bureau of Reclamation, tribes, farmers and ranchers on pioneering wetland restoration projects to improve water quality. We also helped create the Upper Klamath Basin Working Group, a community-based coalition that seeks to balance the needs of all stakeholders.

Williamson River Delta Preserve, with Mt. McLoughlin catching the morning light.

conservation profile

targets yellow rail, migrating waterfowl, Lost River sucker, shortnose sucker, bull trout, freshwater streams and marshlands, freshwater mollusks

stresses degraded water quality, damming and diversions, grazing, invasive species

strategies restore ecosystems, protect water quality, promote compatible development, strengthen local partner organizations

results more than 37,000 acres in conservation management and restoration; diverse working group created to develop solutions that will enhance the environment and promote a sustainable local economy

SKAGIT RIVER
Washington

Healthy annual runs of salmon anchor the web of life in the Skagit, the third-largest river system in the western United States.

location 50 miles northeast of Seattle

ecoregions North Cascades, Willamette Valley-Puget Trough-Georgia Basin

project size 3,200 square miles

public lands Mount Baker-Snoqualmie National Forest, North Cascades National Park, Mount Baker, Noisy-Diobsud, Glacier Peak, Henry M. Jackson and Pasayten wilderness areas

partners U.S. Forest Service, Skagit Watershed Council, Skagit Land Trust, Trust for Public Land, Seattle City Light, Washington state departments of Fish and Wildlife and Natural Resources

conservancy initiatives Freshwater, Invasive Species, Marine

natural events bald eagles feed on chum salmon carrion, winter; largest gathering of snow geese in the Pacific Northwest coincides with thousands of shorebirds and raptors, winter

information Shari Miranda, (206) 343-4345, ext. 361, smiranda@tnc.org; nature.org/washington

An ancient cycle lives on within the Skagit River watershed, where juvenile salmon depart for the sea each year to mature, then return to the fresh water of their birth to spawn and die. The linchpin in this ecosystem, salmon carry the ocean's richness inland 80 miles from Puget Sound to the Cascade Mountains, in the process nourishing an entire river system, its surrounding forests and the wildlife that depend on them. The Skagit is the only river in the lower 48 that is home to all five species of Pacific salmon.

Skagit River and Mount Baker in winter.

The Skagit system encompasses more than 3,000 rivers and streams and produces one-quarter of all the fresh water flowing into Puget Sound. In its lower reaches, the river meanders along low banks, changing its course over time and occasionally flooding, creating gravel bars, backwater sloughs and wetlands that provide habitat for wildlife such as salmon and beaver. One of the four largest winter gatherings of bald eagles occurs on the Skagit, coinciding with chum salmon runs. The eagles roost in cottonwood, alder and bigleaf maple that line the river and feed on fish carcasses washed up onto sandbars.

But signs of distress in the celebrated salmon runs sound a warning for the entire watershed. Damming of the river in five places has tamed its wild nature. The Skagit's banks are increasingly being reinforced with rocks and concrete walls, hindering its natural tendency to wander and flood. Moreover, logging and other activities on adjacent lands degrade the forest and add sediment to the river.

In its highest elevations, large portions of the Skagit watershed are protected in North Cascades National Park; its middle and lower elevations are composed of national forests, private timberlands and other private lands. By bringing together private landowners and public agencies a quarter-century ago, The Nature Conservancy catalyzed efforts to protect this vast system. Together we established the Skagit River Bald Eagle Natural Area partnership, a consortium that has protected more than 8,000 acres to date. Today, we are working to protect private lands in the lower elevations,

Coho salmon.

cooperating with landowners and local communities to meet the needs of the river while promoting compatible management of adjoining lands.

conservation profile

targets river flows, five species of Pacific salmon, bald eagles

stresses residential development, timber harvesting, invasive species, altered hydrological regime

strategies acquire land, modify dam operations, engage community, combat invasive species, encourage conservation management on public and private lands, promote ecologically sound public policies, promote land acquisition by public agencies

results 12,122 acres in conservation management; public-private Skagit River Bald Eagle Natural Area partnership established

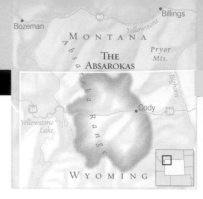

THE ABSAROKAS
Wyoming

In the Greater Yellowstone area—the largest intact ecosystem in the lower 48—keeping rangeland open and unbroken by development is essential to preserve ancient migration routes and wilderness.

location near Cody; 2 hours from Billings, Montana

ecoregion Utah-Wyoming Rocky Mountains

project size more than 3 million acres

preserves Heart Mountain Ranch and Grassbank

public lands Yellowstone National Park, Shoshone National Forest, mixed Bureau of Land Management and state lands

partners U.S. Forest Service, Bureau of Land Management, National Park Service, Wyoming Game and Fish, Draper Museum of Natural History, Audubon Society, Rocky Mountain Elk Foundation, private landowners, Absaroka-Beartooth Ranchland Trust

conservancy initiatives Fire, Invasive Species

natural events sage grouse gather at mating grounds, early spring; elk migrations, spring and fall

information Shawn Smith, (307) 733-8890; shawnsmith@tnc.org; nature.org/wyoming

Lamar Valley near Soda Butte Creek.

The borders of a national park mean nothing to grizzly bears, which move in winter from Yellowstone National Park to the nearby lower elevations of the Absaroka Range.

For migrating herds of elk, the open slopes of a ranch offer a good place to calve in the spring. Although human boundaries do exist, they are rarely apparent in country that remains largely unbroken.

The extraordinary wildlife of this wilderness along the eastern edge of Yellowstone has drawn the likes of Teddy Roosevelt, Buffalo Bill Cody and Ernest Hemingway. Named for the Crow Indians who made their home here, the Absarokas provide vital habitat for wide-ranging species such as wolves, mountain lions and mule deer. Volcanic in origin, the land is dissected by scores of clear creeks that transform into frenzied rivers during summer rainstorms. Glaciers, canyons, dense forests, broad mountain meadows and hundreds of alpine lakes comprise some of the nation's most striking wilderness. It is rugged country where stark beauty meets ageless rituals.

Bernie and Pam Bjornestad, ranchers participating in the Heart Mountain Grassbank.

Maintaining the intact nature of the Absarokas is vital to many species like sage grouse and grizzlies, whose habitat has been greatly reduced elsewhere in the West. Because ranches contain much of the precious open space that connects and buffers conservation areas, keeping local ranches in business and free of subdivision is a primary goal of The Nature Conservancy. At Heart Mountain—a geological puzzle and well-known symbol of the Absarokas—the Conservancy worked with the local community to launch the Heart Mountain Grassbank. The grassbank gives Absarokas ranchers a shared source of livestock forage while they rest and restore the grass of their own rangeland. A revolving "bank" of grass that allows many ranchers to participate, the grassbank is an innovative tool that supports working landscapes while keeping at bay the subdivision common in many Western landscapes.

conservation profile

targets grizzly bear, bighorn sheep, Yellowstone cutthroat trout, ferruginous hawk, wildflowers like aromatic pussytoes, Absaroka goldenweed, Shoshonea, Absaroka biscuitroot

stresses flood of new residents, ranch subdivision, second-home development, alteration of natural fire regime

strategies secure conservation easements, acquire land, restore ecosystems through fire management, encourage conservation management of public land, involve community in management of natural resources

results launched Heart Mountain Grassbank; land exchange with Bureau of Land Management protected 4,000 acres of migratory corridor

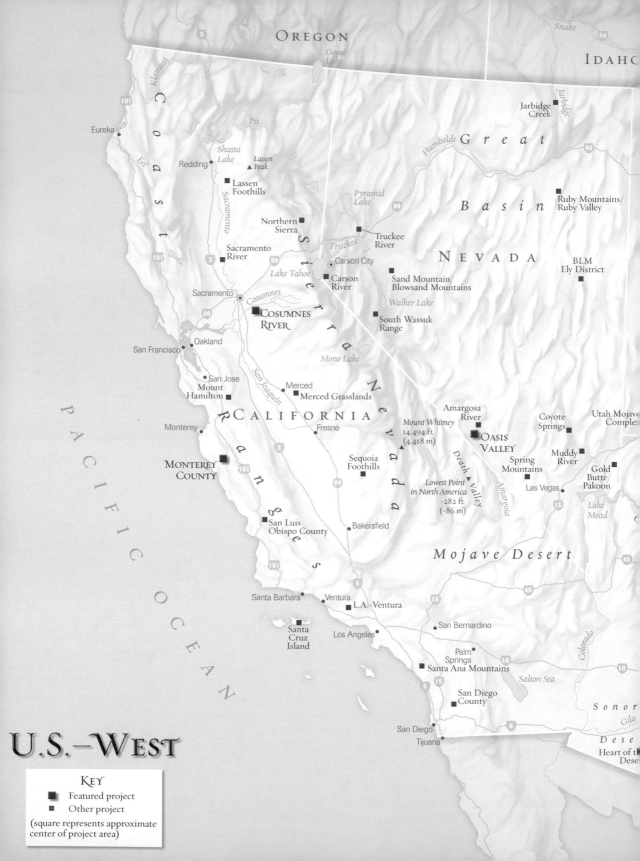

OREGON

IDAHO

Snake

Goose
Lake

Jarbidge
Creek

Eureka

Klamath

Pit

Shasta
Lake

Lassen
Peak

Redding

Lassen
Foothills

Sacramento

C
o
a
s
t

Humboldt

G r e a t

B a s i n

Ruby Mountains/
Ruby Valley

Pyramid
Lake

Northern
Sierra

Sacramento
River

Truckee

Truckee
River

N E V A D A

BLM
Ely District

Carson City

Lake Tahoe

Carson
River

Sand Mountain/
Blowsand Mountains

Sacramento

Cosumnes

COSUMNES
RIVER

S
i
e
r
r
a

Walker Lake

South Wassuk
Range

San Francisco

Oakland

Mono Lake

San Joaquin

San Jose
Mount
Hamilton

Merced

Merced Grasslands

C A L I F O R N I A

N
e
v
a
d
a

Amargosa
River

Coyote
Springs

Utah Mojave
Complex

Monterey

Fresno

Mount Whitney
14,494 ft
(4,418 m)

Oasis
Valley

Muddy
River

MONTEREY
COUNTY

R
a
n
g
e
s

Sequoia
Foothills

Death Valley

Spring
Mountains

Gold
Butte
Pakoon

Lowest Point
in North America
-282 ft
(-86 m)

Las Vegas

Amargosa

San Luis
Obispo County

Bakersfield

Lake
Mead

M o j a v e   D e s e r t

Santa Barbara

Ventura

L.A.-Ventura

San Bernardino

Colorado

Santa
Cruz
Island

Los Angeles

Palm
Springs

Santa Ana Mountains

Salton Sea

S o n o r

San Diego
County

Gila

San Diego

Tijuana

D e s e

Heart of th
Dese

U.S.–WEST

KEY

■ Featured project

■ Other project

(square represents approximate
center of project area)

0   75   150 miles
0   75   150 kilometers

N

WYOMING

NEBRASKA

Cheyenne

GREAT
SALT
LAKE

Salt Lake
City

Great Salt
Lake

Uinta Mts.

Fort Collins

Western
High Plains

Arikaree
River

Yampa River

Denver

S. Fork Republican

Smoky Hill

Book Cliffs
Project

Roan Cliffs

U T A H

South
Park

Colorado Springs

K A N S A S

C O L O R A D O

Chico
Basin

Grand Junction

Glade
Park

Colorado River
Corridor

San Miguel

Gunnison

Pueblo

Arkansas

Gunnison

Dugout/
Canyonlands
Complex

San Miguel
River

SAN LUIS
VALLEY

Rio Grande

Purgatoire

Purgatoire
River

Lake
Powell

San Juan

M
o
u
n
t
a
i
n
s

Sangre de Cristo Mountains

OKLAHOMA

Colorado

Southern
Sangre
de Cristo
Mountains

Jemez
Mountains

Santa Fe

Canadian

San Francisco
Peaks Area

San Francisco Mts.

Flagstaff

Albuquerque

VERDE RIVER
WATERSHED

Rio Grande

A R I Z O N A

Verde

White
Mountains

N E W   M E X I C O

Lubbock

Hassayampa River
Watershed

Salt

Sacramento Mts.

Phoenix

Organ/
San Andres
Mountains

Tularosa
Basin

San Andres Mts.

Pecos

T E X A S

Gila

GILA-
MIMBRES
HEADWATERS

Sacramento
Mountains

San Pedro

San Pedro
River Watershed

Santa Cruz

Tucson

Sonoita Creek
Watershed

San Rafael
Valley

Malpais Borderlands

El Paso

Rio Grande

Pecos

M E X I C O

VERDE RIVER WATERSHED

Arizona

With more people moving into this area of desert and grassland that once supported only a few, water is the pivotal issue for the Verde watershed.

location between Prescott and Flagstaff, including Sedona

ecoregion Apache Highlands

project size 6,600 square miles

preserves Hartwell Canyon

public lands Prescott and Coconino national forests, Dead Horse Ranch State Park, Verde River Greenway, Tuzigoot National Monument, Montezuma's Castle National Monument, Red Rock State Park

partners U.S. Forest Service, Arizona State Parks, Verde River Citizens Alliance, Verde Water Association, Arizona Game and Fish Department, local landowners, Central Arizona Land Trust

conservancy initiatives Freshwater, Global Climate Change

natural events birthing of the pronghorn, May–June; wildflowers and cactus bloom, May–June; bald eagles breed, December

information Sharon Arnold, (602) 322-6993; sharon_arnold@tnc.org; nature.org/arizona

South of the Grand Canyon, off the edge of the pine-forested Mogollon Rim, the Verde River rises in a valley of tawny grass—seven springs watering an arid land. The clear waters gather and flow southward all year round, through the grasslands, through the red-rock desert, to the Verde's confluence with the Salt River 140 miles away.

In this dry region of desert and grassland, life follows the tendrils of water, precious and sacred. The banks, canyons

Cottonwoods line the Verde River, with the Black Hills in the distance.

and valleys of the Verde and its tributaries are awash in petroglyphs, pueblos and other signs of aboriginal cultures. At Montezuma's Well, the Sinagua peoples irrigated their crops more than 800 years ago. Some scholars believe that the well-watered Verde watershed was the scene of inter-tribal celebrations.

People today are still drawn to the balm of the Verde landscape. Near Sedona, where some see only strange rock formations and cliffs, others come to experience energy vortexes and a landscape of spiritual healing. Here New Age meets Old West, the latter in the form of ranchers who, like countless generations before them, gravitated to the watercourses for life and livelihood.

Pronghorn antelope.

Some of the largest individual pronghorn antelope in Arizona live in healthy bands in the upper Verde grasslands, but their wide-open range is becoming increasingly broken by roads and residential sub-divisions as the area's human population swells. Likewise, new development overtaps the watershed's groundwater supply, which in turn decreases surface flow in the Verde itself. At stake are several native desert fishes like the spikedace and razorback sucker—species that have been decimated else-where in the Southwest. In an effort to engage the community in water resource planning, The Nature Conservancy is working with Yavapai County planners to launch a county purchase of development rights program, which aims to leave grassland habitat unbroken and more water in ground and stream.

conservation profile

targets Big Chino Valley grasslands, Verde River, tributaries, cottonwood-willow forests, pronghorn antelope, river otter, southwestern willow flycatcher, spikedace, razorback sucker

stresses habitat loss and fragmentation to rural subdivision and flood-control projects, groundwater pumping, surface water diversions, invasive plants and animals

strategies encourage conservation manage-ment of public and private land, acquire land, secure conservation easements, protect water quantity, engage community, inform policy and management through scientific data

results 1,400 acres protected to date; launched Verde River Citizens Alliance

COSUMNES RIVER
California

The last free-flowing river on the western slope of the Sierra Nevada, the Cosumnes is now threatened by encroaching suburbs and growing demands for water.

location 20 miles south of Sacramento

ecoregion Great Central Valley

project size 800 square miles

preserves Cosumnes River

partners Bureau of Land Management, Ducks Unlimited, California Department of Fish and Game, California Department of Water Resources, State Lands Commission, Sacramento County

conservancy initiatives Fire, Freshwater, Invasive Species

natural events sandhill crane migration, September–March; Sandhill Crane Festival, early November

information Mike Eaton, project director, (916) 683-1699, meaton@tnc.org; nature.org/california

Cosumnes River.

The Cosumnes River is an anomaly in the heart of California's breadbasket—the last undammed river in the heavily irrigated Central Valley. The Cosumnes flows freely from its headwaters in the red fir forests of the Sierra Nevada to its confluence with the Mokelumne River and the marshes of the Sacramento–San Joaquin Delta. Its brown waters mosey sleepily along a broad, shallow course in the valley but are transformed by winter rains, surging and routinely flooding their banks. Ocean tides push nearly 100 miles up the delta, creating freshwater tidal wetlands in the river's lower reaches.

Stretches of the river are today much as they were when described by explorer John C. Fremont in 1844—laced with sloughs, ponds, oak woods and fertile bottomlands. Within the watershed are extensive seasonal wetlands known as vernal pools, which fill with rain in the spring and evaporate in the summer heat. These fleeting oases beget wildflowers and the endangered fairy shrimp, whose eggs lie dormant in the soil until the rains come.

The marshes and grasslands of the Cosumnes are wintering grounds for tens of thousands of migrating birds, songbirds and raptors, among them lesser and greater sandhill cranes, tundra swans and great blue heron. The river itself is home to a number of native fishes, and Chinook salmon are showing signs of rebounding after years of decline.

More than a century ago, settlers discovered the Central Valley's rich soils and began to clear forest and drain wetlands to make way for crops. Today, wedged between the bustling cities of Sacramento and Stockton, the agricultural land flanking the Cosumnes is increasingly targeted for suburban development. The land's continuation as farmland is a key conservation strategy, as it provides habitat for wildlife and helps buffer important streamside areas from the effects of urbanization.

In 1995, The Nature Conservancy and local farmers developed a 1,040-acre organic farm on the Cosumnes River Preserve. Since then, we have protected more than

Valley oak.

20,000 acres of private farmland and rangeland in the watershed through conservation easements, and 10,000 acres more through direct purchase. A new Conservancy subsidiary—Conservation Farms and Ranches, Inc.—will manage day-to-day farming operations and ensure professional management of these critical properties.

conservation profile

targets Cosumnes River, valley oak forest, blue oak forest, vernal pools, salmon, giant garter snake, sandhill crane and other wintering and year-round birds

stresses habitat destruction due to urbanization, groundwater pumping, incompatible agricultural practices

strategies build conservation alliances, promote compatible agricultural practices, influence land-use planning, acquire land, secure conservation easements

results 40,000 acres in conservation management; 1,040-acre organic farm established; 1,500 acres of riparian forest restored

MONTEREY COUNTY
California

Surrounded by encroaching population centers, Monterey County—still rural and wild—lies at the heart one of the world's most threatened ecoregions.

location 125 miles south of San Francisco

ecoregion California Central Coast

project size 3,300 square miles

preserves Elkhorn Slough, Big Creek, Palo Corona Ranch, Arroyo Seco Ranch

public lands Point Lobos State Reserve, Los Padres National Forest, Ventana Wilderness, Carmel River State Beach, Joshua Creek Canyon Ecological Reserve, Garrapata State Park

partners Big Sur Land Trust, Land Trust of Santa Cruz County, Elkhorn Slough Foundation, County of Monterey, California State Coastal Conservancy, California Department of Parks and Recreation, California Wildlife Conservation Board, U.S. Forest Service, Monterey Bay National Marine Sanctuary

conservancy initiatives Marine, Invasive Species

natural events California gray whale migrations, spring and fall; monarch butterflies return to Pacific Grove, winter

information Bill Leahy, project director, (831) 831-1722; bleahy@tnc.org; nature.org/california

Many of California's signature landscapes—towering mist-shrouded redwood forests, dramatic coastlines hemmed in by sheer-faced cliffs, rugged mountains blanketed by forests of evergreens, bucolic farm fields of fruits and vegetables—are found in just one county along the state's Central Coast.

Monterey County is an ecological microcosm of California. Extending from the rich waters of Monterey Bay south to Big Sur, the county's landscape is world-famous, breathtaking in beauty and rich in biological diversity. It has inspired artists ranging from author John Steinbeck to renowned poet Robinson Jeffers.

Pampas grass, Big Sur coast.

Today Monterey is the third-fastest-growing county in California, experiencing a population increase of 35 percent from 1980 to 1999. Scientists have identified the Central Coast as one of the most threatened ecoregions in the world because of its rapid loss of habitat to development and the presence of many rare native species like the endangered California condor. North America's largest bird and one of the continent's rarest, the condor has fewer than 74 individuals remaining in the wild.

Fortunately, vast expanses of Monterey County remain largely undeveloped, unfragmented and connected to nearby wildlands by wildlife corridors. Conservationists currently have a window of opportunity to safeguard the county's most biologically important areas—but that window is closing. Monterey County is at increasing risk from the rapid conversion of ranches, farms and oak woodlands to vineyards and subdivisions; intensive agriculture and a growing population place mounting pressure on regional water supplies. These threats are compounded by the lack of a broadly accepted regional vision for protecting the county's finest natural areas and guiding future growth into less environmentally sensitive places.

To help create a regional vision for Monterey County, The Nature Conservancy is lending scientific expertise, conservation planning capabilities, public opinion research and new policy tools to local community organizations and others grappling with land-use and public policy decisions. Together with public and private partners, we plan to purchase outright or acquire conservation easements on key lands in

highly threatened, biologically rich conservation areas. Some of the properties targeted for conservation action feature vital wildlife corridors linking protected areas.

Sea otter in kelp.

conservation profile

targets San Joaquin kit fox, California condor, California brown pelican, southern sea otter, Menzies' wallflower, Monterey pine

stresses conversion of ranches and agricultural land, unsustainable water use, pollution of streams and offshore waters

strategies acquire land, secure conservation easements, promote ecologically sound public policies and planning, engage community in natural resource management, protect water supply, combat invasive species

results acquired two ranches totaling more than 11,500 acres; voters approved an urban growth boundary in neighboring Santa Cruz County

SAN LUIS VALLEY
Colorado

Water is the highest stake in the San Luis Valley—for farmers, wetlands and wildlife, and for the towering dunes whose sands are continuously replenished by the flow of water itself.

location 150 miles southwest of Colorado Springs

ecoregion Southern Rocky Mountains

project size 9,000 square miles

preserves Medano-Zapata Ranch, Mishak Lakes, Baca Ranch

public lands Great Sand Dunes National Monument, Monte Vista and Alamosa national wildlife refuges, San Luis Lakes State Park, Russell Lakes State Wildlife Area, Rio Grande National Forest, Blanca Wetlands

partners National Park Service, U.S. Fish and Wildlife Service, ranchers, farmers, local land and water trusts, Colorado State Land Board, U.S. Forest Service, Colorado Division of Wildlife, Bureau of Land Management, water conservation districts

conservancy initiatives Freshwater, Invasive Species, Fire

natural events sandhill cranes gather, March and April

information Bowen Gibson, (720) 974-7009; bowen_gibson@tnc.org; nature.org/colorado

Great Sand Dunes National Monument and the Sangre de Cristo Mountains.

To stand in the greasewood flats of the San Luis Valley and look eastward to the Sangre de Cristo Mountains is a fantastic, otherworldly sight: Pale, sinuous sand dunes twist and rise hundreds of feet in the foreground, a startling contrast to the snow-capped mountains looming behind. These are the tallest dunes in North America, shaped and replenished by the dynamic interaction

of sand, wind and water—water from aquifers and that which pours off the mountain slopes in crystal streams.

The San Luis Valley has been called one of the continent's most unusual landscapes. Running 150 miles long and 50 miles wide, flanked by the Sangre de Cristo and San Juan Mountains, it encompasses cottonwood-lined creeks, shrubby expanses of rabbit-brush and sagebrush, shallow lakes, piñon and juniper hillsides, forests of aspen, pine and spruce, and the strange sand dunes themselves.

Underneath the valley floor lies a huge aquifer that feeds ponds, artesian wells, springs and lakes; from the valley flow the headwaters of the Rio Grande. The wetlands draw large concentrations of wildlife, such as the sandhill cranes that come to dance here each spring. The waters also have enabled farmers, many of whose ancestors moved into the valley from the Spanish Southwest generations ago, to make a living. The presence of so much water in the arid West makes the San Luis the envy of many.

In 2001, to thwart a plan that would have exported water from the valley to growing Front Range communities to the east, The Nature Conservancy signed a purchase agreement for the 97,000-acre Baca Ranch, a historic ranch that dates from an 1824 Mexican land grant. The water

rights—and the water itself—remain with the land, ensuring that the hydrologic processes that nurture the sand dunes and myriad life forms will continue. The local community broadly supported the Baca purchase and the creation of the Great Sand Dunes National Park—a rare occurrence in the rural West where new public lands are not always welcome.

Great Sand Dunes tiger beetle.

conservation profile

targets sand dunes, greasewood flats, ephemeral wetlands, wet meadows, slender spiderflower, Great Sand Dunes tiger beetle, sandhill cranes and other migratory shorebirds

stresses exportation and diversion of water, invasive species, inappropriate recreation, oil and gas exploration and development, incompatible residential development, landscape fragmentation

strategies acquire land, secure conservation easements, protect water quantity, influence land-use planning, combat invasive species, prevent or minimize impact of oil and gas exploration and development

results more than 200,000 acres in conservation management

OASIS VALLEY
NEVADA

Lowest Point
in North America
-282 ft.
(-86 m)

Death Valley

Amargosa

Pahrump

Lake
Mead

Las
Vegas

Mojave Desert

CALIFORNIA

OASIS VALLEY
Nevada

Competing demands for water threaten to drain this desert oasis at the headwaters of the Amargosa River, home to more than 50 species found nowhere else on Earth.

location 125 miles northwest of Las Vegas

ecoregion Mojave Desert

project size 3 million acres

preserves Torrance Ranch, Parker Ranch

public lands bulk of project area owned by Bureau of Land Management; Ash Meadows National Wildlife Refuge, Death Valley National Park

partners Bureau of Land Management, National Park Service, U.S. Fish and Wildlife Service, Natural Resources Conservation Service, Nevada Division of Wildlife, University of Nevada-Reno, Nye County, Town of Beatty

conservancy initiatives Invasive Species

natural events neotropical migratory birds, spring and fall; wildflower blooms in the desert uplands, spring

information Caroline Ciocca, (702) 737-8744, cciocca@tnc.org; nature.org/nevada

From its headwaters in Oasis Valley to Death Valley 125 miles away in California, the Amargosa River courses beneath the Mojave Desert, mostly unseen and undetectable. It surfaces only sporadically as springs and seeps—true oases in the country's most arid state. The wetlands engender prolific islands of trees, grasses and creatures uniquely adapted to this system of harsh extremes, including more than 50 fish, snail, amphibian and plant species that exist nowhere else on the planet.

In the Oasis Valley, the Amargosa has long drawn people as well. Paiute and Shoshone tribes have continuously occupied the valley for several centuries, living off its abundance of surface waters, wild grains and game. Their stone tools, arrowheads and petroglyphs are found throughout this part of the forbidding Mojave. In the early 1900s, three major railroad lines intersected here, bringing settlers and miners to the area's booming gold towns, dubbed the "Chicago of the West."

The natural wonders of the Amargosa are now in jeopardy as the precious life-line of underground water is in danger of being siphoned off by two of the nation's fast-growing cities: Las Vegas and Pahrump. The river and its spring oases are key to the survival of the Amargosa toad, whose federal listing as endangered was forestalled in 1996 when The Nature Conservancy led an effort to protect its habitat through a management agreement among seven public agencies.

To address the issue of excessive water withdrawal throughout the river system, the Conservancy is assembling a regional water coalition to influence current and future uses of water in the Amargosa River system. In the Oasis Valley, we are working with the community of Beatty to rid the streams and wetlands of tamarisk and crayfish, invasive species that are harming native ones like the Amargosa toad and the Oasis Valley speckled dace.

Collared lizard.

Torrance Ranch.

conservation profile

targets Mojave Desert, riparian woodland and wetlands, freshwater springs, cactus, desert tortoise, kit fox, Amargosa toad, gila monster, Oasis Valley speckled dace, Oasis Valley springsnail, Devil's Hole pupfish

stresses excessive water withdrawal, invasive species

strategies protect water supply, combat invasive species, engage community in natural resource management, promote ecotourism

results 655 acres in conservation management; Conservation Area Plan completed for larger Amargosa River System

GILA-MIMBRES HEADWATERS

GILA-MIMBRES HEADWATERS
New Mexico

In the shadow of the oldest wilderness area in the country, an experiment aims to balance cattle grazing with the ecological needs of wild creatures.

location near Silver City; 2.5 hours northwest of El Paso, Texas

ecoregion Arizona-New Mexico Mountains

project size 1.9 million acres

preserves Gila Riparian, Mimbres River

public lands Gila National Forest, Gila Cliff Dwellings National Monument, Bureau of Land Management lands, state trust lands

partners U.S. Forest Service, Jornada Experimental Range, Greer & Winston, Ltd., NM Environmental Department, NM Department of Game & Fish, U.S. EPA, U.S. Fish and Wildlife Service, Grinnell College

conservancy initiatives Fire, Freshwater

natural events hummingbirds, mid-July–to early August; monsoon rains bring abundance of frogs, toads and summer wildflowers, July–September

information Bill Waldman, state director, (505) 988-3867, bwaldman@tnc.org; nature.org/newmexico

U p near the continental divide of southwestern New Mexico, where sun-warmed pine and fir needles are pungent underfoot, two rivers rise and flow down opposite sides of the Mogollon Range. The Gila flows west, the Mimbres east. The Gila—free-flowing and wild in its New Mexico reaches—eventually merges with the Colorado. But the Mimbres, a closed-basin desert stream, tumbles downslope only 40 miles before disappearing underground.

Around 1450, an ancient culture bearing the same name as the evanescent river also disappeared mysteriously. Signs of the Mimbres people are everywhere along the two rivers, from

pit houses to shards of black-on-white pottery. Later the Apaches made these mountains and valleys their home— and their hideout. Geronimo, the Chiricahua Apache who was born here, three times fled Arizona reservations to return to the wilds of his birthplace. The maze of rugged canyons hid him and fellow Apaches like Cochise, as well as outlaws like Butch Cassidy.

Gila Cliff Dwellings National Monument.

The wilderness that gave them refuge remains to this day. In 1924, at the urging of Aldo Leopold, whose first assignment out of Yale Forestry School had been in the Gila National Forest, the Gila became the nation's first designated wilderness area. Here, where southern Rockies meet Sierra Madre, Mexican gray wolves, Mexican spotted owls and hundreds of species of nesting birds travel the spine of the sheltering mountains. In the headwaters of the two wild rivers remain the last stronghold of the endangered southwestern willow flycatcher and the sole population of the Chihuahua chub, a native fish that once nourished the Mimbres people.

Although a ranching culture has helped preserve the area's wilderness character, cattle grazing along the rivers have degraded water quality and streamside forests, putting both the flycatcher and the chub in danger. In a collaborative venture to find ecologically sound grazing practices, The Nature Conservancy has teamed with local ranchers to create the 132,000-acre Headwaters Ranch, an experiment that is being monitored and documented by federal agency scientists.

West Fork of the Gila.

conservation profile

targets Mexican spotted owl, southwestern willow flycatcher, Chiricahua leopard frog, Mexican gray wolf, cottonwood-willow forests, Arizona sycamore, native fish like Chihuahua chub, spikedace and Gila trout

stresses altered fire regime, inappropriate grazing, invasive species, river channelization, surface water diversion

strategies acquire land and water rights, improve grazing management, restore ecosystems through fire management, remove levees and water diversions, combat invasive species

results more than 140,000 acres in conservation management

GREAT SALT LAKE
Utah

With its eastern shore bounded by sprawling metropolitan areas, the Great Salt Lake faces development pressures that threaten the system's abundant avian life.

location northwest of Salt Lake City

ecoregion Great Basin Ecoregion

project size 22,000 square miles

preserves Great Salt Lake Shorelands

public lands Bear River Migratory Bird National Wildlife Refuge, Farmington Bay Refuge, Ogden Wildlife Management Area, Howard Slough Waterfowl Management Area

partners Utah Reclamation Mitigation and Conservation Commission, Envision Utah, Great Salt Lake Alliance, Utah Division of Wildlife Resources, Utah Department of Natural Resources, Ducks Unlimited, Davis County, Kennecott Utah Copper, National Audubon Society, Intermountain West Joint Venture

conservancy initiatives Invasive Species

natural events major bird migrations, spring and fall; Great Salt Lake Bird Festival, May

information Heidi Mosburg, (801) 238-2328, hmosburg@tnc.org; nature.org/utah

Vast and enigmatic, the Great Salt Lake fills the nadir of Utah's Great Basin. This inland "sea" is eight times as salty as sea water; Israel's Dead Sea is the only body of water in the world with a higher salt content. But far from dead, the Great Salt Lake is a complex and dynamic ecosystem and a desert oasis to millions of migrating birds each spring and fall.

The Great Salt Lake, itself almost the size of Connecticut, is a relict of the massive Lake Bonneville, which covered most of western Utah some 20,000 years ago. The

Stansbury Island.

hills around the lake reveal distinct benches marking the ancient lake's water levels. The past is also evident in the Bonneville Salt Flats to the west—a broad, salt-covered lake bed that remained when Bonneville's waters evaporated. It is one of the flattest places on Earth.

Native Americans inhabited the lake's shores and islands as far back as 10,000 years ago. In 1843 the first formal exploration was led by prominent surveyor John C. Fremont, who hired fur trapper Kit Carson as a guide on this and other mapmaking expeditions. Fremont's widely read accounts of their travels helped make Carson a national hero of his time.

The Great Salt Lake is a unique natural system. Salt-tolerant plants thrive in seasonally flooded playas and mud flats that support more than 200 bird species in their Pacific Flyway migrations. These avian travelers are nourished by brine flies and brine shrimp that proliferate in saltwater.

Burgeoning Salt Lake City, sandwiched between mountains and lake, puts pressure on the Great Salt Lake and its wetlands. Shoreline development and mineral extraction are key threats to the lake's wildlife. The Nature Conservancy is participating in a citizen-based process in Davis County that is planning for future growth on the shoreline while incorporating the ecological needs of the lake. Local municipalities have already agreed to the

Flock of gulls.

plan's provision to confine development to designated areas. Next steps are the adoption and implementation of conservation measures, such as transfer-of-development rights programs and easements.

conservation profile

targets Great Salt Lake, seasonally flooded wetlands and mud flats, riparian systems, white-faced ibis, long-billed curlew, snowy plover and other nesting and migratory birds

stresses habitat loss to residential and industrial development, surface water diversions, compartmentalization of lake for mineral extraction, water quality degradation

strategies acquire land, secure conservation easements, engage community, influence land-use planning, encourage conservation management of public and private lands, restore ecosystems, promote compatible development

results 3,500-acre preserve established; Davis County Shorelands Plan Phase 1 completed

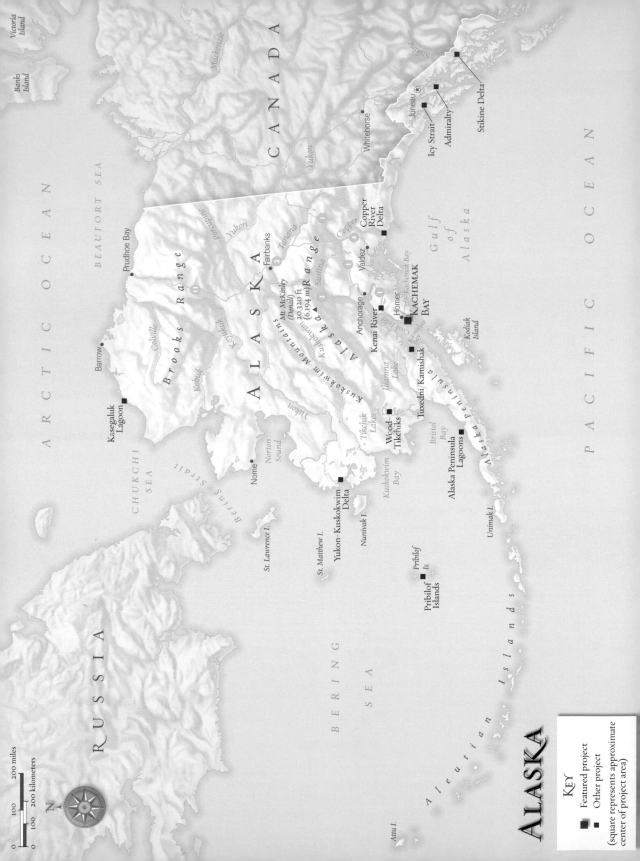

ALASKA

KEY

■ Featured project
▪ Other project

(square represents approximate center of project area)

ARCTIC OCEAN

BEAUFORT SEA

CANADA

Mackenzie

Victoria Island

Banks Island

Porcupine

Prudhoe Bay

Barrow

Kasegaluk Lagoon

CHUKCHI SEA

Brooks Range

Colville

Kobuk

Koyukuk

Noatak

Yukon

Fairbanks

Tanana

ALASKA

Whitehorse

Stikine

Juneau

Icy Strait

Admiralty

Stikine Delta

ALASKA

Alaska Range

Copper

Copper River Delta

Mt. McKinley (Denali) 20,320 ft (6,194 m) ▲

Susitna

Valdez

Kuskokwim Mountains

Anchorage

Kenai River

Kachemak Bay

Homer

KACHEMAK BAY

Cook Inlet

Gulf of Alaska

Kodiak Island

Kusko kwim

Tikchik Lakes

Wood-Tikchiks

Iliamna Lake

Tuxedni / Kamishak

Nome

Norton Sound

Bering Strait

St. Lawrence I.

St. Matthew I.

Nunivak I.

Yukon-Kuskokwim Delta

Kuskokwim Bay

Bristol Bay

Alaska Peninsula Lagoons

Alaska Peninsula

Unimak I.

Pribilof Is.

Pribilof Islands

BERING SEA

RUSSIA

Aleutian Islands

Attu I.

PACIFIC OCEAN

N

0   100   200 miles
0   100   200 kilometers

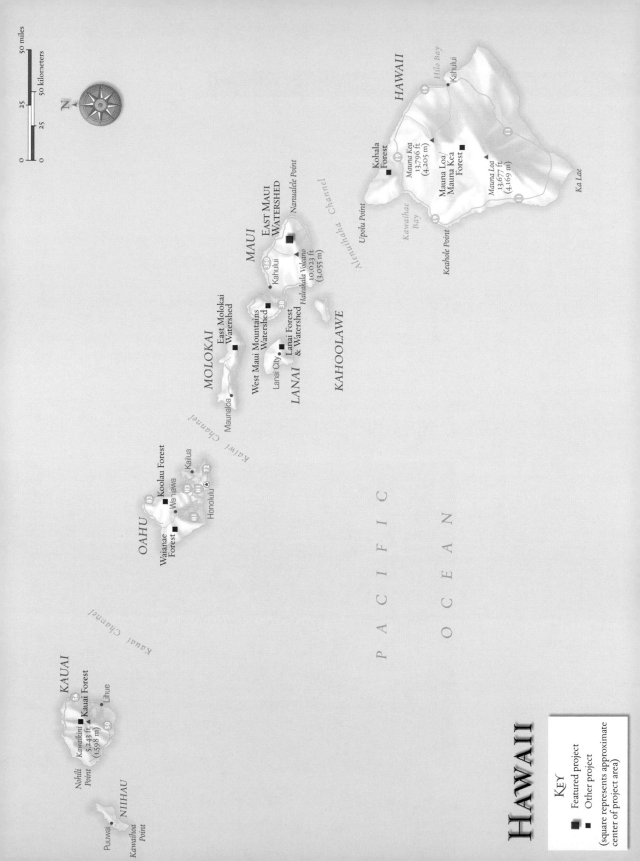

HAWAII

50 miles
50 kilometers
25
25
0
0
N

KAUAI
Kauai Forest
Kawaikini
5,243 ft
(1,598 m)
Lihue
Nohili
Point
NIIHAU
Kawaihoa
Point
Puuwai

Kauai Channel

OAHU
Koolau Forest
Wahiawa
Waianae
Forest
Kailua
Honolulu

Kaiwi Channel

MOLOKAI
East Molokai
Watershed
Maunaloa

West Maui Mountains
Watershed
LANAI
Lanai City
Lanai Forest
& Watershed

MAUI
EAST MAUI
WATERSHED
Nanualele Point
Kahului
Haleakala Volcano
10,023 ft
(3,055 m)

KAHOOLAWE

Kalohi Channel

Alenuihaha Channel

HAWAII
Hilo Bay
Kahului
Kohala
Forest
Mauna Kea
13,796 ft
(4,205 m)
Mauna Loa /
Mauna Kea
Forest
Mauna Loa
13,677 ft
(4,169 m)
Upolu Point
Kawaihae
Bay
Keahole Point
Kawaihae Point
Ka Lae

P A C I F I C   O C E A N

ALASKA

Mt. McKinley
20,320 ft (6,194 m) ▲

Range

Susitna

Anchorage

Valdez

Iliamna
Lake

Kenai
Peninsula

Homer

Gulf of
Alaska

**KACHEMAK
BAY**

Kodiak
Island

KACHEMAK BAY
Alaska

Mounting development pressure along the shoreline of Kachemak Bay threatens the coastal and marine habitats of this unique tidal system.

location 130 miles southwest of Anchorage

ecoregions Cook Inlet Basin, Gulf of Alaska Mountains and Fjordlands

project size 1 million acres of land and water

preserves Stone Steps Lake Wetlands

public lands Kachemak Bay State Park, Kachemak Bay Critical Habitat Area, Kenai National Wildlife Refuge, Alaska Maritime National Wildlife Refuge

partners Kachemak Heritage Land Trust, Seldovia Native Association, Kachemak Bay Research Reserve, City of Homer

conservancy initiatives Invasive Species, Marine

natural events Kachemak Bay Shorebird Festival, early May; extreme tides, daily; seabird colony of 15,000 nesting birds, spring

information Cheryl McGrew, (907) 276-3133, ext. 104, cmcgrew@tnc.org; nature.org/alaska

The waters of Kachemak Bay cut a sapphire channel between two fingers of land at the tip of Alaska's Kenai Peninsula. To the south, glaciers and rugged fjords rise from the sea, giving way to dramatic snow-covered peaks. Across the bay, moose and bear forage among low-lying wetlands, spruce forests and open meadows. In 1778, Captain James Cook sailed into Kachemak Bay in search of the Northwest Passage, but the vast waterway is only an offshoot of a much larger inlet.

Kachemak Bay is one of the Earth's most productive marine systems. The secret to its richness lies in the tides, which can

Humpback whales.

rise as much as 28 vertical feet in six hours. This variation creates gravel bars and salt marshes teeming with life, which beckon hundreds of thousands of shorebirds on their spring migrations. Pods of orcas sweep the sea for prey, and sea otters bob playfully in the choppy currents. The bay and the rivers flowing into it support vigorous runs of five species of salmon that are endangered in the Pacific Northwest.

Humans have inhabited Kachemak Bay for thousands of years, drawn by the same life-sustaining forces that support the bay's abundance of wildlife. The Kenaitze and Dena'ina Indians subsisted for centuries fishing, hunting and gathering plants. Generous deposits of coal drew white settlers in the 1800s, but commercial fishing and processing gradually overtook coal as the local economic driver. Today fishing is fueling a growing tourism industry, as sport-fishing enthusiasts are lured to "the Halibut Capital of the World" to catch specimens weighing as much as 350 pounds.

Although remote and sparsely populated by lower-48 standards, Kachemak Bay's allure is threatening its shoreline. Commercial development has spread into sensitive wetlands, and residential development rings many of the bay's coves. In response, The Nature Conservancy works to acquire critical properties, to influence local land-use planning and to

Bald eagles on driftwood.

strengthen the capacity of a local land trust to acquire lands and secure conservation easements from private landowners.

conservation profile

targets tidal marine/estuarine ecosystem, shorebirds, cliff-nesting seabirds, floodplain ecosystems, coastal spruce forest, wetland complexes, Steller's sea lion, bald eagle, sea otter, orca, humpback whale, Pacific salmon

stresses incompatible residential and commercial development, incompatible logging, marine pollution, especially from oil spills

strategies acquire land, secure conservation easements, influence land-use planning, promote compatible development, build conservation alliances, strengthen local partner organizations, engage community

results largest unfragmented wetland complex on north shore protected; priority floodplain properties acquired

EAST MAUI WATERSHED
Hawaii

Although aggressive invasive species are pushing hundreds of Hawaiian natives to the brink of extinction, collaborative conservation work in East Maui is pushing back.

location 15 miles from Maui's Kahului International Airport

ecoregion High Islands Hawai'i

size 100,000 acres

preserves Waikamoi

public lands Haleakala National Park; Kipahulu, Hana, Makawao, and Ko'olau state forest reserves; Hanawi Natural Area Reserve

partners National Park Service, Hawai'i State Division of Forestry and Wildlife, Hana Ranch Company, Haleakala Ranch Company, County of Maui, East Maui Irrigation Company

conservancy initiatives Freshwater, Invasive Species

natural events East Maui Taro Festival, March; Keanae cultural festival, August

information Janice Nillias, (808) 587-6237, jnillias@tnc.org; nature.org/hawaii

On the eastern side of Maui, native Hawaiian forest of towering 'ohi'a and koa trees stretches across the wet windward slopes of dormant Haleakala Volcano. As with all of the Hawaiian islands, life forms here developed in isolation for millions of years, separated from land by thousands of miles of ocean in all directions. From a few specimens that storm and chance sent by air and sea to the

Waimoku Falls, Haleakala National Park.

Hawaiian archipelago evolved more than 10,000 unique plant and animal species. Fifty-odd species of honeycreeper, for instance—birds of all color, shape and size— evolved from a single common ancestor. Some have curved beaks designed to extract nectar from certain blossoms; others have short beaks made for feeding on insects or seeds.

From the rim of Haleakala's crater to the sea 10,000 feet below, ancient forest envelops a rugged terrain of steep cliffs and deep valleys carpeted with spongy moss and a lush tangle of shrubs, ferns, vines and roots. The misty treetops are spangled with crimson and yellow 'ohi'a blossoms and colorful native birds like the 'i'iwi, amakihi and 'akohekohe, or crested honeycreeper. Copious rains produce 60 billion gallons of fresh water each year— the primary source for island residents and businesses. This forest of East Maui was so sacred to ancient Hawaiians that only those with appropriate spiritual training were allowed to enter.

In 1991 The Nature Conservancy joined forces with the area's six federal, state and private landowners and the county of Maui to form the East Maui Watershed Partnership, bringing 100,000 acres—the core of the watershed—into active conservation management. But the greatest threat to this unique natural system still exists. Non-native species brought to the Hawaiian islands by humans can devastate native forest and birds, which lack natural defenses to fend off non-native predators. Goats and deer denude the landscape; wild pigs plow up the rain forest, spreading weeds and diseases. Invasive weeds like miconia choke out native plants and trees.

Haleakala silversword.

The Conservancy's efforts are now focused on removing these alien pests. To control hoofed animals, we are constructing fences around the most sensitive areas in the steep summit forest. Our goal is to remove all ungulates above an elevation of 3,500 feet, creating a 30,000-acre reserve where East Maui's forest birds can find refuge in a thriving ecosystem.

conservation profile

targets koa and 'ohi'a forest, Haleakala silversword, Maui natives like the crested honeycreeper and Maui parrotbill

stresses invasive plants and animals

strategies combat invasive species, protect water supply, engage community, build conservation alliances, secure conservation easements

results 100,000 acres in conservation management through formation of the East Maui Partnership; five miles of fencing completed; miconia treatment conducted over a 20,000-acre area; community-based hunting program established

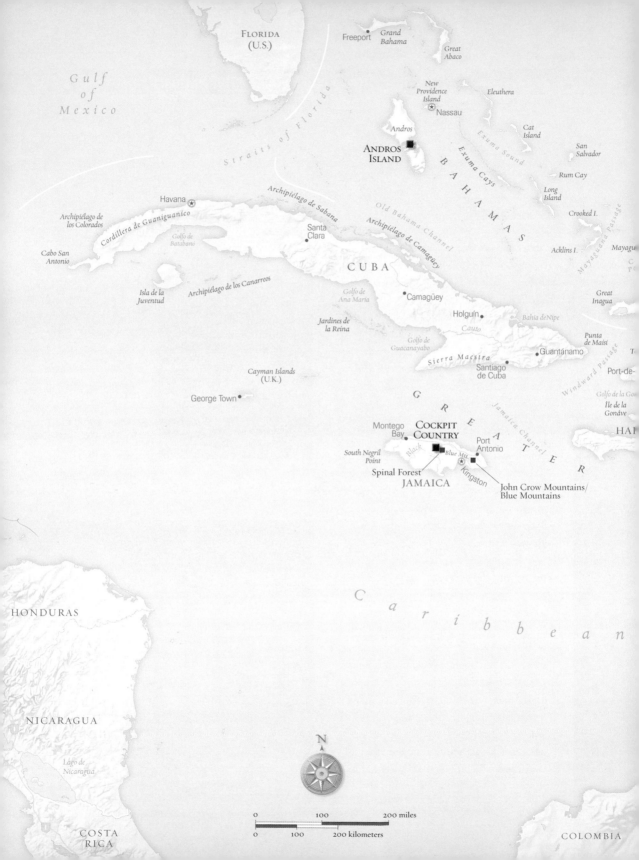

FLORIDA
(U.S.)

Freeport *Grand
Bahama*

*Great
Abaco*

*Gulf
of
Mexico*

*New
Providence
Island*

Eleuthera

⊛ Nassau

Andros

**ANDROS
ISLAND**

*Cat
Island*

*San
Salvador*

*B
A
H
A
M
A
S*

Exuma Cays

Exuma Sound

Rum Cay

*Long
Island*

Crooked I.

Havana ⊛

Archipiélago de Sabana

Old Bahama Channel

*Archipiélago de
los Colorados*

Cordillera de Guaniguanico

Santa
Clara

Archipiélago de Camagüey

Acklins I.

Mayaguana Passage

Mayagua

*Golfo de
Batabanó*

C U B A

*Cabo San
Antonio*

Camagüey

Holguín

*Great
Inagua*

*Isla de la
Juventud*

Archipiélago de los Canarreos

*Golfo de
Ana María*

Bahía de Nipe

Cauto

*Punta
de Maisí*

*Jardines de
la Reina*

*Golfo de
Guacanayabo*

Guantánamo

Port-de-

Sierra Maestra

Santiago
de Cuba

Windward Passage

Golfo de la Go

*Île de la
Gonâve*

*Cayman Islands
(U.K.)*

George Town ∙

*G
R
E
A
T
E
R*

Jamaica Channel

HAI

Montego
Bay ∙

**COCKPIT
COUNTRY**

Port
Antonio

*South Negril
Point*

Black   *Blue Mts.*

⊛
Kingston

Spinal Forest

JAMAICA

**John Crow Mountains/
Blue Mountains**

HONDURAS

C   a   r   i   b   b   e   a   n

NICARAGUA

*Lago de
Nicaragua*

N

0   100   200 miles

0   100   200 kilometers

**COSTA
RICA**

COLOMBIA

THE CARIBBEAN

ATLANTIC

OCEAN

W E S T

I N D I E S

L E E W A R D   I S L A N D S

Turks and Caicos
Islands
(U.K.)
• Grand Turk

DOMINICAN
REPUBLIC

MADRE
DE LAS
AGUAS
■

• Santiago

Lago de
Enriquillo

Mt. La Selle
8,793 ft (2,680 m)

• Santo
Domingo

Isla
Saona

Isla
Mona

Mayagüez •

San
Juan

Puerto Rico
(U.S.)

Isla
Culebra

Isla
Vieques

Virgin
Islands
(U.S.)

VIRGIN ISLANDS
MARINE & COASTAL SYSTEM

Virgin Islands
(U.K.)
Anegada

■ Road Town

Charlotte
Amalie

St. Croix

Anguilla
(U.K.)

The
Valley •

St. Martin
(Fr.)

St. Barthélémy (Fr.)

St. Maarten
(Neth.)
Saba

St. Eustatius
(Neth.)

Barbuda

Basseterre
●

St. John's
●

ANTIGUA
&
BARBUDA

ST. KITTS
& NEVIS

Montserrat
(U.K.)

Guadeloupe
(Fr.)

Basse-Terre
●

Marie-Galante

A N T I L L E S

S e a

Aves
(Venezuela)

L
E
S
S
E
R

A
N
T
I
L
L
E
S

DOMINICA

Roseau ●

Martinique
(Fr.)

Fort-de-France ●

Castries ● ST. LUCIA

GRENADINES
MARINE & COASTAL
SYSTEM
■

ST. VINCENT
& THE
GRENADINES

Kingstown
●

GRENADA

St. George's ●

W
I
N
D
W
A
R
D

I
S
L
A
N
D
S

BARBADOS

Bridgetown ●

Aruba
(Neth.)

Oranjesad ●

L E S S E R   A N T I L L E S

Netherlands
Antilles

Curaçao

Willemstad ●

Bonaire

Islas Los Roques

Islas
Las Aves

Islas
Orchila

Isla Blanquilla

Golfo de Venezuela

Caracas ●

VENEZUELA

Isla
La Tortuga

Islas de
Margarita

Los Testigos

Canaan ●

Tobago

TRINIDAD
&
TOBAGO

Port of
Spain ●

Trinidad

ANDROS ISLAND
Bahamas

An anomaly in the Caribbean, Andros Island is big, forested and unspoiled—
a rare Bahamian wilderness teeming with opportunities for conservation.

location 20 miles west of
Nassau; 60 miles east of Miami

ecoregion Bahamian
Archipelago

project size 2,300 square miles
of land; 7,500 square miles of
marine environment

public lands Central Andros
National Park, Crown lands

partners Andros Conservancy
and Trust, Bahamas National Trust,
Department of Fisheries, Bahamas
Reef Environment Educational
Foundation, Ministry of Tourism,
local businesses

conservancy initiatives
Fire, Marine

natural events storm-triggered
crab migration and festival, June;
full-moon fish spawning aggregations, monthly

information
Aleksandra Stankovic,
(703) 841-7189,
astankovic@tnc.org;
nature.org/bahamas

Love Hill Reef.

L ying just above the Tropic of
Cancer, Andros is the largest and
yet least discovered and developed
island in the Bahamian Archipelago. Forty
miles wide by 100 miles long, Andros hosts
only 9,000 residents. Inland, beyond
white beaches and mangrove flats
renowned for bonefish, most of the island
remains forested. Tropical pines, hardwoods, dry broadleaf evergreens and

freshwater marshes offer a glimpse of what peninsular Florida, 60 miles to the west, once looked like. In the community of Red Bays lives another link to Florida's past: Seminole Indians who trace their roots on Andros to an exodus from the mainland centuries ago.

Cutting perfect circles into the forest are 200 blue holes—small, deep pools in the island's limestone skeleton formed when a subterranean cavern collapsed. At first the holes were flooded with seawater; but after countless seasons of storms, fresh water collected, settling atop the heavier saltwater. Living in the thin freshwater lens are hundreds of species unique to each blue hole. The secrets of these evolutionary laboratories have intrigued scientists, including the late Jacques Cousteau, for decades.

Cousteau also led expeditions to explore Andros's 170-mile-long barrier reef, the third-longest coral reef in the world. Near the reef the turquoise waters of the Caribbean turn dark blue as a deep channel curves within a mile of the island's eastern shore. In this "Tongue of the Ocean," as it is known locally, where the shallows give way to a precipitous drop of thousands of feet, huge aggregations of grouper spawn on nights of the full moon. Here, from the ocean's depths, sea turtles, barracudas and other creatures emerge onto the near-shore flats.

Already tanker ships arrive daily to export 6 million gallons of the island's fresh water to Nassau, posing a severe threat to Andros's ecosystems. Sensing a sea change facing their island, many Androsians and The Nature Conservancy came together to incorporate the Andros Conservancy and Trust, and soon after helped create the island's first protected area—the 300,000-acre Central Andros National Park.

Tiger grouper.

conservation profile

targets coral reefs, pine woodlands, blue holes, Nassau grouper, queen conch, rock iguana, West Indian flamingo, hawksbill turtle, spotted dolphin, shearwater, Kirtland's warbler

stresses unsustainable harvest of marine resources, freshwater depletion, destruction of mangrove and coastal habitats, altered fire regime

strategies designate marine and terrestrial protected areas, strengthen local partner organizations, restore ecosystems through fire management, foster sustainable fishing practices

results created Central Andros National Park

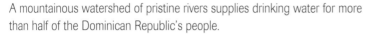

MADRE DE LAS AGUAS CONSERVATION AREA
Dominican Republic

A mountainous watershed of pristine rivers supplies drinking water for more than half of the Dominican Republic's people.

location east from the Haitian border; 30 miles from Santo Domingo

ecoregion Hispaniola Pine Forest, Hispaniola Broadleaf Forest

project size 1.4 million acres

public lands Armando Bermúdez, Juan B. Pérez Rancier (Valle Nuevo), José del Carmen Ramírez, Nalga de Maco and Eugenio de Jesus Marcano (Humeadora) national parks: Ebano Verde Scientific Reserve

partners Fundación Moscoso Puello, Federación de Campesinos hacia el Progreso, Junta Yaque, Plan Cordillera, Asociación de Agricultores de los Dajaos, Fundación Lomas Verdes, Asociación de Mujeres Nueva Esperanza

conservancy initiatives Freshwater, Global Climate Change

natural events Valle Nuevo in January and February: springlike mornings, hot noons, damp and chilly afternoons, and cold starry nights.

information Aleks Stankovic, (703) 841-7189, astankovic@tnc.org; nature.org/dominicanrepublic

A mong the islands of the Caribbean, soaring slopes like those of the Dominican Republic's Central Mountains are a rarity. Christopher Columbus avoided these formidable peaks—the highest, Pico Duarte, towers above the clouds at more than 10,000 feet—when he explored the island of Hispaniola in 1492.

Nestled within these mountains are the headwaters of 17 important rivers that provide energy, irrigation and drinking

Bridge over Rio Tablones, Armando Bermúdez National Park.

water for more than half of the country's population. Madre de las Aguas—"mother of the waters"—takes its name from these waterways. Spanning seven separate protected areas, the watershed covers one-fifth of the Dominican Republic's land area and nurtures the nation both physically and spiritually.

Many of its species, including more than 90 percent of its amphibians, reptiles and butterflies, are uniquely Dominican and found nowhere else on Earth. Cloud forests draw fresh water from the skies to fortify the rivers, which rush downward through pine, palm and broadleaf forests filled with hundreds of bird and butterfly species. More unusual creatures inhabit these woods as well, such as the small, shrewlike solenodon, which first appeared 30 million years ago and now exists only on the island of Hispaniola.

Cloud forest, Cordillera Central.

Today deforestation, uncontrolled fires, hunting, slash-and-burn agriculture and erosion from hillside farming threaten this wilderness and, along with it, the country's irreplaceable freshwater supply. In response, The Nature Conservancy and partner group Fundación Moscoso Puello are working to expand and link Madre de las Aguas' network of protected areas. Plans call for hiring and training park rangers, reforesting abandoned farmland and training local agricultural collectives in methods of low-impact farming and sustainable forest harvesting.

conservation profile

targets Bicknell's thrush, solenodon, Hispaniolan woodpecker, narrow-billed tody, highland aquatic systems, cloud forests, montane broadleaf and manacla forests, Hispaniolan pine, juniper and magnolia

stresses unsustainable logging, uncontrolled fires, slash-and-burn agriculture, expansion of coffee fields and hillside farming

strategies protect water quality and supply, engage community, strengthen local partner organizations, secure conservation easements

results helped expand Valle Nuevo National Park by more than 100,000 acres; visitor centers and ranger stations built for two national parks; 1,300 small farmers participating in sustainable farming practices

COCKPIT COUNTRY
Jamaica

With 5,000 hillocks and valleys rippling across the land, Cockpit Country has been nearly impenetrable for humans—good news for Jamaica's most pristine forests.

location 130 miles northwest of Kingston

ecoregion Jamaican Tropical Moist Broadleaf Forest

project size 372 square miles

public lands Cockpit Country Forest Reserve

partners Jamaica Forestry Department, South Trelawny Environmental Agency, Windsor Research Centre

conservancy initiatives Freshwater, Invasive Species

information Aleks Stankovic, (703) 841-7198, astankovic@tnc.org; nature.org/jamaica

The distinctive terrain and unique inhabitants of Cockpit Country are products of the passage of time. Millions of years of limestone erosion in the region have sculpted a topography of rounded peaks and steep-sided valleys underlain by a complex network of caves. Because of the island's biogeographic isolation during most of its geologic history, this strange terrain harbors a highly diverse array of plants and animals found nowhere else on Earth.

Cockpit Country's thousands of depressions—dubbed "cockpits" by the

The rolling hillocks and valleys of Cockpit Country.

British in the 17th century for their resemblance to cock-fighting arenas—drain abundant rainfall through porous bedrock and sinkholes. Spring-fed streams wind through caverns, emerging at the coast as three major rivers—the Great, Black and Martha Brea—collectively the source of two-thirds of Jamaica's fresh water. Native bats like the imperiled Jamaican flower bat roost in the region's 300 caves, some housing colonies of 50,000 creatures.

The largest remaining stand of moist broadleaf forest that once blanketed Central Jamaica is found in the hillocks and valleys of Cockpit Country. The interior bursts with a profusion of ferns, orchids and bromeliads; overhead, the air is filled with rare butterflies and 79 species of birds like the black-billed parrot, seldom seen outside Cockpit Country. The island's largest land predator, the Jamaican boa, steals along the forest floor in search of the rodents, insects and reptiles that are its prey.

Cockpit Country's rugged terrain and thick vegetation have made much of it inaccessible to humans, and today the ecosystem remains largely intact. The Jamaica Forestry Department manages most of the area as a forest reserve. But economic ventures such as yam cultivation and limestone and bauxite mining are toppling forests and causing soil to erode into waterways, degrading water quality. Working with community partners, The Nature Conservancy is exploring alternative sources of income that are less environmentally damaging, such as ecotourism, butterfly farming and growing plants for the horticultural industry.

Giant swallowtail butterfly

conservation profile

targets tropical moist broadleaf forest, Jamaican flower bat, orchids, bromeliads, black-billed parrot, ring-tailed pigeon, Jamaican boa, black racer, Jamaica kite, blue and giant swallowtail butterflies

stresses unsustainable agricultural practices, habitat destruction due to mining and a planned highway

strategies foster sustainable forestry practices on public and private lands, reduce soil erosion, promote ecotourism and other compatible development, engage community

results 200,000 acres in conservation management; legislation supporting private lands conservation introduced; first site selected by USAID for Parks in Peril program

Map caption (top right): ATLANTIC OCEAN — VIRGIN ISLANDS MARINE & COASTAL SYSTEM — San Juan, Puerto Rico (U.S.), Isla Vieques, Virgin Islands (U.S.), Charlotte Amalie, St. Croix, Virgin Islands (U.K.), Anegada, Caribbean Sea, Anguilla (U.K.), St. Martin (Fr.), St. Maarten (Neth.), Saba, St. Eustatius (Neth.), Basseterre, ST. KITTS & NEVIS

MARINE AND COASTAL SYSTEM
Virgin Islands

The Virgin Islands' tourism-based economy depends entirely upon a healthy environment, making conservation essential for local communities.

location east of Puerto Rico

ecoregions Leeward Moist Forest, Leeward Xeric Scrub Forest, Lesser Antilles Mangroves

project size 3,500 square miles

preserves Jack and Isaac Bays, Magens Bay Watershed

public lands St. John National Park, Salt River National Historical Park and Ecological Reserve, Sandy Point and Green Cay national wildlife refuges

partners U.S. Fish and Wildlife Service, National Park Service, U.S. Forest Service, University of the Virgin Islands, St. Croix Environmental Association, St. John Land Trust, The Ocean Conservancy, British Virgin Islands National Parks Trust

conservancy initiatives Invasive Species, Marine

natural events leatherback turtle nesting, April–June; hawksbill and green turtle nesting, July–October

information Jennifer Amerling, (340) 774-7633, jamerling@tnc.org; nature.org/usvirginislands

Trunk Bay, St. John.

The Virgin Islands rise from turquoise waters, their white sand beaches and mangroves giving way to forested ravines and arid mountainsides. These island gems were named by Christopher Columbus on his second voyage, a comparison to the legendary beauty of St. Ursula's 11,000 virgin martyrs.

Seven different European flags have flown over the islands at different times since Columbus' landing on St. Croix. Divided today between U.S. and British control, the Virgin Islands comprise nearly 90 islands and cays encircled by coral reefs and sea-grass meadows, including one of the largest barrier reefs in the Western Hemisphere. The reefs bustle with myriad brilliantly colored fish such as parrotfish and blue tangs.

Three species of endangered sea turtle—green, leatherback and hawksbill—also swim here, climbing up the beaches to dig holes in the sand and lay eggs.

Tourism is the number-one industry in the Virgin Islands today as travelers from around the globe seek a bit of paradise. Although vital to the local economy, heavy-handed tourism damages reefs and degrades marine and coastal waters; divers and boat anchors chip corals, and new development causes sediment erosion that degrades the reefs.

The Nature Conservancy is working with government partners to promote the islands' natural assets while minimizing impacts on local habitat and wildlife. Federal and national parks are being expanded, territorial parks are being created and the U.S. Fish and Wildlife Service has launched a remarkably successful turtle recovery project. We are also exploring the potential for ecotourism at our preserves. In one such program, small groups of tourists, guided by Conservancy researchers, may tour

Green sea turtle.

protected turtle nesting sites and view the hatchlings from a safe distance.

conservation profile

targets coral, mangroves, seagrass meadows, salt ponds, sea turtles, sharks, barracuda; terns, shearwaters, boobies, frigatebirds and other sea birds; wood warbler and other migratory birds; Antillean nighthawk, green-throated carib

stresses upland development, overfishing, heavy marine recreation

strategies designate marine and terrestrial protected areas, acquire land, secure conservation easements, engage community, promote compatible development, restore ecosystems

results Salt River National Historical Park and Ecological Reserve created 1992; Magens Bay Watershed Preserve and East End St. Croix Marine Park created 2002

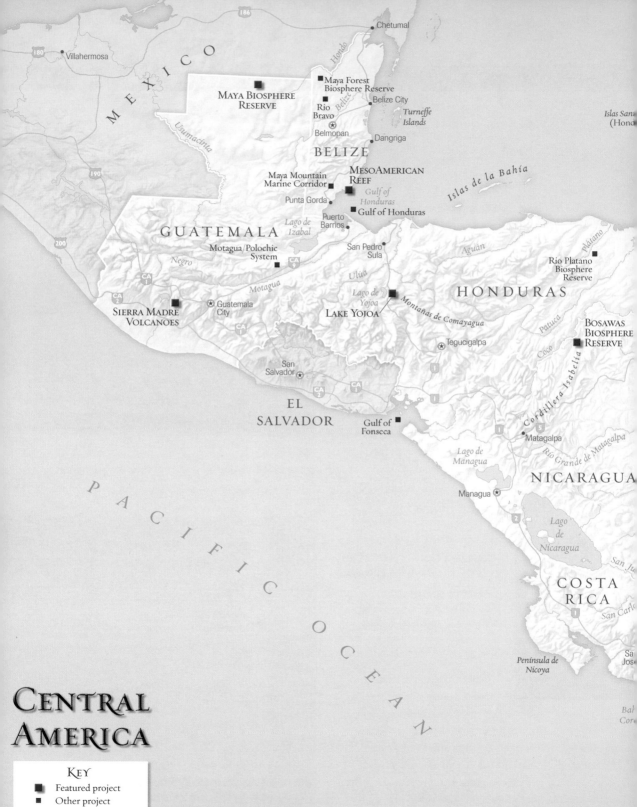

Chetumal

186

180

● Villahermosa

MEXICO

Hondo

■ Maya Forest
Biosphere Reserve

MAYA BIOSPHERE
RESERVE

Río
Bravo ●

Belize City ●

Belize

Turneffe
Islands

191

Usumacinta

190

● Belmopan

BELIZE

● Dangriga

Islas San...
(Hond...

200

GUATEMALA

Maya Mountain
Marine Corridor

Punta Gorda ●

Lago de
Izabal

MesoAmerican
Reef

Puerto
Barrios ●

Gulf of
Honduras

Gulf of Honduras

Islas de la Bahía

Negro

Motagua/Polochic
System

CA
1

San Pedro ●
Sula

Aguán

Ulúa

Río Plátano
Biosphere
Reserve

Plátano

CA
1

Motagua

Lago de
Yojoa

Montañas de Comayagua

HONDURAS

Pátuca

CA
2

SIERRA MADRE
VOLCANOES

⊛ Guatemala
City

LAKE YOJOA

BOSAWAS
BIOSPHERE
RESERVE

Coco

Cordillera Isabelia

Río Grande de Matagalpa

CA
1

⊛ Tegucigalpa

EL
SALVADOR

San
Salvador ⊛

CA
2

CA
1

1

1

1

Gulf of
Fonseca ■

Matagalpa ●

5

Lago de
Managua

NICARAGUA

2

PACIFIC

Managua ⊛

Lago
de
Nicaragua

San Ju...

OCEAN

COSTA
RICA

San Carl...

Península de
Nicoya

1

Sa...
Jose

Bal...
Cor...

CENTRAL
AMERICA

KEY

■ Featured project

■ Other project

(square represents approximate
center of project area)

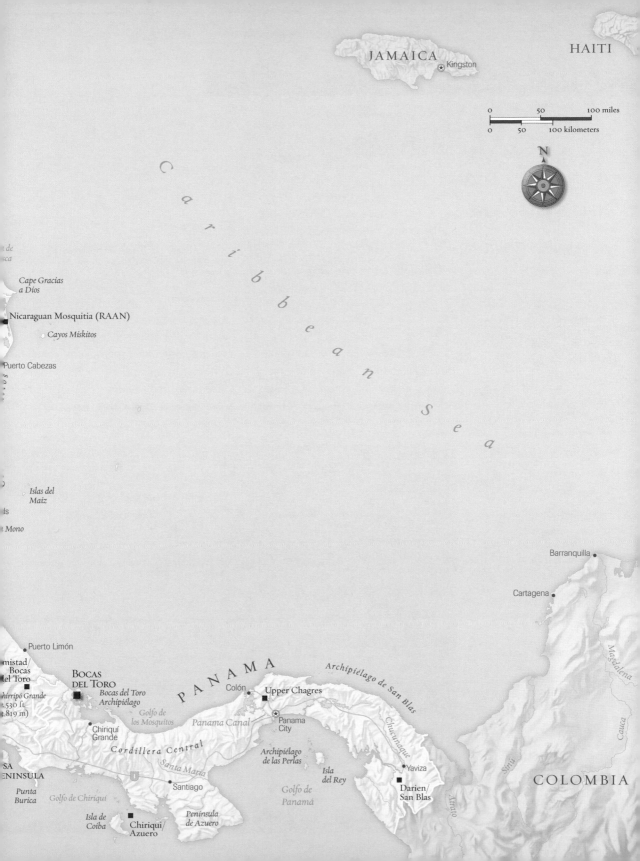

JAMAICA
Kingston

HAITI

0   50   100 miles
0   50   100 kilometers

N

C a r i b b e a n   S e a

Cape Gracias
a Dios

Nicaraguan Mosquitia (RAAN)

Cayos Miskitos

Puerto Cabezas

Islas del
Maíz

Mono

Barranquilla

Cartagena

Puerto Limón

mistad/
Bocas
el Toro

BOCAS
DEL TORO

PANAMA

Colón

Upper Chagres

Archipiélago de San Blas

hirripó Grande
2,530 ft
3,819 m)

Bocas del Toro
Archipiélago

Panama Canal

Panama
City

Magdalena

Chiriquí
Grande

Golfo de
los Mosquitos

Cordillera Central

Santa María

Archipiélago
de las Perlas

Chucunaque

Yaviza

Cauca

SA
ENINSULA

Isla
del Rey

Darien/
San Blas

COLOMBIA

Punta
Burica

Golfo de Chiriquí

Santiago

Golfo de
Panamá

Sinú

Atrato

Isla de
Coiba

Chiriquí/
Azuero

Península
de Azuero

MesoAmerican Reef
Belize

Pinpointing the exact location where reef fish spawn—on the full moon off the reef's steep coral cliffs—is pivotal to the recovery of declining Caribbean and Gulf of Mexico fisheries.

location running 250 miles from Yucatán Peninsula to Honduras

ecoregion Central Caribbean Sea

project size 180 miles in Belize

preserves 15,000 acres of adjacent coastline (owned by partner TIDE)

public lands marine protected areas and reserves (Port Honduras, Gladden Spit, Laughing Bird Caye, Sapodilla Cayes, Half Moon Caye)

partners Toledo Institute for Development and Environment, Friends of Nature, Belize Audubon Society, Belize Department of Fisheries, Wildlife Conservation Society, USAID, World Bank, World Wildlife Fund, Smithsonian, UN Programs, World Resources Institute

conservancy initiatives Marine, Freshwater, Fire

natural events spawning aggregations of snapper, full moons, March–June

information Erica Bailey, (703) 841-2088, ebailey@tnc.org; nature.org/belize

More than a million years ago tiny marine organisms began laying the foundations of the MesoAmerican Reef, a long spine of coral hugging the shore of present-day Mexico, Belize, Guatemala and Honduras. Through the ages their fanciful castles, spires and grottoes grew taller and bigger with each wave of calcium carbonate and skeleton laid down by coral polyps, coralline algae, tube worms and mollusks. Their construction continues to this day, making the

Cays, Glover Reef.

MesoAmerican Reef the second largest reef in the world after Australia's Great Barrier Reef.

Lining the reef are hundreds of cays, small islands of coral and sand once inhabited by the Maya. On their leeward side mangrove swamps shelter lagoons—perfect habitat for West Indian manatees.

On the windward side of the reef, where the coral shelf drops off into the deep Caribbean trench, full moons trigger huge spawning aggregations of reef fish. In the upwelling currents along these cliffs, spiraling columns of cubera snapper, dog snapper and other reef fish release opaque clouds of sperm and eggs. Plankton-eating whale sharks, the largest fish in the ocean, circle in to feast on the spawn. A marine biologist working for The Nature Conservancy only recently witnessed this spectacle of nature and has since been able to pinpoint the exact timing and location of the spawning aggregations—a critical step in the protection of endangered fish like Nassau grouper.

Working with Friends of Nature, the Toledo Institute for Development and Environment and others, the Conservancy helped secure marine protected area status for Gladden Spit—one of the spawning aggregation sites— and Port Honduras, a large section of sea that spans 10 percent of Belize's coastline. To address the overfishing that

Cubera snapper spawning.

has depleted their waters, local fishermen have voluntarily called for no-take zones and a ban on gill-net fishing to help the fisheries rebound. The Conservancy has also helped retrain former fishermen as saltwater fly-fishing, scuba and kayak guides and as rangers who patrol the protected areas.

conservation profile

targets whale shark, Nassau grouper, snapper, spawning aggregations of reef fish, coral reefs, manatee, mangroves, seagrass beds

stresses overfishing, hunting of manatees, sedimentation and polluted runoff from agriculture and unregulated development, damage to corals from boat anchors and nets

strategies identify spawning aggregation sites, designate marine protected areas, engage community in natural resource management, promote compatible economic development, protect water quality, promote ecologically sound public policies, identify sites resilient to coral bleaching

results Port Honduras and Gladden Spit declared marine reserves in 2000

Puerto Limón

San José

COSTA RICA

Chirripó Grande
12,530 ft
(3,819 m)

Bahía de Coronado

OSA PENINSULA

Archipiélago de Bocas del Toro

PANAMA

PACIFIC OCEAN

Punta Burica

Golfo de Chiriquí

OSA PENINSULA
Costa Rica

Twenty-five years after the country's first national park was created here, the Osa Peninsula remains Costa Rica's last wild frontier.

location 220 miles southeast of San José

ecoregion Montane Isthmiam Pacific Forest

project size 1 million acres

public lands Corcovado National Park, Piedras Blancas National Park, Marine Ballena National Park, Caño Island Biological Reserve, Golfito Wildlife Refuge, Golfo Dulce Forest Reserve, Terraba-Sierpe Wetland and Mangrove Reserves

partners Costa Rican Ministry of Environment, National Protected Areas System, Osa Biological Corridor Coalition, Costa Rica-USA Foundation, Conservation International

natural events turtle nesting, whale migration and breeding, fall and winter

information Erica Bailey, (703) 841-2088, ebailey@tnc.org; nature.org/costarica

Rain forest, Osa Peninsula.

The Osa Peninsula juts into the Pacific Ocean off the Costa Rican coast, a remote paradise harboring a diversity of habitats and biological richness rarely found in such a small geographic area. Here the jungle meets the sea: Lowland tropical rain forest lines pristine white-sand beaches, and mangroves front freshwater lagoons. Known as the last wild frontier in Costa Rica, the peninsula's inaccessibility spared it from development for many years.

The Osa Peninsula was once an island that later connected to the mainland of the Central American Isthmus. As a result, it has an extraordinary rate of endemism—of species found nowhere else on Earth. The canopy of the rain forest—with the greatest

Double-crested basilisk.

tree species diversity in all of Central America—harbors not only the country's largest population of scarlet macaws but also 50 species of nocturnal bats feeding on some 6,000 types of insects. Large cats such as jaguar and puma share the forest floor with tapir and anteaters while howler monkeys chatter overhead. Offshore, the deep blue waters of the Pacific and Golfo Dulce host migrating humpback whales and sea turtles that nest on Osa's shores.

In 1975 The Nature Conservancy helped create Corcovado National Park, now the crown jewel in Costa Rica's park system. Although the park today protects one-third of the Osa Peninsula, exploitation of natural resources, often inside Corcovado and other national parks, continues to degrade the forest. Gold mining, once the primary economic driver on the peninsula beginning with a gold rush in the 1930s, brought dams and tunnels to the area and polluted rivers and streams. Logging, both legal and illegal, poses the principal threat to Osa's natural assets.

Today the Conservancy is acquiring private land still held within the borders of Piedras Blancas National Park. On the nearly 60 percent of the peninsula that is in private hands, we have targeted those lands that serve as corridors between protected areas and are purchasing conservation easements to ensure safe passage for wildlife.

conservation profile

targets lowland tropical forest, jaguar, puma, scarlet macaw, howler monkey, giant anteater, four species of sea turtles, whales, dolphins

stresses fragmentation and destruction of habitat, deforestation from logging and poor land-use planning, hunting, illegal extraction of natural resources

strategies consolidate disparate public lands, encourage conservation management of public and private lands, strengthen local partner organizations

results Corcovado National Park established and expanded to 100,000 acres; Piedras Blancas National Park established

MAYA BIOSPHERE RESERVE
Guatemala

The Maya Forest, nearly destroyed by ancient Mayan civilization a thousand years ago, faces a new wave of overuse from modern-day settlers.

location north of Guatemala City; 30 minutes by plane, plus one hour by car

ecoregion Petén-Veracruz Moist Forest

project size 4 million acres

public lands Maya Biosphere Reserve, which includes Tikal National Park, Sierra del Lacandón National Park, Laguna del Tigre National Park, Mirador-Rio Azul National Park, three wildlife preserves, several multiple-use areas

partners Defensores de la Naturaleza, Consejo Nacional de Areas Protegidas, Instituto de Antropología e Historia

natural events at the Mayan ruins of Uaxactun, observe equinoxes and solstices at the temples of the Astronomical Complex

information Erica Bailey, (703) 841-2088, ebailey@tnc.org; nature.org/guatemala

From a bird's-eye view, the Maya Biosphere Reserve appears as a vast sea of leafy green stretching across northern Guatemala. Dense thickets of chicle, mahogany and Spanish cedar sprout from karstic soil on higher ground. When the rains come, large lakes of standing water form in lowland areas. These swampy, seasonal freshwater wetlands, or *bajos,* can cover as much as 40 percent of the reserve at the height of spring rains.

The Maya Biosphere Reserve is part of the greater Maya Forest, which blankets thousands of miles of Guatemala, Mexico

Temples, Tikal National Park.

and Belize—all told, the Americas' largest contiguous tropical forest north of the Amazon. In Guatemala, the 4 million acres of forest corridor in the reserve guard habitat for jaguar, puma, ocelot, giant anteater and some 90 other mammals. Bright flashes of color glimpsed through the canopy and a constant cacophony of sound reveal the presence of scarlet macaws, quetzals, toucans and as many as 400 bird species.

The Maya established some of their most powerful cities here beginning more than 2,500 years ago. Within the embrace of the Maya Biosphere Reserve are Tikal, a World Heritage Site, and several other important archeological sites. Although some have been excavated, many structures remain obscured by the dense forest, only the crumbling ruins of temple towers escaping roots and vines to peek through the upper canopy.

Scientists believe that widespread deforestation and the associated depletion of soils likely caused the collapse and abandonment of these Mayan cities in A.D. 930, only 1,500 years after the first settlements were established. A thousand years later, people are following the same path of the ancient Mayans, clearing the land for agriculture and ranching and threatening to unravel the forest ecosystem. The Nature Conservancy is working with a local partner organization, Defensores de la Naturaleza, to improve the management and protection of Sierra del Lacandón, a national park within the reserve. We also helped Defensores purchase 22,500 acres within the park and are developing a master plan for Tikal National Park.

Jaguar.

conservation profile

targets mature tropical forests, seasonal wetlands, jaguar, ocelot, puma, jaguarundi, tigrillo, giant anteater, howler and spider monkeys, tapir, great curassow, scarlet macaw, jabiru stork

stresses forest fires, oil exploration and drilling, incompatible farming and ranching practices, road and dam construction, unplanned human settlements, looting of cultural resources

strategies promote ecologically compatible land-use practices, improve protected area planning and management capacity, promote regional land-use planning, facilitate relocation of human settlements

results 4 million acres in conservation management; 22,500 acres in Sierra del Lacandón National Park acquired

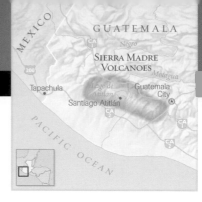

SIERRA MADRE VOLCANOES
Guatemala

With more and more tourists drawn to Lake Atitlan's stunning peak-and-crater land-scape every year, its future depends on careful planning to ensure local culture and forests are not lost.

location near Atitlan; three hours northwest of Guatemala City

ecoregion Central American montane and pine forest

project size 763 square miles

public lands numerous small municipally and nationally owned lands

partners Universidad del Valle, Vivamos Mejor, National Protected Areas Council, local municipalities, community groups

natural events sulphur seeps from the top of Volcan Pacaya, year-round

information Erica Bailey, (703) 841-2088, ebailey@tnc.org; nature.org/guatemala

At the northern end of Guatemala's Sierra Madre range, cradled among three towering volcanic cones, lies a vast crater lake reflecting the sky and summits. On the steep slopes surrounding the lake, huge conifers mingle with tropical oak and some 750 plants to form a textured green mosaic interspersed with basaltic fields, caves, waterfalls and geysers.

Mount Atitlan, a dormant volcano, rises from the southern shore of Lake Atitlan.

Thirty-seven volcanic peaks, some reaching heights of 12,500 feet above sea level, stretch the length of Guatemala's southern border from El Salvador into Mexico. Isolated and rugged, the Sierra Madre harbors many rare plants and animals. The last remaining population of highland margay—a subspecies of the margay, the only cat with the ability to rotate its hind legs 180 degrees and hang from branches by one foot—survives here as a result of widespread destruction of its arboreal habitat elsewhere.

The largest indigenous population in all of Central America lives among the mountains and crater lakes of the Sierra Madre. Tzutujil and Cakchiquel Maya focus many of their rituals and celebrations around Lake Atitlan and the surrounding volcanoes. Fiercely independent, the native peoples have survived and adapted to thousands of years of oppression and colonization. In response to the latest invasion by tourists, local Maya sell traditional crafts, act as guides and have built lodging to meet visitor demand.

But unplanned growth and tourism are taking their toll on Mayan culture as well as on the forests that have sustained local communities for centuries. Lake Atitlan and the whole Sierra Madre volcanic range lack the legal enforcement and planning needed to contain development and prevent the fragmentation of

Resplendent quetzal.

villages and forests. In early 2002 The Nature Conservancy established a presence here, bringing financial aid through the Parks in Peril program to plan for the future of this increasingly popular tourist destination.

conservation profile

targets pine-oak forests, tropical pine forests, broadleaf cloud forests, azure-rumped tanager, resplendent quetzal, horned guan, golden cheeked warbler, highland margay, howler monkey, cougar, northern naked-tailed armadillo

stresses illegal logging, unsustainable firewood extraction, forest fires, inappropriate land use, uncontrolled development, mismanaged tourism, illegal hunting

strategies establish legally protected areas, build conservation alliances, influence land-use planning, promote ecologically compatible land-use practices, engage community in natural resource management

results Lake Atitlan Watershed Protected Area incorporated into Parks in Peril program

BELIZE
Gulf of Honduras
Puerto Barrios
GUATEMALA
San Pedro Sula
LAKE YOJOA
Ulúa
Lago de Yojoa
Montañas de Comayagua
HONDURAS
Tegucigalpa
EL SALVADOR

LAKE YOJOA
Honduras

Modern-day land protection methods are being tested on a Honduran landscape containing cultural artifacts dating to the beginning of the first millennium.

location 80 miles northwest of Tegucigalpa, 50 miles south of San Pedro Sula

ecoregion Central American Pine-Oak Forest

project size 192,247 acres

public lands Cerro Azul Meambar National Park, Santa Bárbara Mountain National Park

partners Association of Municipalities for the Protection of Lake Yojoa (AMUPROLAGO)

natural events dry season, verano, January–May; wet season, invierno, June–December

information Erica Bailey, (703) 841-2088, ebailey@tnc.org; nature.org/honduras

The calm waters of Lake Yojoa.

In the Central American isthmus, seasons are defined by rainfall rather than temperature. The wet season, *invierno,* can dump up to 200 inches of rain across Honduras.

Here in the rainiest western reaches of the country, Lake Yojoa is a product of the climate. Stretching for 10 miles and reaching depths of 50 feet, it is the largest natural lake in Honduras. Towering mountains surround the lake, trailing brooks and waterfalls from their slopes. Three kinds of forests—tropical, pine and cloud—blanket the lake's steep shore to the east, hosting motmots, toucans and parrots. The marshy western shore provides ideal habitat for tiger herons, wood storks, snail kites, black ducks and dozens of other water loving species.

Signs of the ancient Lenca people, who populated Lake Yojoa's shores as long ago as A.D. 200, abound. Ruins found here, including unexcavated pyramids, are attracting archeologists from all over the world and are expected to shed light on a period of pre-Columbian history that may be older than any explored to date. Although their native language disappeared long ago, the descendents of the Lenca still dance the *guancasco* to celebrate friendship, build homes out of bamboo and clay, and observe other customs from a time when they coexisted with the great Mayan civilization.

Lake Yojoa today faces a battery of threats from expanding and unsustainable agriculture, forestry and development. In 2001, The Nature Conservancy and our partner AMUPROLAGO, an association of local municipalities, began working to safeguard at-risk private lands through conservation easements—a U.S.-born conservation tool that is new to Latin America.

Snail kite.

Eight landowners have agreed to limit development of their land in exchange for financial benefits from the local municipalities. Because working with municipalities is new to our work here, and the Lake Yojoa region is the first place in Honduras where conservation easements are being used, this will be a test case for the entire country.

conservation profile

targets jaguar, spider monkey, kingfisher, motmot, Mahonia glauca bush, several species of orchid found only in the Lake Yojoa region

stresses unsustainable agriculture, forestry and grazing, pesticide use, natural resource extraction, development

strategies secure conservation easements, promote ecologically compatible land-use practices, engage community in natural resource management, strengthen local partner organizations

results created the first conservation easements in Honduras with eight landowners; concluded conservation planning that will guide a management plan for the entire watershed

HONDURAS

BOSAWAS
BIOSPHERE
RESERVE

NICARAGUA

Estelí

BOSAWAS BIOSPHERE RESERVE
Nicaragua

Lacking official records of ancestral rights to their land, indigenous peoples
race to claim and protect a landscape containing unrealized treasures.

location north-central Nicaragua,
on border with Honduras

ecoregion Central America
Moist Atlantic Forest

project size 1.8 million acres

partners CEDAPRODE, Alistar
Nicaragua, Bosawas Technical
Secretariat

natural events annual migration of birds including the wood
thrush, cerulean warbler and the
Canada warbler, late summer–
early spring

information Erica Bailey,
(703) 841-2088, ebailey@tnc.org;
nature.org/nicaragua

In the mountains of north-central
Nicaragua, the Bosawas Biosphere
Reserve takes its name from three
natural features—the *Bo*cay River, Mount
*Sa*slaya and the *Wa*spuk River. The
Coco River carves out the border with
neighboring Honduras. The 1.8 million-
acre Bosawas reserve contains 7 percent

On the Rio Coco.

of Nicaragua's land and its richest reservoir of natural resources.

Most of this isolated terrain has not been studied, although Bosawas is known to harbor large populations of endangered species such as Baird's tapir, jaguar and the harpy eagle. Mahogany, ceiba, Spanish cedar, rosewood and rubber provide fruit for keel-billed toucans and a haven for the scarlet tanager and other songbirds migrating from North America. Howler monkeys play among the branches, their screeches heard for several miles. Gaudy leaf frogs cling to the moist leaves of rare orchids and bromeliads.

Also inhabiting this secluded corner of Central America are Mayangna and Miskito Indians, who live in villages scattered throughout the reserve. Numerous petroglyphs attest to their long history in these tropical forests. Although the Mayangna and Miskito claim this land through ancestral heritage, they have no official title of land ownership. But recently, as timber, ranching and agriculture interests have begun moving their activities into this "unclaimed" land, promising to turn a profit for a country that is deeply in debt, the conflict between traditional and exploitative uses of the land has grown.

Since 1993, as an essential part of efforts to protect the Bosawas reserve, The Nature Conservancy has helped docu-

ment the historical presence of Mayangna and Miskito in the region. We are using this information to assist them in applying for legal title to their ancestral lands. We've also

Baird's tapir.

provided technical support in the mapping of their territories and the creation of land-use management plans.

conservation profile

targets Baird's tapir, jaguar, harpy eagle, wood thrush, cerulean warbler

stresses agriculture, deforestation, colonization

strategies strengthen local partner organizations, build conservation alliances, undertake scientific research, promote ecologically compatible land-use practices

results established a federation that ensures inclusion of Mayangna and Miskito Indians in government decision-making related to the Bosawas Biosphere Reserve

BOCAS DEL TORO
Panama

At "Mouths of the Bull," a lush coastal paradise supports a robust fishing and tourism economy—but unchecked, both could unravel the very ecosystem on which they depend.

location northwest Panama, 465 miles from Panama City

ecoregions Talamanca Montane Forests, Atlantic and Pacific Humid Isthmian Forests

project size 6,200 square miles

public lands Bastimentos Marine Park, San San Pond Sack Wetlands, La Amistad International Park, Volcán National Park, Palo Seco and Fortuna forest reserves

partners National Environmental Authority, ANCON, ADEPESCO (alliance of 11 indigenous fishing communities), ADESBO (alliance of local organizations and government agencies)

conservancy initiatives Freshwater, Marine

natural events raptor migrations, August-October; birds like the three-wattled bellbird migrate locally from lowlands to mountains, March-September; turtle nesting: leatherback, May-June; loggerhead, April-September; green, July-August; hawksbill, July-September

information Erica Bailey, (703) 841-2088, ebailey@tnc.org; nature.org/panama

From mountain ridges to coral reefs—and all the cloud forest, coastal swamps, mangrove cays, islands and seagrass beds in between—Bocas del Toro unfolds over northwest Panama. The forested slopes of the Talamanca Mountains descend to low-lying wetlands—an important link in the flyway for migratory birds such as the wood thrush and magnolia warbler. Sloths

Sunrise over Bocas del Toro.

hang in the treetops of swampy coastal forests, and manatees cruise sheltered lagoons.

Bocas del Toro's archipelago is an expanse of turquoise waters dotted with lushly forested islands. Much of it today is a 32,700-acre national marine park. Ngöbe Indians navigate the watery maze between islands and the mainland in dugout canoes called *pangas*. Four species of sea turtles nest on white-sand beaches and inhabit reefs laden with tropical fish. Throaty chirps heard within the dense jungles of Isla Bastimentos betray poison dart frogs. The skin of these brilliantly colored, thumbnail-sized frogs produces a venom used by pre-Columbian Indians to poison their arrows.

Christopher Columbus landed here on his fourth and final New World voyage. His presence still looms large: The principal island and the bay itself bear his name, and legend has it that he gave the region its name upon seeing a large rock on Isla Bastimentos shaped like a bull. The province's capital city was a bustling port around the turn of the 20th century when United Fruit, now Chiquita Bananas, was headquartered on Isla Colón. Today the economy is driven by commercial fishing and a robust tourism industry—both of which require healthy coastal and marine ecosystems.

But the clearing of trees to make way for agriculture and development is destroying native forest and releasing sediment and pollution into rivers, coastal swamps and the sea. Overfishing has led to the decline of populations of lobster, crabs and octopus, disrupting the marine food chain and signaling trouble for the local economy.

The Nature Conservancy is working with ADEPESCO, an alliance of 11 indigenous fishing communities, to develop fishing regulations that will be approved by the Panama Maritime Authority and self-imposed by ADEPESCO members. We are also exploring alternative income-generating activities such as fish farming and guiding ecotours for these fishermen to pursue during no-take periods.

Poison dart frogs.

conservation profile

targets cloud forests, tapir, jaguar, white-lipped peccary, mangrove forests, manatees, coral reefs, sea turtles

stresses deforestation, habitat destruction, overfishing, turtle poaching, unregulated tourism

strategies strengthen local partner organizations, encourage expansion and improved management of public land, foster sustainable fishing and agriculture practices

results Bastimentos National Marine Park expanded to include critical coral reefs; local communities given information on minimum catch size and weight of lobsters for sustainable harvesting

500 miles
500 kilometers
250
250
0
0

N

ATLANTIC

OCEAN

Recife

Salvador

Serra das Almas (Caatinga) Nature Reserve

São Francisco

Grande Sertão Veredas National Park

BRAZIL

Brazilian Highlands

Tocantins

Xingu

Ilha de Marajó

Cayenne

FRENCH GUIANA

SURINAME

Paramaribo

Georgetown

GUYANA

Guiana Highlands

Branco

Amazon

Tapajós

Juruena

Noel Kempff Mercado National Park

Mato Grosso Plateau

AMAZON

Amazon

Negro

Madeira

Amazon Basin

AMBORÓ CARRASCO CONSERVATION AREA

BOLIVIA

Mamoré

Madre de Dios

Lago Titicaca

PUERTO RICO

DOMINICAN REPUBLIC

HAITI

Caribbean Sea

BAHAMAS

CUBA

JAMAICA

Los Roques National Park

Islas Los Roques

Avila National Park

Caracas

Llanos Aguaro-Guariquito National Park

Sierra Nevada de Santa Marta

Lago de Maracaibo

Sierra Nevada National Park

Corales de Rosario National Park

VENEZUELA

Llanos

CANAIMA NATIONAL PARK

Guiana Highlands

Orinoco

Orinoco

Meta

CACHALÚ/ EASTERN ANDES

Bogotá

COLOMBIA

Magdalena

Medellín

Cali

Putumayo

Amazon

Juruá

Purus

PACAYA-SAMIRIA NATIONAL RESERVE

Ucayali

SERRA DO DIVISOR NATIONAL PARK

Central Selva Protection Area

PERU

Marañón

Andes

Lima

Paracas National Reserve

CONDOR BIORESERVE

Quito

ECUADOR

Podocarpus National Park

Machalilla National Park

GALÁPAGOS ISLANDS

UNITED STATES

Gulf of Mexico

MEXICO

BELIZE

GUATEMALA

HONDURAS

EL SALVADOR

NICARAGUA

COSTA RICA

PANAMA

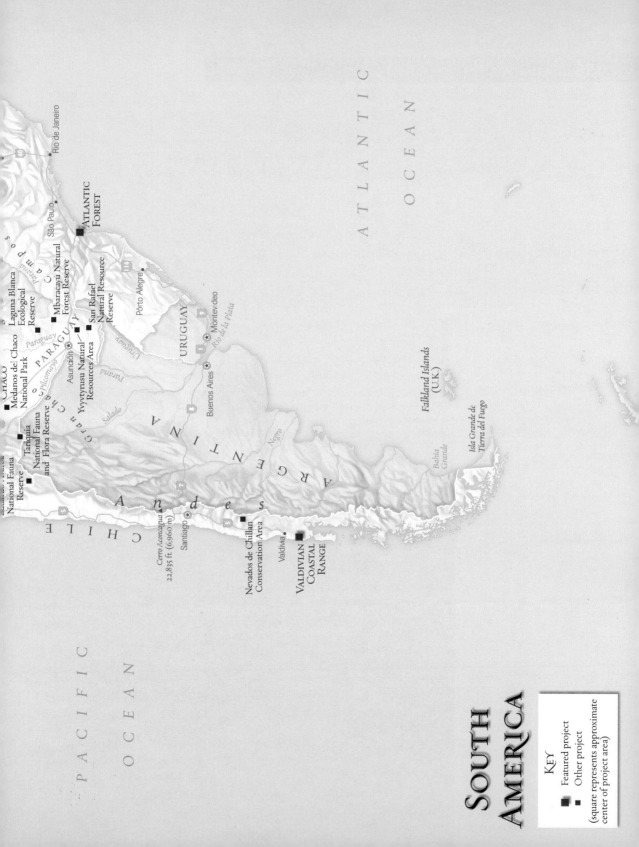

Rio de Janeiro

São Paulo

ATLANTIC
FOREST

Laguna Blanca
Ecological
Reserve

Mbaracayú Natural
Forest Reserve

San Rafael
Natural Resource
Reserve

Pôrto Alegre

CHACO

Medanos del Chaco
National Park

Asunción

PARAGUAY

Yvytyrusú Natural
Resources Area

Montevideo

URUGUAY

Río de la Plata

Buenos Aires

Tariquia
National Fauna
and Flora Reserve

National Fauna
Reserve

Negro

ARGENTINA

Salado

Falkland Islands
(U.K.)

Bahía
Grande

Isla Grande de
Tierra del Fuego

CHILE

Andes

Cerro Aconcagua
22,835 ft (6,960 m)

Santiago

Nevados de Chillán
Conservation Area

Valdivia

VALDIVIAN
COASTAL
RANGE

PACIFIC

OCEAN

ATLANTIC

OCEAN

SOUTH
AMERICA

KEY
■ Featured project
■ Other project
(square represents approximate
center of project area)

AMBORÓ CARRASCO CONSERVATION UNIT
Bolivia

Time seems to disappear in this little-known jungle, where it is still possible to experience virgin rain forest like that which sustained the Incas centuries ago.

location between the cities of Santa Cruz and Cochabamba

ecoregions Bolivian Yungas, Southwestern Amazonian Moist Forest, Central Andean Puna

project size 3.1 million acres

public lands Amboró and Carrasco national parks

partners Fundación Amigos de la Naturaleza, Centro Integrado para la Defensa Ecologica y el Desarrollo Rural, Fundación para el Turismo y Desarrollo de la Mancomunidad Sara e Ichilo, Asociación Ecologica del Oriente, Servicio Nacional de Areas Protegidas

information Anna Gibson, (703) 841-4109, agibson@tnc.org; nature.org/bolivia

Few adventurers come to Bolivia looking for rain forest. Those who do, however, are rewarded by Amboró and Carrasco national parks, 3 million acres of true mythic jungle.

The two contiguous parks span evergreen and cloud forests, high-alpine grasslands, whitewater rivers and dramatic waterfalls. They encompass pure, spring-fed streams and some of the last virgin rain

Amboró National Park.

forest on Earth. The rich, humid region, bordered by the cities of Santa Cruz and Cochabamba, known as the "Valley of the Eternal Spring," has sustained indigenous communities for centuries. Mysterious ruins and ceremonial grounds near the city of Samaipata hint at the religious life of the Incas and other cultures before them to reveal a long history of pre-Columbian settlement.

The landscape bursts with color, noise and life. Shrill-voiced toucans announce the day, jaguars prowl the forest, and howler and capuchin monkeys swing from the trees. Ground-feeding birds like horned curassows hunt for food on the forest floor, while vibrant cock-of-the-rock soar above. Brilliant native orchids of every size, shape and color imaginable illuminate a lush sea of green; ferns abound, some even sporting leaves large enough to shelter a human. The ancient puya raimondii, the world's largest bromeliad, bursts into bloom once every 80 to 100 years, then dies.

Large rural communities live in and around the parks and subsist on the natural bounty. However, activities like logging, hunting, fishing and agriculture sometimes encroach on park boundaries. To meet the needs of local people and still keep this pristine wilderness intact, The Nature Conservancy began working in Amboró and Carrasco national parks in 2002, as part of the

Andean cock-of-the-rock.

Parks in Peril program with the U.S. Agency for International Development. Our aim is to improve the parks' management and enforcement of park regulations, increase awareness of the parks' benefits, promote non-destructive activities such as ecotourism, and work with local communities to develop more sustainable approaches to natural resource use.

conservation profile

targets endemic orchids, spectacled bear, horned curassow, cock-of-the-rock, jaguar, capybara, howler and capuchin monkeys, puya raimondii, mahogany; puna, páramo and Bolivian yungas communities

stresses colonization, road-building, illegal logging, grazing, hunting, mining and oil exploration

strategies promote ecotourism, promote ecologically compatible land-use practices, strengthen local partner organizations, engage community in natural resource management

results hired park guards; helped create new methods of collaboration among public and private institutions working in both parks

THE AMAZON
Brazil

In the Amazon Basin, indigenous lands hold the key to the future of the largest remaining expanse of tropical forest on Earth.

location Amazônia covers half of Brazil; Acre state and Serra do Divisor are in far western Brazil, on the border with Peru

ecoregion Southwest Amazon

project size 5 million acres (Serra do Divisor National Park and associated indigenous and extractive reserves)

public lands Serra do Divisor National Park

partners SOS Amazônia, IBAMA (Brazilian EPA)

natural events rivers of Serra do Divisor flood the forest, annually

information Cathy Kerkam, (703) 841-2082, ckerkam@tnc.org; nature.org/brazil

Mists enshroud the Amazon's riotous vegetation.

The Amazon Basin covers an area almost the size of the contiguous United States. Beginning just 100 miles from the Pacific Ocean in the ice fields of the Andes, the Amazon River rolls 4,000 miles eastward to the Atlantic—in volume nearly one-quarter of the world's freshwater flow. So mighty is this outflow of fresh water into the ocean that a Spanish explorer in 1500 named it the "Sweet Sea," failing to comprehend that it might be a river.

The cause célèbre of the conservation movement, Amazônia is recognized as the planet's greatest reserve of life forms. Here the largest continuous expanse of tropical forest on Earth harbors approximately one-third of her species. Despite three centuries of scientific study, only a small fraction of its biological richness has been revealed. On a single tree in western Amazônia, biologist E.O. Wilson once found 43 species of ants—the equivalent of the entire ant fauna of the British Isles. New discoveries are revealed monthly. A four-week-long rapid ecological assessment in 1997 in Brazil's far western state of Acre revealed three new species of birds; in summer 2002, two new species of monkeys were discovered. Its creatures are fantastic and multi-hued, from the 7-inch-wide blue Morpho butterfly to the pink river dolphins that, in the local mythology, can assume human form and seduce young girls.

But the Amazon is being rapidly deforested as roads are built into the interior and as ranchers turn forest into pasture. To effect conservation on such a challenging scale, The Nature Conservancy gives priority to the most threatened landscapes, such as that of Serra do Divisor National Park, on Brazil's border with Peru. The park spreads across 2 million acres of the state of Acre, the homeland of rubber tree tapper Chico Mendes, who was killed trying to protect these forests.

Surrounding the park are some 3 million acres of indigenous and extractive reserves, set aside for the exclusive use of forest peoples—perhaps the best hope for long-term conservation of the forest. The reserves are the result of a long struggle on the part of indigenous

Red uakari.

communities to own and manage their lands. In the 1990s they won legal title, and indigenous lands now represent 25 percent of the Brazilian Amazon. The Conservancy is working with the federal government and indigenous communities to create community-based, community-supported environmental management plans for the reserves.

conservation profile

targets primates, tapir, jaguar, palm and bamboo forests, bromeliads, freshwater turtles

stresses deforestation, irregular logging and overhunting

strategies strengthen local partner organizations, work with indigenous communities to create community-supported environmental management plans, promote ecologically compatible land-use practices, work with ranchers to minimize impact of grazing

results program to purchase park inholdings launched; personnel added to northern sector of Serra do Divisor in 2000; 50 jobs being created for local people to monitor conservation targets

ATLANTIC FOREST
Brazil

Climate action projects and other methods of placing economic value on standing forests are helping protect one of the world's most imperiled ecosystems.

location near Curitiba in the state of Parana; 38,000 square miles along the Atlantic coast

ecoregion Atlantic Forest

project size 77,000 acres

preserves Guaraqueçaba Environmental Protection Area, Morro da Mina

public lands Serra dos Órgãos National Park, Superagui National Park, Tijuca National Park, Morro do Diabo State Park, Poço das Antas Biological Reserve

partners Sociedade de Pesquisa em Vida Selvagem e Educaçao (SPVS), Fundaçáo Boticário

conservancy initiatives Global Climate Change

natural events arrival of hundreds of red-tailed parrots to roost, Bay of Guaraqueçaba at sunset

information Cathy Kerkam, (703) 841-2082; ckerkam@tnc.org; nature.org/brazil

What remains of the Atlantic Forest today is a living relict of another time. Five centuries ago, the *Mata Atlântica,* as it is known, stretched seamlessly inland for hundreds of miles from Brazil's coast all the way to Paraguay and Argentina. Today, less than 7 percent of the original forest remains, much of it in isolated fragments. By contrast, the more celebrated Amazon is still 90 percent intact.

Despite its diminished state, the Atlantic Forest still ranks among the top five protection priorities worldwide for many conservation organizations. To understand why, consider just one statistic: Its

Granite Mountain, Serra dos Órgãos National Park.

forests contain more tree diversity on a two-and-a-half-acre plot than the entire eastern seaboard of the United States. Jaguars, tapirs and yellow-throated caimans roam amid this richness, carefully watched by endangered red-tailed parrots, gilt-edged tanagers and hundreds of other birds.

Humans are drawn to the Atlantic Forest as well: Roughly 70 percent of Brazil's population lives here. As a result, habitat fragmentation and land conversion are serious threats. Unsustainable logging, forestry, cattle ranching and agriculture are also widespread.

To protect what remains of this extraordinary forest, The Nature Conservancy has joined with our Brazilian partner SPVS to operate the country's first climate action project at the Guaraqueçaba Environmental Protection Area, the largest remaining tract of contiguous Atlantic Forest in Brazil. Several U.S. energy corporations have funded extensive climate action reforestation efforts here, viewing the forests, which absorb carbon dioxide, as a means to offset carbon dioxide emissions from their core businesses. Scientists calculate that protecting some 17,000 acres of forest can offset the emissions of roughly 750,000 cars in one year.

Climate action projects recognize that standing forests have economic as well as biodiversity value. Our hope is that, 10 to 20 years from now, intact forest will equal or exceed cleared land in value.

Red-tailed parrots.

conservation profile

targets jaguar, tapir, river otter, woolly spider monkey, black-faced tamarin, red-tailed parrot and more than 100 other endangered birds, tropical evergreen forest, *restinga* (sand forest)

stresses habitat fragmentation and conversion, unsustainable logging, plantation forestry, cattle ranching, agriculture, urban sprawl, invasive species

strategies undertake climate action projects, restore ecosystems, promote ecologically compatible land-use practices, strengthen local partner organizations

results helped create private reserves totaling more than 60,000 acres; launched the first climate action project in Brazil

VALDIVIAN COASTAL RANGE
Chile

In this temperate rain forest now threatened with deforestation, relict species like small marsupials are living reminders of a primordial world when southern Chile was linked to New Zealand and Australia.

location just north of Valdivia south to the Gulf of Ancud

ecoregions Valdivian Temperate Forest, Araucanian Marine, Valdivian Freshwater

project size 600,000 acres

preserves Punta Curiñanco

public lands Reserva Forestal Valdivia, Reserva de Alerce Costero, public lands held by Army and forest service

partners Comité Nacional Pro Defensa de la Fauna y Flora, Senda Darwin Foundation, World Wildlife Fund, Austral University, Coastal Range Coalition

conservancy initiatives Freshwater, Global Climate Change, Marine

natural events Magellanic penguin migration, December–January; red-legged cormorant nesting, year round; murtilla and calafate berries, April–May

information Anna Gibson, (703) 841-4109, agibson@tnc.org; nature.org/chile

Autumn tints the trees of the Valdivian Coastal Range.

The Valdivian Coastal Range runs in a narrow strip along Chile's southern coast, stretching north from the Gulf of Ancud to a promontory just beyond the city of Valdivia. Remote beaches and rocky shorelines harbor sea lions, red-legged cormorants and a healthy population of endangered marine otter.

Rolling hills are blanketed in evergreen forests—one of only five temperate rain forests in the world. Two marsupials unique to South America and many woody plants are "living fossils" of an ancient time when this land was part of a larger land mass linked to New Zealand and Australia.

During the last ice age, glaciers covered areas to the east and south, forcing many species to take refuge in the Valdivian Coastal Range. Here they evolved in isolation from the rest of the continent and the world, resulting in a proliferation of many species that exist nowhere else. The majority of Valdivian amphibians and seed plants are globally unique, as are half of its freshwater fish and 33 percent of its mammals.

For hundreds of years Chile's indigenous Mapuche people defended their forests from Inca and Spanish invaders. When the Spanish succeeded in colonizing southern Chile late in the 19th century, 250 miles of the Valdivian coastline were still largely forested. Today, however, logging, agriculture and commercial uses are rapidly shrinking the Mapuche's traditional resources. Local environmentalists use the term "false green" to describe the deceiving, lush growth of exotic tree plantations now threatening to replace native temperate rain forest. At the same time, native trees are being overharvested for firewood, and highway construction threatens the only known habitat for olivillo trees, 65-foot evergreens that can live as long as 400 years.

In 2001 The Nature Conservancy helped our Chilean partner Comité Nacional Pro Defensa de la Fauna y Flora establish the 200-acre Punta Curiñanco Reserve to demonstrate private land conservation and protect olivillo trees. Efforts planned for the future include establishing new protected areas—given that the Valdivian Coastal Range has no national parks—and developing native tree nurseries for forest restoration and alternative sources of fuel wood and income for local residents.

conservation profile

targets coastal old-growth olivillo forests, marine otter, pudú deer, mountain monkey, alerce tree

stresses deforestation, coastal highway construction, overfishing, water pollution

strategies promote ecologically compatible land-use practices, engage community in natural resource management and private land protection, establish new protected areas

results Punta Curiñanco Reserve established; marine park designation pending to protect endangered marine otter

CACHALÚ/EASTERN ANDES
Colombia

High rates of slash-and-burn deforestation have made the oak forests of Colombia one of the rarest ecosystems in the tropical Andes.

location Department of Santander, 250 miles northeast of Bogotá

ecoregion Eastern Cordillera Montane Forest

project size 300,000 acres

preserves Cachalú Biological Reserve (owned by partner Fundación Natura)

public lands Guanentá National Flora and Fauna Sanctuary

partners Fundación Natura, Colombian National Park Service, Ministry of Environment

information Tracey Yuditsky, (703) 841-4890; tyuditsky@tnc.org; nature.org/colombia

Cachalú Biological Reserve.

In the local indigenous language—of which there are some 200 in Colombia—*Cachalú* means "land of the sky." Here the peaks of the Cordillera Oriental, Colombia's eastern mountain range, reach heights of more than 8,000 feet. On the west side of the mountains are valleys and *páramo*—the Andes signature high-elevation grasslands of wildflowers and wind. To the east lie the torrid, sparsely populated lowlands of Amazônia. Between these two worlds the mountains seemingly float, terra firma of the air.

Cachalú is also the name given to the private biological reserve that harbors Colombia's largest remaining stand of the endangered oak forest, *Quercus humboldtii*. The genus *Quercus*, which includes familiar trees like the white oak and live oak, reaches the southern-most extent of its range in Colombia. With nearly 70 percent of the tropical Andes in Colombia already cleared for cattle and agriculture, the rich forests of Cachalú and the surrounding landscape are high on conservationists' list for protection.

At the crossroads of two continents, Colombia is a land of great biological diversity. It ranks first in the world for the number of bird species, with more than 1,700 recorded, and first for amphibian species, with more than 550 recorded. But in a country also renowned for its political instability, the conservation imperative presents a steep challenge to those who would protect that diversity.

Despite Colombia's notorious turmoil, conservation flourishes in the Cordillera Oriental, even amid the civil strife and danger that plague much of the rural highlands. Partners Fundación Natura and The Nature Conservancy are working together to protect more than 300,000 acres in the eastern Andes, radiating outward from Cachalú.

Puma.

With an influx of Colombian immigrants arriving in the highlands, the pressure to clear the land is growing. The conservation challenge is helping subsistence farmers meet their needs for living without destroying the forest and other natural resources that sustain them.

conservation profile

targets oak forest, high-elevation grasslands (*páramo*), Andean cock-of-the-rock, collared peccary, spectacled bear, red howler monkey, puma, mountain tapir, black-billed mountain toucan, black inca

threats deforestation, driven by cattle ranching and agriculture and fueled by rapid population growth

strategies promote ecologically compatible land-use practices, encourage conservation management of public and private lands, use Cachalú as a demonstration site, influence land-use planning, encourage scientific research

results conservation planning methodology adopted by municipality of Encino

CONDOR BIORESERVE
Ecuador

From the Andes to the Amazon Basin, the Condor Bioreserve provides water to millions and refuge to its endangered namesake—the Andean condor, national symbol of Ecuador.

location 65 miles east of Quito

ecoregions Northern Andean Páramo, Eastern Cordillera Real Montane Forest, Napo Moist Forest

project size 3.6 million acres

public lands Cayambe-Coca, Antisana and Cofán-Bermejo ecological reserves; Sumaco-Napo Galeras, Cotopaxi and Llanganates national parks

partners Ministry of Environment, Fundación Antisana, Fundación Rumicocha, EcoCiencia

conservancy initiatives Freshwater

natural events lava flows from Antisana Volcano, year-round; bird migrations, September–November and March–May

information Anna Gibson, (703) 841-4109, agibson@tnc.org; nature.org/ecuador

The jagged peaks of the northern Andes brush the clouds in the Condor Bioreserve, reaching 19,730 feet at snow-capped Cotopaxi Volcano. Atop the high plateaus lies the *páramo*, a rolling grassland unique to the Andes, where indigenous people grow potatoes and where *chagras*—Andean cowboys— graze cattle and sheep. The endangered spectacled bear, the only bear native to South America, forages on the forested slopes of the Andes, venturing onto the *páramo* to feed on puya bromeliads. To the east spreads the rain forest of the Amazon.

Páramo and Cayambe Volcano, Cayambe-Coca Ecological Reserve.

The bioreserve is home to the largest community of the endangered Andean condor in the world. With a wingspan of up to 12 feet, the condor is the largest flying bird on Earth, using its great wings to ride thermal air currents to heights of 16,000 feet.

More than 20 rivers originate in the bioreserve and drain into both the Pacific and Atlantic oceans. The Andean highlands and forests are dotted with clear lakes and lagoons; waterfalls are abundant in the Amazon foothills. These systems are the principal source of drinking water for Ecuador's capital, Quito, and provide hydroelectric power to much of the country.

The Condor Bioreserve encompasses six protected areas interspersed with private lands. Two indigenous communities, the Oyacachi and the Sinangóe, live inside the bioreserve and depend on its natural resources for their livelihood. But newcomers and market forces are altering their traditional way of life. The area is readily accessible via the Pan-American Highway, and new roads cut increasingly deeper into the reserve's heart. As new settlers strive to earn a living, forest is razed for agriculture, ranching and timber; hunters routinely burn the *páramos* to flush game.

Conservation efforts are focused on eliminating ecologically harmful activities on public parkland and establishing corridors for wildlife to travel between reserves. The Nature

Andean condor.

Conservancy has teamed up with local organizations to train residents to become park rangers and equip them with guard stations, two-way radios and patrol vehicles. The rangers work to reduce poaching, illegal logging and fire within the parks' boundaries. We are also using funds raised by schoolchildren through our Adopt An Acre program to purchase a pocket of privately owned land nestled between Cayambe-Coca and Antisana ecological reserves, a key step in consolidating protection of the Condor Bioreserve.

conservation profile

targets Andean *páramo*, Amazon foothills, cloud forest, Andean forest, spectacled bear, mountain tapir, mountain frogs, river otter

stresses habitat destruction, incompatible agricultural and forestry practices, poorly planned infrastructure projects, illegal hunting

strategies engage community, strengthen local institutions, restore ecosystems, promote ecologically compatible land-use practices, encourage conservation management of public and private lands

results water conservation trust fund established and generating $350,000 annually; 26 park guards trained; private lands conservation program initiated; spectacled bear-tracking program designed and implemented

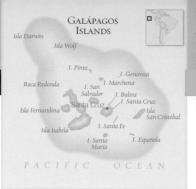

GALÁPAGOS
ISLANDS

Isla Darwin

Isla Wolf

I. Pinta
I. Genovesa
I. Marchena
Roca Redonda
I. San
Salvador
I. Baltra
Isla Fernandina
Santa Cruz
I. Santa Cruz
Isla
San Cristóbal
Isla Isabela
I. Santa Fe
I. Santa
María
I. Española

PACIFIC   OCEAN

GALÁPAGOS ISLANDS
Ecuador

In this historic living laboratory where Darwin's theory of natural selection was born, only human intervention can undo the damage caused by people and invasive species.

location 620 miles off the coast of Ecuador

ecoregions Galápagos Island xeric scrub; marine habitats including mangroves, coral reefs

project size 18.8 million acres

public lands Galápagos National Park

partners Galápagos National Park, the Charles Darwin Foundation, Fundación Natura

natural events climate turns tropical, January–May

information Anna Gibson, (703) 841-4109, agibson@tnc.org; nature.org/ecuador

Sea lions in the waters of the Galápagos.

Upon approach, the Galápagos Islands hardly evoke paradise. The parched and seemingly barren islands of volcanic debris appear hostile to life itself. But as you draw nearer, you see sea lions sunbathing on the shore, iguanas diving from boulders into the sea and blue-footed boobies wheeling in the azure sky above. Farther inland, famed giant tortoises lumber across the landscape as delicate flamingos feed at an inland pond. And Darwin's renowned finches, along with vermilion flycatchers, flit among the sheltering mangroves.

Perhaps no other place on Earth better represents the science of biodiversity and the need for conservation than the Galápagos Islands. When Charles Darwin pub-

lished *The Origin of Species by Natural Selection* in 1859, using the Galápagos as his primary laboratory, this remote and uninhabited volcanic archipelago of 128 islands, including 13 major islands, was forever changed. Most of the documented wildlife still inhabits the islands today, but so do more than 16,000 permanent human residents (up from zero in Darwin's day) with more than 70,000 annual visitors. All bring traffic, pollution, resource depletion and invasive alien species—the latter a plague for the isolated islands' native species.

After years of supporting local Ecuadorian partners and the Charles Darwin Research Institute, The Nature Conservancy is now playing a more active role in creating a long-term, comprehensive strategy for conservation in the Galápagos. Already we have conducted several workshops on conservation planning, ecotourism and conflict resolution with partners responsible for managing the marine reserve and the terrestrial park. Soon the Galápagos reefs will be a demonstration site for how El Niño phenomena and climate change affect relatively undamaged coral systems. In urbanized areas, such as those on Santa Cruz Island, the Conservancy will also spearhead a private lands initiative through which land will be kept in private ownership while legal restrictions prevent development and ecologically harmful activities.

Giant tortoise and thermal vents.

conservation profile

targets coastal lagoons and mangroves, giant tortoise, coral communities, 600 species of orchids, blue-footed booby, frigate bird, hammerhead shark, sea lion, iguana, whales, sparrow hawk

stresses invasive species, unsustainable use of natural resources, urbanization, global climate change

strategies combat invasive species, influence land-use planning, restore ecosystems, foster sustainable fishing practices, encourage conservation management of public lands, establish a private lands conservation program

results locally based network of conservation groups created; law enacted to keep marine reserve usage fees in local hands for park management

CHACO
Paraguay

A proposed biological corridor would connect this 2-million-acre wilderness with protected areas totaling more than 8 million acres, safeguarding habitat in one of South America's fiercest landscapes.

location 370 miles north of Asunción

ecoregions Chaco and Humid Chaco

project size roughly 11 million acres spanning Paraguay and Bolivia

public lands Defensores del Chaco National Park and Cerro Cabrera-Timane National Park, Paraguay; Kaa Iya National Park, Bolivia

partners Fundación DeSdel Chaco, U.S. Agency for International Development, Paraguayan government

natural events lapacho trees produce beautiful yellow blooms, September

information Cathy Kerkam, (703) 841-2082, ckerkam@tnc.org nature.org/paraguay

A sprawling, varied and often unforgiving wilderness, Paraguay's Chaco bridges more than 100,000 square miles between the grassy Argentine Pampa, the towering Andes Mountains and the Pantanal, the world's largest wetland.

The name "Chaco" comes from Quechua natives, who were so impressed by vast herds of mammals that they called

Seasonal wetlands in the Chaco.

the region "great hunting ground." The Chaco remains a safe haven for roaming predators including puma, jaguar and the maned wolf, one of the world's most threatened species. It also serves as a mecca for birds, including the pink flamingo and the ostrich-like nandu, as well as a handful of species found nowhere else on Earth.

Although a refuge for wildlife, the Chaco is less hospitable to humans. Mennonite settlers arriving from Canada in the 1920s dubbed the region a "green hell" because of its scissor-sharp brushland, scarce water and extreme temperatures. Even today, few Paraguayans venture west of the Paraguay River. The Chaco spans 60 percent of Paraguay but supports just 3 percent of the country's population. Only one partially paved road, the Ruta Trans Chaco, traverses the region. Yet even the remote Chaco faces pressure from unsustainable cattle ranching and population growth.

The Nature Conservancy has been working in the Chaco since the late 1990s, when we helped hire park guards, created a local conservation group and provided infrastructure for the protection of the 2-million-acre Defensores del Chaco National Park. We are currently working with Fundación DeSdel Chaco to create a biological corridor linking Chaco National Park to 8.6 million acres of protected areas in Bolivia and

Maned wolf.

Paraguay. By protecting this area, we would create the largest dry, tropical protected area in Latin America.

conservation profile

targets seasonal freshwater springs and wetlands, jaguar, tagua, trebol tree, night monkey, Chacoan fairy armadillo, Chacoan peccary, and birds such as the Quebracho crested-tinamou and greater rhea

stresses habitat fragmentation, unsustainable ranching, damming of rivers, illegal hunting

strategies promote ecologically compatible land-use practices, protect water supply, strengthen local partner organizations, staff park guard stations, engage community

results secured concrete protection for 2 million acres; completed rapid ecological assessment and management plan for the park

Pacaya-Samiria National Reserve
Peru

In Peru's largest national reserve, which is also home to thousands of people, community leaders must be the catalysts for a sustainable way of life.

location 93 river miles from Iquitos

ecoregion Iquitos Varzea

project size 5 million acres

public lands Pacaya-Samiria National Reserve

partners Pro Naturaleza, Peruvian Society of Environmental Law, Conservation Data Center, National Institute of Renewable Natural Resources

conservancy initiatives Freshwater

natural events annual flood leaves much of the reserve under water, November–April; river turtle eggs hatch, September

information Anna Gibson, (703) 841-4109, agibson@tnc.org; nature.org/peru

A five-hour boat ride from Iquitos is the only path into this remote jungle. Water defines landscape and life here in the Peruvian Amazon. Pacaya-Samiria is named for the two rivers that wind their way through this flooded forest. The wide waterways converge into the larger Marañón and Ucayali rivers, whose confluence at the northeast tip of the reserve marks the headwaters of the mighty Amazon.

The Amazon River forms where the Ucayali and Marañon rivers merge.

Pacaya-Samiria, declared a national reserve in 1968 and enlarged to its present size in 1982, spans an area twice the size of Yellowstone National Park. Its natural systems are driven by a giant pulse of water that washes down from the Andes each November, flooding the river banks and confining humans and animals alike to patches of high, dry ground for many months. In May, when water levels drop more than 30 feet and fish are concentrated in narrow waterways, hunting season ends and fishing season begins.

Although they appear muddy, the waters of these rivers are easily navigated by pink river dolphin and manatees; water lilies large enough to hold a small child float on the surface. Under the dense canopy of the rain forest, 440 species of tropical birds share the tree branches with howler and spider monkeys while jaguars stalk prey on the jungle floor.

Some 100,000 *ribereños,* or "river people," live in villages in and around the reserve, relying on its resources for nourishment and livelihood. No other protected area in the country is as directly linked to the survival of so many people. Although their overharvesting of fish, wildlife and trees threatens the system, the *ribereños* have a strong stake in the forest's continued well-being. The Nature Conservancy and our Peruvian partner Pro Naturaleza have trained local people as volunteer park

Walking palm tree.

rangers and are working with community leaders to develop management plans for fisheries, palm forests and river turtles. Lessons learned here now inform conservation work throughout the region.

conservation profile

targets Peruvian flooded forest, Moriche palm forest, rivers, pink river dolphin, manatee, giant river otter, caiman, river turtle, giant water lily, jaguar, tapir, macaw and other birds

stresses illegal logging of hardwoods, overfishing, overharvesting of fruits and trees, overhunting of large mammals, petroleum extraction

strategies engage community, promote ecotourism and other compatible development, foster sustainable fishing practices, restore ecosystems

results Peru's largest community park ranger program established; turtle management program established

CANAIMA NATIONAL PARK
Venezuela

In a landscape larger than Belgium, residents hope that a shift from agriculture to ecotourism will protect their unique homeland and accommodate a growing population.

location southeast Venezuela, close to the border with Brazil and Guyana

ecoregions Guianan Savannas, Pantepui, Guianan Highlands Moist Forest, Llanos

project size 36 million acres

public lands Canaima National Park; Cerro Venamo, Illu Tramen Tepui, Karaurín Tepui, Wadakapiapué Tepui, Yuruaní Tepui and Kukenán (Matawi) Tepui natural monuments

partners EcoNatura, Venezuelan National Institute of Parks (INPARQUES), National Experimental University of Guayana, National General Directorate of Indigenous Affairs of the Education, Culture and Sports Ministry

natural events flowering season, late October–November; migration of more than a million fish, many of which congregate at the base of rapids and waterfalls, June–mid-August

information Catherine Kerkam, (703) 841-2082, ckerkam@tnc.org; nature.org/venezuela

Vertical sandstone walls emerge abruptly out of the rolling grasslands of southeastern Venezuela's *Gran Sabana*. Water drains from the flat and isolated summits of these table mountains, called *tepui* by the native Pemón, cascading in hundreds of waterfalls. From Auyantepui, Angel Falls drops 3,250 feet, making it the highest waterfall in the world. The legendary *tepuis* are part of the Guiana Shield,

Angel Falls tumbles 3,250 feet from the tepui.

a geological formation extending from Venezuela into Brazil, Guyana and Colombia. Characterized by uplifted igneous and metamorphic rocks, the Guiana Shield formed more than 3 billion years ago, before Africa and the Americas broke apart.

Beneath the ethereal *tepuis*, the living landscape of Canaima National Park unfolds. Majestic rivers cross open savannas, groves of moriche palm, meadows and dense forest. Exotic wildlife and plants abound, including jaguar, giant anteaters, ocelots, osprey, broad-winged hawk and 500 species of orchids. At Canaima's higher elevations, one-third of the species are endemic, found nowhere else on Earth.

Nearly all of the human residents of this region are Pemón, living in small villages where grasslands meet wooded jungle. With no legal claim to land as their property, much of their ancestral land has been lost to development. Canaima National Park, which prohibits extracting natural resources within its ecologically fragile boundaries, has become a refuge for the Pemón. But here they continue to employ slash-and-burn agriculture, where small plots of forest are cleared and cultivated for a short time before the nutrients released from the scorched vegetation are depleted. Unfortunately, the needs of a growing Pemón population have shortened the fallow periods when forest is left to regenerate, leaving soils unsuitable for agriculture and a fragile ecosystem in jeopardy.

The Nature Conservancy and our partners are working to help the Pemón find economic alternatives that will support their growing population and sustain their spectacular landscape. If managed responsibly, ecotourism is one possible solution. We are

River guide, Cherun River.

conducting a study of tourism's impact on Canaima and training community members in nature- and adventure-tourism as a means of improving their local economy and avoiding overuse of the park's natural resources.

conservation profile

targets jaguar, giant river otter, giant anteater, giant armadillo, harpy eagle, fiery-shouldered parakeet, tepui parrotlet, moriche palm swamp, riparian and cloud forests

stresses fire, desertification, depletion of game and fisheries, pollution, mining, logging, unmanaged ecotourism

strategies encourage conservation management of public lands, engage community in management of natural resources, strengthen local partner organizations, build conservation alliances, promote ecotourism and compatible development

results conducted training workshops for indigenous leaders; published books on Canaima and Pemón oral tradition

PACIFIC

OCEAN

Sea of Okhotsk

Hokkaido

Sea of Japan

NORTH
KOREA

SOUTH
KOREA

JAPAN

Tokyo

Kyushu

Pyongyang

Seoul

Okinawa

*Yellow
Sea*

Shanghai

*East
China
Sea*

Taipei

TAIWAN

*Philippine
Sea*

NORTHERN
MARIANA
ISLANDS
(U.S.)

Beijing

C H I N A

Huang

Hong Kong

Hainan

Luzon

Manila

Sea

Lanzhou

Yangzi

YUNNAN GREAT
RIVERS PROJECT

Kunming

Red

Hanoi

VIETNAM

Mekong

LAOS

Vientiane

THAILAND

Bangkok

Gobi Desert

Ulaanbaatar

M O N G O L I A

Altay Mountains

K A Z A K H S T A N

Ürümqi

*Taklimakan
Desert*

Tian Shan

KYRGYZSTAN

Bishkek

*Lake
Balkash*

R U S S I A

*Lake
Baikal*

S i b e r i a

New Delhi

I N D I A

Ganges

NEPAL

Kathmandu

Mt. Everst
29,028 ft
(8,848 m)

Brahmaputra

BHUTAN

Thimphu

BANGLADESH

Dhaka

Indus

H i m a l a y a

MYANMAR
(BURMA)

Rangoon

Irrawaddy

Salween

*Bay
of
Bengal*

Andaman

1,000 miles

500

1,000 kilometers

500

0

0

N

MALDIVES
Male

LANKA

FEDERATED STATES OF
MICRONESIA

Caroline Islands

REPUBLIC
OF PALAU

Koror

Pohnpei ⊙ Palikir

ARNAVON ISLANDS ⊛

SOLOMON ISLANDS

Honiara ⊛
Guadalcanal

KIMBE BAY

New
Britain

Adelbert
Mountains

PAPUA
NEW GUINEA

Irian
A Jaya

Port Moresby ⊛

Coral
Sea

Tasman
Sea

NEW
ZEALAND

Tasmania

Sydney ●

Canberra ⊛

Melbourne ●

AUSTRALIA

Darling

Murray

MALAYSIA

Sarawak

Borneo
(Kalimantan)

EAST
KALIMANTAN

Ulu Mahakam

Lore Lindu
National Park

I N D O N E S I A

Darwin ●

EAST
TIMOR

Dili ⊛

Flores

Pulau
Komodo

Komodo
National
Park

Bali

J a v a

GONDWANA
LINK

Perth ●

BRUNEI

Begawan
⊛

Kuala Lumpur ⊛

SINGAPORE

Jakarta ⊛

S u m a t r a

Strait of Malacca

I N D I A N

O C E A N

ASIA, AUSTRALIA
& THE PACIFIC

KEY

■ Featured project
■ Other project

(square represents approximate
center of project area)

GONDWANA LINK
Australia

Rapid expansion of agriculture has fragmented Western Australia's eucalypt bushlands, habitat for the ground-nesting malleefowl and the greatest vascular plant diversity on Earth.

location south of Perth, stretching the width of the state of Western Australia

ecoregions Southwest Australia Woodlands, Jarrah-Karri Forest and Woodlands, Southwest Australia Savanna, Esperance Mallee, Coolgarlie Woodlands

project size 20 million acres

preserves Chereninup Creek Reserve (owned by Australian Bush Heritage Fund)

public lands Fitzgerald River National Park, Stirling Ranges National Park, state forests and other unallocated federal lands

partners Australian Bush Heritage Fund, Fitzgerald Biosphere Group, Friends of the Fitzgerald River National Park, Greening Australia, Malleefowl Preservation Group, The Wilderness Society of Western Australia

natural events magnificent wildflower blooms, July–November; whale watching, May–December; migratory birds, August–November

information Maria Ferreira, (703) 841-5992, mferreira@tnc.org; nature.org/australia

Stirling Ranges.

You are likely to see more kangaroos and sheep than people as you traverse the rolling terrain of southwestern Australia. This landscape is believed to be an extant chunk of Gondwanaland—the primordial land mass that, before breaking apart, hypothetically connected the Indian subcontinent and lands of the Southern Hemisphere. One of the oldest and most isolated land surfaces on the planet, this combination of semi-arid scrubland and wet forest has evolved over hundreds of millions of years with little catastrophic disturbance. As a result, pockets of species found nowhere else have evolved in close proximity across the landscape, creating a biodiversity "hotspot."

In addition to kangaroos, other ubiquitous hopping marsupials and the occasional emu, the land harbors such unusual creatures as the hedgehog-esque echidna, the frilled lizard and the prairie chickenlike malleefowl, which constructs huge nesting mounds more than 3 feet high and twice as wide. But the 12,000 plant species—ranging from rare eucalypts and orchids to the primitively beautiful banksia—give this area its global biological significance.

Royal hakea, Fitzgerald River National Park.

Gondwana Link is a visionary effort by six grassroots Australian organizations and The Nature Conservancy to connect existing national parks and reserves with new private and public conservation lands, creating an unbroken band of protected bush across the state of Western Australia— from the Indian Ocean to the edge of the country's Red Center. When fully established, the link will include two major national parks—Fitzgerald River and Stirling Ranges—and stretch more than 620 miles.

In the past century, this sparsely populated region has been transformed into Australia's breadbasket—with devastating results for biodiversity and the land itself. Massive land conversion for farming and ranching has destroyed wildlife habitat and fragmented what remains, isolating plant and animal populations. But an unforeseen phenomenon has begun stripping the landscape of its agricultural value as well. As the native ground cover of thirsty, deep-rooted eucalypts is replaced with seasonal wheat and other crops, the water table has risen, pushing ancient salt deposits to the surface and resulting in ghostly barren moonscapes.

conservation profile

targets jarrah and marri forests, eucalypt woodlands, Mediterranean scrubland, echidna, frilled lizard, malleefowl

stresses agricultural conversion and habitat fragmentation, climate change

strategies acquire land, secure conservation easements, restore ecosystems, promote ecologically sound public policies, encourage conservation management of public land

results Gondwana Link coalition established; first 1,400 acres acquired

YUNNAN GREAT RIVERS PROJECT
China

Working with the Chinese government and local people enables the Conservancy to have an impact in a conservation project of unprecedented reach.

location bordering Sichuan Province and Tibet Autonomous Prefecture and Myanmar (Burma)

ecoregions Nujiang-Lancang Gorge, Hengduan Mountains

project size 25,000 square miles

public lands all land in China is public land

partners more than 40 government and institutional partners including the Yunnan Provincial Government, the State Department and Planning Commission, State Environmental and Protection Administration, U.S. Park Service, Yunnan Poverty Alleviation Bureau

conservancy initiatives Global Climate Change

natural events extraordinary flower blooms including more than 160 species of rhododendron and azalea, primroses, gentians, native magnolias, lilacs and hydrangeas, spring–fall

information Maria Ferreira, (703) 841-5992, mferreira@tnc.org, nature.org/china

Kawagebo Peak, Meili Mountains.

Geologic collisions permanently wrinkled China's Yunnan Province into soaring mountain ranges and deep gorges. Four of Asia's greatest rivers—the Yangtze, Irrawaddy, Salween and Mekong—sparkle and dance between the mountains, at times flowing within 60 miles of one another. Snow-capped peaks, rhododendron-covered mountain slopes, old-growth forests and glaciers combine to create a landscape so remote and timeless that many historians believe it inspired the fictional paradise of Shangri-la in James Hilton's classic novel *Lost Horizon*.

For millennia, humans have been part of Yunnan's natural tapestry. Its highest mountain, Meilixueshan, is among the most sacred in Tibetan Buddhism, and thousands of pilgrims arrive every fall to make a two-week trek around its base. Fourteen of China's ethnic minorities live in the region, including the Naxi, who have lived in harmony with nature for more than a thousand years.

Yunnan's forests provide vital erosion control and flood prevention downstream. Its rivers supply approximately one in 10 people on Earth with food, water, transportation and trade. But poverty, development and pressures from burgeoning energy needs threaten the region's resources.

Yangtze River.

In response, in 1998 China invited The Nature Conservancy to help create the Yunnan Great Rivers Project, a joint effort to protect the region's natural and cultural resources and to improve the livelihood of local communities. This project promises, in the words of Chinese Premier Jiang Zemin, to "serve as a model for all of China's conservation efforts." To promote effective long-term planning, the Conservancy signed a memorandum of understanding with China's natural resource agency to train nature reserve managers from every Chinese province in our conservation methodology, Conservation by Design. Training workshops are already under way. We also develop and promote alternative energy projects, such as biogas and solar power, that meet fuel requirements without taxing the forest.

conservation profile

targets Yunnan golden snub-nosed monkey, snow leopard, evergreen broadleaf forest, rhododendron shrublands, high-elevation spruce-fir forest

stresses poverty, unsustainable agriculture, logging and fuel wood collection, unplanned tourism, unsustainable levels of harvesting and grazing, population growth

strategies establish a system of durable protected areas, promote alternative energy sources, promote ecologically compatible land-use practices, influence land-use planning, build conservation alliances, promote ecotourism

results plan recommending the creation of 3.4 million acres of new nature reserves adopted by the Chinese government

FEDERATED STATES OF
MICRONESIA

*Senyavin
Islands* POHNPEI
Palikir
Pohnpei

C a r o l i n e   I s l a n d s *Kosrae*

P A C I F I C
O C E A N

POHNPEI
Federated States of Micronesia

Flush with plants and animals found nowhere else on Earth, this Pacific island
paradise is an incubator of community-based conservation techniques that
could be applied throughout Oceania.

location Western Pacific;
10-hour flight from Honolulu

ecoregion Micronesia

project size 133 square miles

public lands Pohnpei
Watershed Forest Reserve

partners Conservation Society of
Pohnpei, municipal and state governments, traditional Pohnpeian
leaders

conservancy initiatives
Freshwater

natural events huge spawning
aggregations of grouper,
February–April

information Maria Ferreira,
(703) 841-5992,
mferreira@tnc.org
nature.org/micronesia

Sunset near Sokehs Rock.

With the largest intact upland rain forest in all of Micronesia, the island of Pohnpei is one of the greenest, wettest places in the world. The native forest overflows with species of plants and animals found nowhere else on Earth. The forest is also vital to the island's water quality, a growing tourism industry and the cultural and spiritual lives of Pohnpeians.

But over the past three decades, Pohnpei's native forest has been dramatically reduced from 42 percent to 15 percent of the island's area. The culprit: the clearing

of forest to grow *sakau,* or kava, a plant that produces an earthy, mildly intoxicating beverage.

Sakau has been the elixer of choice for islanders for generations. In Nan Madol, Pohnpei's 700-year-old basalt-block fortress, a stone worn smooth by centuries of pounding *sakau* reveals its deep cultural roots. Yet today, with *sakau* the premier cash crop and a major source of employment on Pohnpei, the volume of its cultivation has degraded the forests and other ecosystems. Planting this shallow-rooted crop on steep slopes leads to soil erosion, which smothers mangroves, lagoons and the coral reefs that ring the island.

Since 1990 The Nature Conservancy has helped craft a watershed management strategy that recognizes the authority of local villagers and traditional leaders to manage their own forest and marine resources— a first for the island nation. As a result, they created a new forest reserve and placed a ban on crop cultivation and settlement in the upland forest. The reserve encompasses nearly a third of the island. Our work in Pohnpei has fostered local participation in watershed management and created a new spirit of cooperation among government and community leaders, producing results that can be exported and implemented across other islands of Micronesia and the Pacific.

Ginger blooms, Kepirohi Falls.

conservation profile

targets upland rain forest, coral reefs, mangroves, fish like Pohnpei greater white-eye, Pohnpei mountain starling, short-eared owl

stresses destruction of native forest for agriculture, sedimentation and runoff, incompatible development, unsustainable fishing practices

strategies promote ecologically compatible land-use practices, promote ecologically sound public policies, engage community in natural resource management, designate marine protected areas, launch local partner organizations

results Pohnpei Watershed Forest Reserve created; watershed strategy gives management authority to local people

EAST KALIMANTAN
Indonesia

The hope of saving one of the last healthy populations of endangered orang-utans hinges on the success of local efforts to protect Borneo's forests from logging and wildfires.

location 250 miles north of Samarinda

ecoregion East Borneo Rain Forest

project size 3.2 million acres

partners National Protected Areas and Conservation Directorate, Berau District Land-Use Planning Agency, Berau District Environmental Monitoring Agency, Sumalindo Timber Concession, Gunung Timber Concession, Long Gie village, Long Duhung village, Long Boi village, Sido Bangun community

natural events wild boar migration, May; green turtle nesting and hatching, year-round; giant manta migration, year-round; trees fruit and fill the air with a sweet smell, January–February

information Maria Ferreira, (703) 841-5992; mferreira@tnc.org; nature.org/indonesia

The dense forests of northeastern Borneo, in the province of East Kalimantan, conceal an other-worldly realm. Among the mist-shrouded trees and limestone spires hung thick with ferns, orchids and vines roam strange and colorful creatures like the honey-chested sun bear and the clouded leopard. Long-armed gibbons and langurs swing from high branches, and large horn-billed pheasants scavenge the forest floor.

Wallace's line runs just east of Borneo, through the Makassar Strait, marking the divide between islands that

Lowland rain forest, East Kalimantan, Borneo.

were once connected to Asia and those of Australian origin. Many of Borneo's Asian-derived but Australian-influenced species are unique in the world. Because large sections of the isolated rain forests of East Kalimantan have never been explored, it is likely that some inhabitants remain to be discovered.

In 2002 The Nature Conservancy and a team of local villagers discovered a large population of orangutans in East Kalimantan. Borneo and Sumatra are the only two places on Earth where these red-haired primates are found in the wild, and the newly discovered East Kalimantan group could represent as much as 10 percent of remaining native populations. Orangutans live their entire lives high above the ground, building their nests in trees. East Kalimantan was spared the devastating fires of the early 1980s and late 1990s and today survives as one of Indonesia's last pristine wilderness—one of only a few forest refuges large enough to support viable populations of orangutans.

But Borneo's forests are being lost at record pace. Widespread fires are set to clear the land for agriculture, and Indonesia's economic depression fuels the cycle of logging and forest degradation. Despite its remoteness and relative wildness, East Kalimantan is not immune to these threats. Working with the local government, forest industry and forest-dependent indigenous

Orangutans.

groups, the Conservancy is seeking protected status for orangutan habitat. We have also established a timber certification program with Home Depot, which promotes the purchase of timber that has been harvested using sustainable techniques and creates strong economic incentives in East Kalimantan to protect the forest.

conservation profile

targets orangutan, proboscis monkey, leaf monkey, sun bear, gibbon, banteng, hawksbill turtle, green turtle, hornbill, Bornean peacock pheasant, Storm's stork, Berau barrier reef

stresses deforestation, wildfires, destructive fishing practices, illegal logging, poaching

strategies promote ecologically compatible land-use practices, engage community in natural resource management

results secured commitment from Home Depot for forest certification program (timber bought from region must be sustainably harvested); facilitated commitments from local and national governments in Indonesia to protect newly discovered orangutan habitat

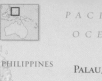

PALAU
Republic of Palau

Palau is one of the seven underwater wonders of the world, with dugongs, saltwater crocodiles, 550 coral species, 300 species of sponges and 1,300 varieties of reef fish.

location 470 miles southeast of the Philippines; approximately 8 hours from Hawaii

ecoregions Micronesia

project size 177 square miles

public lands 16 national and state conservation areas

partners Palau Conservation Society, state and national governments, local communities

conservancy initiatives Marine, Invasive Species

natural events snorkel among stingless jellyfish in the Rock Islands' Jellyfish Lake; turtle nesting and hatching, May–August; coral spawning, year-round

information Maria Ferreira, (703) 841-5992, mferreira@tnc.org, nature.org/palau

Diving among jellyfish, Palau Marine Lakes.

Scuba enthusiasts journey from around the globe to explore the reef riches surrounding Palau's 586 islands, one of the top underwater destinations in the world. Divers drift down coral walls past colorful anemones, schools of triggerfish, towering sea fans and giant clams. They might see a lone wrasse, manta ray or sunken ship from World War II. Above the water, the strange Rock Islands—uninhabited mushroom-shaped islets topped with dense green

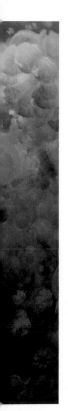

foliage—create a prized maze for sea-kayakers and ideal habitat for myriad sea life.

Although much of Palau's human history is shrouded in mystery, there is evidence of habitation here from as early as 1000 B.C. Following European contact in the late 18th century, Palau passed from Spanish to German to Japanese rule, becoming a protectorate of the United States after World War II. One of the world's youngest nations, Palau gained its independence in 1994.

The Nature Conservancy was the first international conservation organization to build a presence in Palau, playing a key role in establishing the Palau Conservation Society, today the country's leading non-profit organization. Both organizations have aided the government in designating a dozen new marine and terrestrial conservation areas—the cornerstone of a nationwide network of conservation areas that the Conservancy is helping design. After the president of Palau asked the Conservancy to become more involved in developing the country's environmental policy, we began helping create comprehensive "ridges to reefs" conservation strategies and management plans.

In 1998 Palau's corals were severely damaged by climate change–related bleaching, whereby warmed ocean currents and too much sunlight penetrating the water turned corals white, brittle and lifeless. Nearly 99 percent of corals on some reefs died. Their subsequent recovery, however, and the study of those reefs that proved resilient to coral bleaching helped spark a new Conservancy-wide program. The Transforming Coral Reef Conservation Program aims to

Rock Islands at Seventy Islands National Park.

mitigate future coral bleaching by designing and managing marine protected areas that can survive climate-change events and replenish damaged corals. Palau is one of the pilot sites for this exciting new initiative.

conservation profile

targets coral reefs, rock islands and lagoons, coastal mangroves, interior forests, hawksbill turtle, dugong, manta ray

stresses overexploitation of marine resources, unsustainable development, inadequate solid waste and sewage disposal, coastal dredging, spread of invasive species, climate change

strategies designate marine protected areas, influence land-use planning, promote ecologically sound public policies, strengthen local partner organizations

results 12 new conservation areas designated; Palau Conservation Society established; founding president of PCS, Noah Idechong, received Goldman Environmental Prize and is now a member of the Palau National Congress

KIMBE BAY
Papua New Guinea

Kimbe Bay, boasting more than 60 percent of the coral species of the entire Indo-Pacific, is a prime target for exploitation by the destructive international live reef fish trade.

location north coast of New Britain in the Bismarck Archipelago; 1.5-hour flight from Port Moresby

ecoregions Papua

project size 9,500 square miles

public lands Kimbe Bay's reefs are community owned

partners Mahonia na Dari, Walindi Plantation Resort, Australia's James Cook University, the University of Papua New Guinea

conservancy initiatives Marine

natural events whales and dolphins migrate through, year-round

information Maria Ferreira, (703) 841-5992, mferreira@tnc.org; nature.org/papuanewguinea

Active volcanic cones encircle tranquil Kimbe Bay on the island of New Britain. Blue-eyed cockatoos and the world's largest moths fill the air, while bandicoots and wallabies share the landscape with one of the world's greatest arrays of orchids. But it was the underwater world of Kimbe Bay that first attracted The Nature Conservancy in 1993. The bay had largely escaped the destruction that the live reef fish trade—with its use of cyanide and dynamite to catch prized species alive, for sale in Hong Kong's markets—has brought to coral reefs elsewhere in Southeast Asia.

Offshore coral reefs play an important role in local culture and mythology, even though they are rarely visited by islanders

and biologically misunderstood. On New Britain, as in many other places, coral was commonly considered to be lifeless rock, not a fragile living organism crucial to the survival of fish and other marine life. As a result, reefs were thought to be indestructible and no premium was put on their protection. It became clear that any grassroots conservation effort would require citizen education.

Teaming up with the Walindi Plantation Resort—Kimbe Bay's primary sport diving center—the Conservancy helped establish Mahonia Na Dari ("Guardians of the Sea" in the local language). The conservation organization sponsors a marine research, conservation and education center to aid scientists and teach islanders about their ecosystems. Historically, the people of New Britain have had a limited relationship with their marine environment. Few children learn to swim, and residents of inland villages often have never seen the ocean.

Mahonia Na Dari's marine education program is developing a future generation of conservation leaders to safeguard Kimbe Bay and has been instrumental in building community support for conservation work. Several villages have established community-managed marine protected areas, closing many reefs to allow them to recover from overharvesting. The education program is so successful that it is being integrated into Papua New Guinea's National School Teaching Curriculum. The marine conservation and research center now hosts scientists from Australia's James Cook

Islanders in outrigger canoes.

Spine-cheek anemonefish in anemone.

University and the University of Papua New Guinea, whose research and monitoring help inform conservation work. The Conservancy is planning to expand its marine conservation efforts to the nearby provinces of New Ireland and Manus.

conservation profile

targets mangroves, seagrasses, coral reefs, reef fish, panda clown fish, turtles, orca, bottle-nosed dolphin, spinner dolphin, pilot whale

stresses runoff from oil palm plantations, overfishing and destructive fishing practices, boat anchor damage to coral reefs, rapid population growth

strategies designate marine protected areas, strengthen local partner organizations, educate and engage community, construct mooring buoys for reef protection, promote marine research

results Mahonia na Dari and marine research facility established; 80 mooring buoys constructed; marine education classes have reached more than 5,000 children, adults and community leaders

ARNAVON ISLANDS
The Solomon Islands

Home to one of the world's largest nesting populations of endangered hawksbill turtles, the Arnavon Islands represent the first community-managed marine conservation project in the South Pacific.

location between northern Santa Isabel and southern Choiseul islands; 200 miles from the capital of Honiara

ecoregions Papua

project size 311,000 acres

public lands Arnavon Marine Conservation Area is community-owned

partners provincial government, village leaders, community members, Lauru Land Conference

conservancy initiatives Marine

natural events hawksbill turtle nesting, June–August

information Maria Ferreira, (703) 841-5992, mferreira@tnc.org; nature.org/solomonislands

Dense emerald forests blanket the islands and crystal-blue water surrounds them. Occasional clusters of stilted, thatched-roof huts hug the shorelines, and villagers ply the waters in dugout canoes. Scattered amid the forests and harbors are rusting remains of bombers, troop ships and tanks. Known mostly by World War II historians for the battle of Guadalcanal and now by scuba divers, the Solomon Islands are off the radar screen for most of the world.

But the islands are very much *on* the radar screen for endangered hawksbill turtles, which return each year from foraging grounds on the Great Barrier Reef in record numbers to lay

their eggs on the smooth-sand beaches of the Solomons. The islands are also an important nesting ground for rare Sanford's sea eagles, Brahmany kites, ospreys and ground-nesting megapodes. There is no other island group in the world where natural selection has produced such a dramatic diversity in bird populations. With creatures like giant clams, bêche-de-mer, trochus and gold-lip pearl oysters, the Solomon Islands is ranked among the top 10 most biologically diverse nations in the world. The diverse species are also among the world's most imperiled.

In a group of islands in the Solomons chain known as the Arnavons, three communities have taken charge of their fragile resources and are setting an example for their South Pacific neighbors to follow. In 1995, at the invitation of these communities and in partnership with the Solomon Islands government, The Nature Conservancy helped establish the Arnavon Marine Conservation Area, the first community-managed marine conservation project in the South Pacific. Villagers patrol beaches during nesting season to prevent turtle and egg poaching, and community leaders have voluntarily established fishing limits and new methods to rebuild stocks and maintain sustainable seafood harvesting. Efforts are also under way to combat cyanide fishing and other destructive practices that have accompanied the live reef fish trade elsewhere in the region.

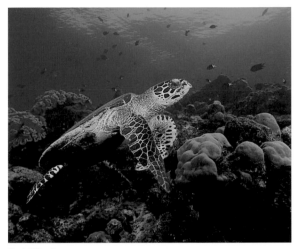
Hawksbill turtle.

Barrel sponge.

conservation profile

targets hawksbill turtle nesting beaches, marine breeding grounds, forests, commercially valuable species such as trochus, sea cucumber, black and gold-lip pearl oysters and giant clams

stresses overharvesting of marine resources, destructive fishing practices, logging

strategies designate marine and terrestrial protected areas, foster sustainable fishing practices, undertake scientific research, strengthen local partner organizations, engage community in natural resource management

results Arnavon Marine Conservation Area established; hundreds of turtles tagged

ECOREGIONAL MAPS

The Nature Conservancy plans for conservation within and across ecoregions. An ecoregion is a large unit of land and water typically defined by climate, geology, topography and associations of plants and animals. These distinct divisions in the natural landscape, such as the Sonoran Desert along the U.S.-Mexico border, follow nature's borders not geopolitical lines.

The following ecoregional maps depict the ecoregions of the countries and continents where we work. They were created by The Nature Conservancy's Global Priorities Group using a variety of sources.

Terrestrial ecoregions of the United States, Alaska and Hawaii were revised/modified by The Nature Conservancy, USDA Forest Service and U.S. Geological Survey, based on Bailey, Robert G. 1995. Description of the ecoregions of the United States (2nd ed.). Misc. Pub. No. 1391, Map scale 1:7,500,000. USDA Forest Service. 108 pp.

Terrrestrial ecoregions of Canada were based on Bailey (1995) at the U.S. borders and Wiken, E.B. (compiler). 1986. "Terrestrial ecozones of Canada." Ecological Land Classification Series No. 19. Environment Canada, Hull, Que. 26 pp. + map.

The world's 867 terrestrial ecoregions were devised by Olson, D.M., E. Dinerstein, E.D. Wikramanayake, N.D. Burgess, G.V.N. Powell, E.C. Underwood, J.A. D'Amico, H.E. Strand, J.C. Morrison, C.J. Loucks, T.F. Allnutt, J.F. Lamoreux, T.H. Ricketts, I. Itoua, W.W. Wettengel, Y. Kura, P. Hedao, and K. Kassem. 2001. "Terrestrial ecoregions of the world: A new map of life on Earth." BioScience 51(11):933-938.

Asia, Australia &
the Pacific

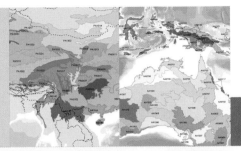

Canada &
United States

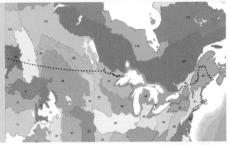

Caribbean

Mexico &
Central America

South America

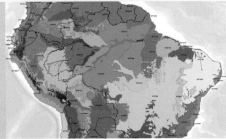

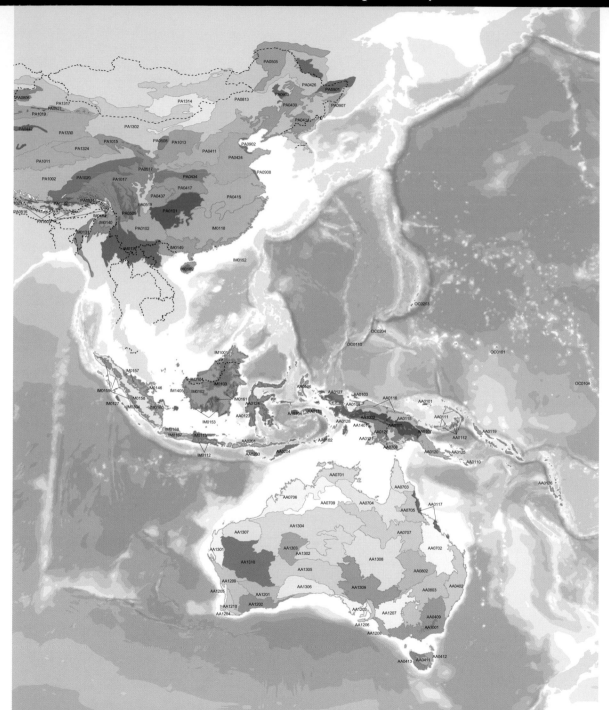

- The World's 867 Terrestrial Ecoregions obatined from Olson, D.M., E. Dinerstein, E.D. Wikramanayake, N.D. Burgess, G.V.N. Powell, E.C. Underwood, J.A. D'Amico, H.E. Strand, J.C. Morrison, C.J. Loucks, T.F. Allnutt, J.F. Lamoreux, T.H. Ricketts, I. Itoua, W.W. Wettengel, Y. Kura, P. Hedao, and K. Kassem. 2001. Terrestrial ecoregions of the world: A new map of life on Earth. BioScience 51(11):933-938.

Tropical & Subtropical Moist Broadleaf Forests

AA0101. Admiralty Islands lowland rain forests
AA0102. Banda Sea Islands moist deciduous forests
AA0103. Biak-Numfoor rain forests
AA0104. Buru rain forests
AA0105. Central Range montane rain forests
AA0106. Halmahera rain forests
AA0107. Huon Peninsula montane rain forests
AA0108. Japen rain forests
AA0110. Louisiade Archipelago rain forests
AA0111. New Britain-New Ireland lowland rain forests
AA0112. New Britain-New Ireland montane rain forests
AA0115. Northern New Guinea lowland rain and freshwater swamp forests
AA0116. Northern New Guinea montane rain forests
AA0117. Queensland tropical rain forests
AA0118. Seram rain forests
AA0119. Solomon Islands rain forests
AA0120. Southeastern Papuan rain forests
AA0121. Southern New Guinea freshwater swamp forests
AA0122. Southern New Guinea lowland rain torests
AA0123. Sulawesi lowland rain forests
AA0124. Sulawesi montane rain forests
AA0125. Trobriand Islands rain forests
AA0126. Vanuatu rain forests
AA0127. Vogelkop montane rain forests
AA0128. Vogelkop-Aru lowland rain forests
IM0102. Borneo lowland rain forests
IM0103. Borneo montane rain forests
IM0104. Borneo peat swamp forests
IM0112. Eastern Java-Bali montane rain forests
IM0113. Eastern Java-Bali rain forests
IM0118. Jian Nan subtropical evergreen forests
IM0127. Mentawai Islands rain forests
IM0131. Mizoram-Manipur-Kachin rain forests
IM0137. Northern Indochina subtropical forests
IM0140. Northern Triangle subtropical forests
IM0146. Peninsular Malaysian rain forests
IM0149. South China-Vietnam subtropical evergreen forests
IM0152. Southern Annamites montane rain forests
IM0153. Southwest Borneo freshwater swamp forests
IM0157. Sumatran freshwater swamp forests
IM0158. Sumatran lowland rain forests
IM0159. Sumatran montane rain forests
IM0160. Sumatran peat swamp forests
IM0161. Sundaland heath forests
IM0167. Western Java montane rain forests
IM0168. Western Java rain forests
IM0169. Hainan Island monsoon rain forests
OC0101. Carolines tropical moist forests
OC0104. Eastern Micronesia tropical moist forests
OC0110. Palau tropical moist forests
PA0101. Gizhou Plateau broadleaf and mixed forests
PA0102. Yunnan Plateau subtropical evergreen forests

Tropical & Subtropical Dry Broadleaf Forests

AA0201. Lesser Sundas deciduous forests
AA0203. Sumba deciduous forests
AA0204. Timor and Wetar deciduous forests
OC0203. Marianas tropical dry forests
OC0204. Yap tropical dry forests

Tropical & Subtropical Coniferous Forests

IM0304. Sumatran tropical pine forests

Temperate Broadleaf & Mixed Forests

AA0402. Eastern Australian temperate forests
AA0409. Southeast Australia temperate forests
AA0411. Tasmanian Central Highland forests
AA0412. Tasmanian temperate forests
AA0413. Tasmanian temperate rain forests
IM0402. Northern Triangle temperate forests
PA0411. Central China loess plateau mixed forests
PA0414. Changbai Mountains mixed forests
PA0415. Changjiang Plain evergreen forests
PA0417. Daba Mountains evergreen forests
PA0424. Huang He Plain mixed forests
PA0426. Manchurian mixed forests
PA0430. Northeast China Plain deciduous forests
PA0434. Qin Ling Mountains deciduous forests
PA0437. Sichuan Basin evergreen broadleaf forests
PA0442. Tarim Basin deciduous forests and steppe

Temperate Conifer Forests

IM0501. Eastern Himalayan subalpine conifer forests
PA0505. Da Hinggan-Dzhagdy Mountains conifer forests
PA0508. Helanshan montane conifer forests
PA0509. Hengduan Mountains subalpine conifer forests
PA0514. Northeastern Himalayan subalpine conifer forests
PA0516. Nujiang Langcang Gorge alpine conifer and mixed forests
PA0517. Qilian Mountains conifer forests
PA0518. Qionglai-Minshan conifer forests
PA0521. Tian Shan montane conifer forests

Tropical & Subtropical Grasslands, Savannas & Shrublands

AA0708. Trans Fly savanna and grasslands
AA0701. Arnhem Land tropical savanna
AA0702. Brigalow tropical savanna
AA0703. Cape York tropical savanna
AA0704. Carpentaria tropical savanna
AA0705. Einasleigh upland savanna
AA0706. Kimberly tropical savanna
AA0707. Mitchell grass downs
AA0709. Victoria Plains tropical savanna

Temperate Grasslands, Savannas & Shrublands

AA0802. Eastern Australia mulga shrublands
AA0803. Southeast Australia temperate savanna
PA0806. Emin Valley steppe
PA0813. Mongolian-Manchurian grassland

Flooded Grasslands & Savannas

PA0901. Amur meadow steppe
PA0902. Bohai Sea saline meadow
PA0903. Nenjiang River grassland
PA0907. Suiphun-Khanka meadows and forest meadows
PA0908. Yellow Sea saline meadow

Montane Grasslands & Shrublands

AA1001. Australian Alps montane grasslands
AA1002. Central Range sub-alpine grasslands
IM1001. Kinabalu montane alpine meadows
PA1002. Central Tibetan Plateau alpine steppe
PA1003. Eastern Himalayan alpine shrub and meadows
PA1011. North Tibetan Plateau-Kunlun Mountains alpine desert
PA1013. Ordos Plateau steppe
PA1015. Qilian Mountains subalpine meadow
PA1017. Southeast Tibet shrublands and meadow
PA1019. Tian Shan montane steppe and meadow
PA1020. Tibetan Plateau alpine shrublands and meadows
PA1021. Western Himalayan alpine shrub and Meadows
PA1022. Yarlun Tsangpo arid steppe

Mediterranean Forests, Woodlands & Scrub

AA1201. Coolgardie woodlands
AA1202. Esperance mallee
AA1203. Eyre and York mallee
AA1204. Jarrah-Karri forest and shrublands
AA1205. Kwongan heathlands
AA1206. Mount Lofty woodlands
AA1207. Murray-Darling woodlands and mallee
AA1208. Naracoorte woodlands
AA1209. Southwest Australia savanna
AA1210. Southwest Australia woodlands

Deserts & Xeric Shrublands

AA1301. Carnarvon xeric shrublands
AA1302. Central Ranges xeric scrub
AA1303. Gibson desert
AA1304. Great Sandy-Tanami desert
AA1305. Great Victoria desert
AA1306. Nullarbor Plains xeric shrublands
AA1307. Pilbara shrublands
AA1308. Simpson desert
AA1309. Tirari-Sturt stony desert
AA1310. Western Australian Mulga shrublands
PA1302. Alashan Plateau semi-desert
PA1314. Eastern Gobi desert steppe
PA1317. Junggar Basin semi-desert
PA1324. Qaidam Basin semi-desert
PA1330. Taklimakan desert

Mangroves

AA1401. New Guinea mangroves
IM1405. Sunda Shelf mangroves

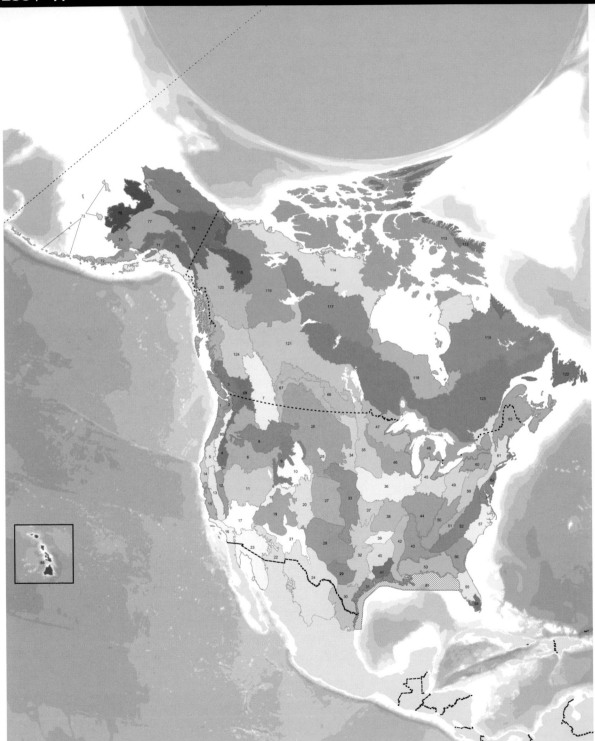

Tundra

- 72. Alaska Peninsula
- 73. Bering Sea and Aleutian Islands
- 74. Bristol Bay Basin
- 75. Beringian Tundra
- 79. Brooks Range Tundra Coastal Plain
- 112. Arctic Cordillera
- 113. Northern Arctic
- 114. Southern Arctic

Subarctic

- 71. Cook Inlet Basin
- 76. Alaska Range
- 77. Interior Alaska Taiga
- 78. Yukon Plateau and Flats
- 115. Taiga Cordillera
- 116. Taiga Plains
- 117. Western Taiga Shield
- 118. Hudson Plains
- 119. Eastern Taiga Shield
- 121. Boreal Plains
- 122. Atlantic Maritime
- 123. Boreal Shield

Warm Continental

- 47. Superior Mixed Forest
- 48. Great Lakes
- 60. High Allegheny Plateau
- 63. Northern Appalachian-Boreal Forest
- 64. St. Lawrence-Champlain Valley
- 120. Boreal Cordillera

Hot Continental

- 38. Ozarks
- 39. Ouachita Mountains
- 44. Interior Low Plateau
- 45. North Central Tillplain
- 46. Prairie-Forest Border
- 49. Western Allegheny Plateau
- 50. Cumberlands and Southern Ridge and Valley
- 51. Southern Blue Ridge
- 59. Central Appalachian Forest
- 61. Lower New England/Northern Piedmont
- 62. North Atlantic Coast

Subtropical

- 31. Gulf Coast Prairies and Marshes
- 40. Upper West Gulf Coastal Plain
- 41. West Gulf Coastal Plain
- 42. Mississippi River Alluvial Plain
- 43. Upper East Gulf Coastal Plain
- 52. Piedmont
- 53. East Gulf Coastal Plain
- 55. Florida Peninsula
- 56. South Atlantic Coastal Plain
- 57. Mid-Atlantic Coastal Plain
- 58. Chesapeake Bay Lowlands

Prairie

- 32. Crosstimbers and Southern Tallgrass Prairie
- 36. Central Tallgrass Prairie
- 35. Northern Tallgrass Prairie
- 37. Osage Plains/Flint Hills Prairie

Marine

- 1. Pacific Northwest Coast
- 2. Puget Trough - Willamette Valley - Georgia Bay
- 3. North Cascades and Pacific Ranges
- 4. Modoc Plateau and East Cascades
- 69. Alaska Coastal Forest and Mountains
- 70. Gulf of Alaska Mountains and Fjordlands
- 80. West Cascades
- 81. Northern Gulf Coast

Mediterranean

- 5. Klamath Mountains
- 12. Sierra Nevada
- 13. Great Central Valley
- 14. California North Coast
- 15. California Central Coast
- 16. California South Coast

Tropical / Subtropical Steppe

- 19. Colorado Plateau
- 28. Southern Shortgrass Prairie
- 29. Edwards Plateau
- 30. Tamaulipan Thorn Scrub

Tropical / Subtropical Desert

- 17. Mojave Desert
- 21. Arizona-New Mexico Mountains
- 22. Apache Highlands
- 23. Sonoran Desert
- 24. Chihuahuan Desert

Temperate Steppe

- 33. Central Mixed-Grass Prairie
- 34. Dakota Mixed-Grass Prairie
- 26. Northern Great Plains Steppe
- 27. Central Shortgrass Prairie
- 66. Aspen Parkland
- 67. Fescue-Mixed Grass Prairie
- 124. Montane Cordillera

Temperate Desert

- 6. Columbia Plateau
- 7. Canadian Rocky Mountains
- 8. Middle Rockies - Blue Mountains
- 9. Utah-Wyoming Rocky Mountains
- 10. Wyoming Basins
- 11. Great Basin
- 18. Utah High Plateaus
- 20. Southern Rocky Mountains
- 25. Black Hills
- 68. Okanagan

Savanna

- 54. Tropical Florida

Rainforest

- 65. Hawaiian High Islands

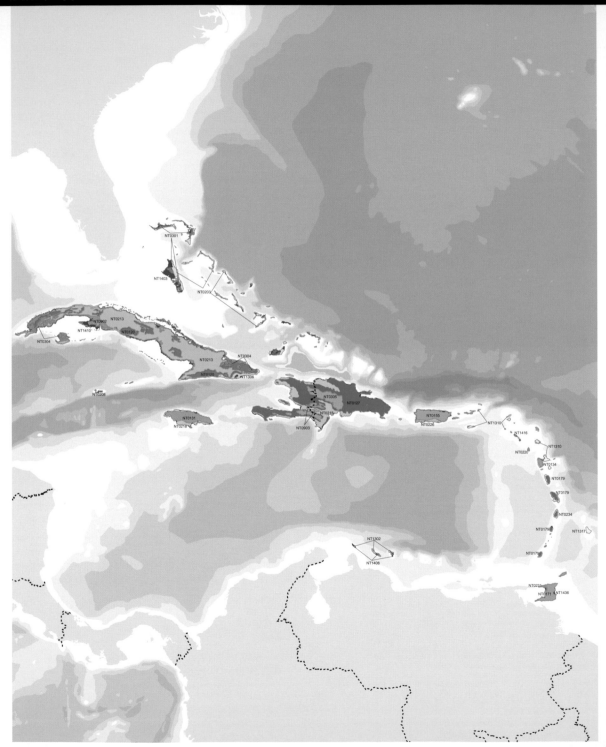

Tropical & Subtropical Moist Broadleaf Forests

NT0120. Cuban moist forests
NT0127. Hispaniolan moist forests
NT0131. Jamaican moist forests
NT0134. Leeward Islands moist forests
NT0155. Puerto Rican moist forests
NT0171. Trinidad and Tobago moist forests
NT0179. Windward Islands moist forests

Tropical & Subtropical Dry Broadleaf Forests

NT0203. Bahamian dry forests
NT0208. Cayman Islands dry forests
NT0213. Cuban dry forests
NT0215. Hispaniolan dry forests
NT0218. Jamaican dry forests
NT0220. Leeward Islands dry forests
NT0226. Puerto Rican dry forests
NT0231. Trinidad and Tobago dry forests
NT0234. Windward Islands dry forests

Tropical & Subtropical Coniferous Forests

NT0301. Bahamian pine forests
NT0304. Cuban pine forests
NT0305. Hispaniolan pine forests

Flooded Grasslands & Savannas

NT0902. Cuban wetlands
NT0903. Enriquillo wetlands

Deserts & Xeric Shrublands

NT1302. Aruba-Curacao-Bonaire cactus scrub
NT1306. Cuban cactus scrub
NT1310. Leeward Islands xeric scrub
NT1317. Windward Islands xeric scrub

Mangroves

NT1403. Bahamian mangroves
NT1408. Coastal Venezuelan mangroves
NT1410. Greater Antilles mangroves
NT1416. Lesser Antilles mangroves
NT1436. Trinidad mangroves

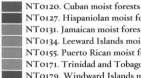

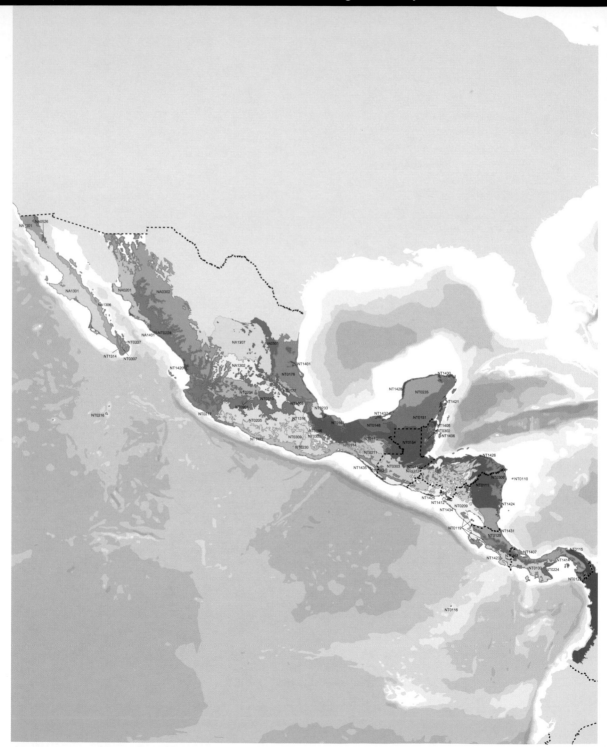

Tropical & Subtropical Moist Broadleaf Forests

NT0110. Cayos Miskitos-San Andrés & Providencia moist forests
NT0111. Central American Atlantic moist forests
NT0112. Central American montane forests
NT0113. Chiapas montane forests
NT0114. Chimalapas montane forests
NT0115. Chocó-Darién moist forests
NT0116. Cocos Island moist forests
NT0119. Costa Rican seasonal moist forests
NT0122. Eastern Panamanian montane forests
NT0129. Isthmian-Atlantic moist forests
NT0130. Isthmian-Pacific moist forests
NT0146. Oaxacan montane forests
NT0148. Pantanos de Centla
NT0154. Petén-Veracruz moist forests
NT0161. Sierra de los Tuxtlas
NT0162. Sierra Madre de Chiapas moist forest
NT0167. Talamancan montane forests
NT0176. Veracruz moist forests
NT0177. Veracruz montane forests
NT0181. Yucatán moist forests

Tropical & Subtropical Dry Broadleaf Forests

NA0201. Sonoran-Sinaloan transition subtropical dry forest
NT0204. Bajío dry forests
NT0205. Balsas dry forests
NT0209. Central American dry forests
NT0211. Chiapas Depression dry forests
NT0216. Islas Revillagigedo dry forests
NT0217. Jalisco dry forests
NT0224. Panamanian dry forests
NT0227. Sierra de la Laguna dry forests
NT0228. Sinaloan dry forests
NT0230. Southern Pacific dry forests
NT0233. Veracruz dry forests
NT0235. Yucatán dry forests

Tropical & Subtropical Coniferous Forests

NA0302. Sierra Madre Occidental pine-oak forests
NA0303. Sierra Madre Oriental pine-oak forests
NT0302. Belizian pine forests
NT0303. Central American pine-oak forests
NT0306. Miskito pine forests
NT0307. Sierra de la Laguna pine-oak forests
NT0308. Sierra Madre de Oaxaca pine-oak forests
NT0309. Sierra Madre del Sur pine-oak forests
NT0310. Trans-Mexican Volcanic Belt pine-oak forests

Temperate Conifer Forests

NA0526. Sierra Juarez & San Pedro Martir pine-oak forests

Flooded Grasslands & Savannas

NT0901. Central Mexican wetlands

Montane Grasslands & Shrublands

NT1009. Zacatonal

Mediterranean Forests, Woodlands & Scrub

NA1201. California coastal sage and chaparral

Deserts & Xeric Shrublands

NA1301. Baja California desert
NA1302. Central Mexican matorral
NA1306. Gulf of California xeric scrub
NA1307. Meseta Central matorral
NT1312. Motagua Valley thornscrub
NT1314. San Lucan xeric scrub
NT1316. Tehuacan Valley matorral

Mangroves

NA1401. Northwest Mexican Coast mangroves
NT1401. Alvarado mangroves
NT1405. Belizean Coast mangroves
NT1406. Belizean Reef mangroves
NT1407. Bocas del Toro-San Bastimentos Island-San Blas mangroves
NT1412. Gulf of Fonseca mangroves
NT1414. Gulf of Panama mangroves
NT1420. Marismas Nacionales-San Blas mangroves
NT1421. Mayan Corridor mangroves
NT1422. Mexican South Pacific Coast mangroves
NT1423. Moist Pacific Coast mangroves
NT1424. Mosquita-Nicaraguan Caribbean Coast mangroves
NT1425. Northern Dry Pacific Coast mangroves
NT1426. Northern Honduras mangroves
NT1428. Petenes mangroves
NT1430. Rio Lagartos mangroves
NT1431. Rio Negro-Rio San Sun mangroves
NT1434. Southern Dry Pacific Coast mangroves
NT1435. Tehuantepec-El Manchon mangroves
NT1437. Usumacinta mangroves

Tropical & Subtropical Moist Broadleaf Forests

NT0101. Araucaria moist forests
NT0102. Atlantic Coast restingas
NT0103. Bahia coastal forests
NT0104. Bahia interior forests
NT0105. Bolivian Yungas
NT0106. Caatinga Enclaves moist forests
NT0107. Caqueta moist forests
NT0108. Catatumbo moist forests
NT0109. Cauca Valley montane forests
NT0115. Chocó-Darién moist forests
NT0117. Cordillera La Costa montane forests
NT0118. Cordillera Oriental montane forests
NT0121. Eastern Cordillera real montane forests
NT0123. Fernando de Noronha-Atol das Rocas moist forests
NT0124. Guayanan Highlands moist forests
NT0125. Guianan moist forests
NT0126. Gurupa varzeá
NT0128. Iquitos varzeá
NT0132. Japurá-Solimoes-Negro moist forests
NT0133. Juruá-Purus moist forests
NT0135. Madeira-Tapajós moist forests
NT0136. Magdalena Valley montane forests
NT0137. Magdalena-Urabá moist forests
NT0138. Marajó Varzeá forests
NT0139. Maranhao Babaçu forests
NT0140. Mato Grosso seasonal forests
NT0141. Monte Alegre varzeá
NT0142. Napo moist forests
NT0143. Negro-Branco moist forests
NT0144. Northeastern Brazil restingas
NT0145. Northwestern Andean montane forests
NT0147. Orinoco Delta swamp forests
NT0149. Guianan Freshwater swamp forests
NT0150. Alta Paraná Atlantic forests
NT0151. Pernambuco coastal forests
NT0152. Pernambuco interior forests
NT0153. Peruvian Yungas
NT0156. Purus varzeá
NT0157. Purus-Madeira moist forests
NT0158. Rio Negro campinarana
NT0159. Santa Marta montane forests
NT0160. Serra do Mar coastal forests
NT0163. Solimoes-Japurá moist forest
NT0165. Southern Andean Yungas
NT0166. Southwest Amazon moist forests
NT0168. Tapajós-Xingu moist forests
NT0169. Tepuis
NT0170. Tocantins/Pindare moist forests
NT0172. Trindade-Martin Vaz Islands tropical forests
NT0173. Uatuma-Trombetas moist forests
NT0174. Ucayali moist forests
NT0175. Venezuelan Andes montane forests
NT0178. Western Ecuador moist forests
NT0180. Xingu-Tocantins-Araguaia moist forests

Tropical & Subtropical Dry Broadleaf Forests

NT0201. Apure-Villavicencio dry forests
NT0202. Atlantic dry forests
NT0206. Bolivian montane dry forests
NT0207. Cauca Valley dry forests
NT0210. Chaco
NT0212. Chiquitano dry forests
NT0214. Ecuadorian dry forests
NT0219. Lara-Falcón dry forests
NT0221. Magdalena Valley dry forests
NT0222. Maracaibo dry forests
NT0223. Marañón dry forests
NT0225. Patia Valley dry forests
NT0229. Sinú Valley dry forests
NT0232. Tumbes-Piura dry forests

Temperate Broadleaf & Mixed Forests

NT0401. Juan Fernandez Islands temperate forests
NT0402. Magellanic subpolar forests
NT0403. San Felix-San Ambrosio Islands temperate forests
NT0404. Valdivian temperate forests

Tropical & Subtropical Grasslands, Savannas & Shrublands

NT0701. Arid Chaco
NT0702. Beni savanna
NT0703. Campos Rupestres montane savanna
NT0704. Cerrado
NT0706. Córdoba montane savanna
NT0707. Guyanan savanna
NT0708. Humid Chaco
NT0709. Llanos
NT0710. Uruguayan savanna

Temperate Grasslands, Savannas & Shrublands

NT0801. Argentine Espinal
NT0802. Argentine Monte
NT0803. Humid Pampas
NT0804. Patagonian grasslands
NT0805. Patagonian steppe
NT0806. Semi-arid Pampas

Flooded Grasslands & Savannas

NT0905. Guayaquil flooded grasslands
NT0906. Orinoco wetlands
NT0907. Pantanal
NT0908. Paraná flooded savanna
N10909. Southern Cone Mesopotamian savanna

Montane Grasslands & Shrublands

NT1001. Central Andean dry puna
NT1002. Central Andean puna
NT1003. Central Andean wet puna
NT1004. Cordillera Central paramo
NT1005. Cordillera de Merida paramo
NT1006. Northern Andean paramo
NT1007. Santa Marta paramo
NT1008. Southern Andean steppe

Mediterranean Forests, Woodlands & Scrub

NT1201. Chilean matorral

Deserts & Xeric Shrublands

NT1301. Araya and Paria xeric scrub
NT1303. Atacama desert
NT1304. Caatinga
NT1307. Galapagos Islands xeric scrub
NT1308. Guajira-Barranquilla xeric scrub
NT1309. La Costa xeric shrublands
NT1313. Paraguana xeric scrub
NT1315. Sechura desert
NT1318. St. Peter and St. Paul Rocks

Montane Grasslands & Shrublands

NT1402. Amapa mangroves
NT1404. Bahia mangroves
NT1408. Coastal Venezuelan mangroves
NT1409. Esmeraldes/Chocó mangroves
NT1411. Guianan mangroves
NT1413. Gulf of Guayaquil-Tumbes mangroves
NT1414. Gulf of Panama mangroves
NT1415. Ilha Grande mangroves
NT1417. Magdalena-Santa Marta mangroves
NT1418. Manabi mangroves
NT1419. Maranhao mangroves
NT1427. Para mangroves
NT1429. Piura mangroves
NT1432. Rio Piranhas mangroves
NT1433. Rio Sao Francisco mangroves

CONSERVATION BY DESIGN
A Primer

Conservation by Design is The Nature Conservancy's strategy for generating conservation results. It is a systematic, science-based approach to identifying and protecting priority conservation areas. It allows us to achieve meaningful, lasting conservation results, and it sets the framework for measuring their impact on our biodiversity mission.

Our vision is to conserve a set of places that, if managed appropriately, will ensure the long-term survival of all their native life and natural communities, not just those that are threatened.

Through Conservation by Design, we are developing the Conservation Blueprint, a map of the areas most critical for the long-term protection of ecosystems, plants and wildlife. The blueprint is composed of *portfolios* of conservation areas within and across *ecoregions.*

- An *ecoregion* is a large unit of land and water typically defined by climate, geology, topography and associations of plants and animals.

- We target for protection big, relatively intact conservation areas—landscapes and seascapes that still retain the basic ecological processes that shaped them, such as fire, grazing and flooding, as well as those with promise for restoration.

- Like well-diversified stock portfolios, we want our *portfolios* of conservation areas to have some of everything, enough to last over the long term, and not too much of any one thing. If managed appropriately, this set of places will ensure the long-term survival of all native life and natural communities, not just threatened species and communities.

the conservation approach

1. Setting Priorities
We define our conservation priorities through ecoregional planning. Teams of Conservancy staff and outside experts first gather information about the species, natural communities and ecosystems of an ecoregion and identify targets for protection. Next, teams set long-term survival goals for each target (i.e., a population or type of ecosystem), taking care to plan for the target's health and distribution across the landscape. Computer models are used to design an efficient network of conservation areas—the portfolio.

2. Developing Strategies
We use "conservation area planning" to develop place-based strategies.

- We first look at an area's *systems*—its species, natural communities and ecosystems, as well as the ecological processes such as fire and floods that influence them.

- By examining *stresses* and *sources of stress,* we determine the environmental threats, such as habitat loss and invasive species, that affect systems and targets, and what is causing them.

- We then create practical and innovative *strategies* to reduce or eliminate those threats, such as land acquisition, restoration and amendment of public policy. An understanding of the cultural, political and economic situation behind the threats is essential for developing sound strategies.

- We then assess our *success*—our progress in reducing threats and improving the biodiversity and ecological health of a conservation area.

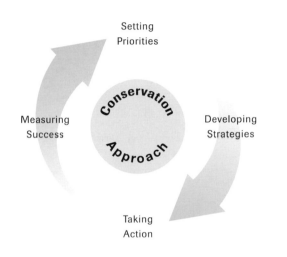

Setting
Priorities

Measuring
Success

Developing
Strategies

Taking
Action

3. Taking Action

Our tool kit of innovative conservation tools is broad and varied (see page 246). Some examples include land acquisition, working with resource-based industries to alter business practices and negotiating conservation easements and management agreements. Increasingly, we act behind the scenes as a facilitator to bring together other groups to accomplish these actions on their own.

4. Measuring Success

Because we define conservation success as the long-term reduction of critical threats and the sustained maintenance or enhancement of biodiversity health, we measure both regularly.

conservation by design: key messages

It creates a blueprint for conservation that can be followed not only by the Conservancy but by other conservation organizations, governments and businesses. It is the locus that can bring together diverse parties to protect a set of conservation areas. The blueprint also can be instrumental in balancing conservation and development, helping guide the siting of highways and expansion of towns, for instance.

It's a message of hope. Amid so many huge environmental challenges, Conservation by Design systematically and thoughtfully defines what's possible—functioning, vibrant, ecologically rich landscapes that can persist amid compatible economic and cultural pursuits.

It's a unifying strategy—an integrated expression of continuity and purpose that ties together our highly decentralized organization.

It puts local actions in a broader context, allowing staff, trustees, donors and partners to see how individual efforts contribute to the whole—to the fulfillment of the blueprint's vision.

It's about doing, not just planning.

It serves as the framework for making rational resource-allocation decisions within the Conservancy.

It allows us to measure performance against the Conservancy's mission.

GLOSSARY
of Commonly Used Conservation Tools

acquisition Procurement of lands or waters or interests in lands or waters by purchase, exchange, donation or other agreement.

ballot measure A binding or non-binding public policy or public funding question submitted to the general public for approval by vote. Typically used by the Conservancy to generate public funding for conservation activities.

biosphere reserve Areas of terrestrial and coastal ecosystems where efforts are under way to achieve both biodiversity conservation and sustainable use objectives. Designated by the UN Man and the Biosphere Programme, biosphere reserves are internationally recognized, nominated by national governments and remain under sovereign jurisdiction of the states where they are located.

climate action project A project where forest and other ecosystems are protected and/or restored with the goal of reducing atmospheric concentrations of carbon dioxide. Funding is usually provided by investors, such as private energy companies, that are interested in offsetting or mitigating their carbon emissions.

community outreach Building relationships within the communities where we work in order to gain community support for strategies to conserve local natural areas and resources.

compatible development Activities that seek to harness the power of the market for conservation projects by pursuing for-profit ventures that will maintain or restore functional landscapes and conserve biodiversity while enhancing the local economy and community.

Conservation Blueprint A map of the places most critical for the long-term protection of ecosystems, plants and wildlife within a defined geographic area or ecoregion. Developed by The Nature Conservancy through ecoregional planning.

conservation buyer A private party willing to purchase a biologically significant property and commit to maintain its ecological integrity in perpetuity. The buyer enters into a conservation easement (see below) agreement with the Conservancy, limiting development and defining compatible use.

Conservation by Design The Nature Conservancy's framework for mission success. Through the CbD methodology, we set conservation priorities, develop strategies, take action and measure success.

conservation easement A legal agreement between a landowner and a land trust or government agency that permanently protects open space by limiting the amount and type of development that can take place, but leaves the land in private ownership and allows for uses of the land that are compatible with specified conservation purposes.

debt-for-nature swap Public or private debt owed by a foreign government is cancelled or reduced in exchange for the permanent protection of parks or other natural areas within the debtor country. The Conservancy often helps broker debt-for-nature swaps. Can also be used between private parties and conservation groups for private land conservation.

ecoregional plan A conservation plan that is developed using the best available scientific information and methods and that is used to identify and protect a portfolio of conservation areas within an ecoregion.

ecotourism Environmentally responsible travel to natural areas to enjoy and appreciate nature (and any accompanying cultural features, both past and present). Ecotourism promotes conservation, has a low visitor impact on a place and provides beneficially active socioeconomic involvement of local peoples.

government co-op A project in which the Conservancy acquires land or interests in land in cooperation with a government agency before the agency itself is able to acquire the land, with the understanding or intent that the property will be conveyed to that agency at a later date. It is an organizational policy that when assisting any government agency in acquiring conservation land, the Conservancy recovers only direct and indirect expenses incurred in such a transaction and, unless the president makes an exception, in no event realizes a profit on such transactions.

habitat conservation plan A conservation plan developed by non-federal parties, including local governments and private landowners, under the auspices of the U.S. Endangered Species Act, for the purpose of allowing development to move forward while providing a mechanism to mitigate the "take" or loss of threatened

and endangered species or their habitats in the areas to be developed.

joint management agreement A contract or memorandum of understanding in which the parties to the agreement, which are generally agencies or organizations with land management programs and resources, specify their respective roles and responsibilities in implementing a common plan for the management of specified lands and/or waters. By entering into such agreements, the parties usually intend to leverage each other's resources in order to manage an area in accordance with a mutually agreed upon plan and vision for the area.

Land Preservation Fund An internal revolving loan fund available to Conservancy chapters that provides access to ready cash to purchase land and waters in a timely manner. Conservancy policy requires that chapters later repay such loans with interest within two years through private fund raising or when the property is sold to a public agency or private conservation buyer.

Parks in Peril A program of the U.S. Agency for International Development, in partnership with The Nature Conservancy, that improves national park systems in developing countries. The program provides funding for activities such as hiring and training park rangers, conserva-

tion planning and building the capacity of parks to protect natural areas.

purchase of development rights An agreement by which private property owners voluntarily sell all future rights to develop their land to a government agency (in jurisdictions where a PDR program exists) or to a private conservation organization. Property owners are usually paid the difference between the value of the land as restricted and the value of the land for its "highest and best use" (generally residential or commercial development), and retain other rights of use and ownership as laid out in the agreement.

Ridges to Reefs® Approach A holistic approach to protecting marine ecosystems that recognizes the interconnectedness of land, coast and sea. To preserve the health of marine life and coral reefs, the Conservancy works to safeguard upland corridors that drain sediment and pollutants from mountains into river systems, through estuaries into the ocean.

MILESTONES

1915

The Ecological Society of America formed.

1946

Scientists intent on preserving natural areas splinter from the ESA, forming the Ecologists Union and resolving to take "direct action"to save threatened places.

Early Conservancy leaders Dick Goodwin [above] and Richard Pough.

1950

The Ecologists Union changes its name to The Nature Conservancy.

1951

The Nature Conservancy officially incorporates in Washington, D.C.

1955

Land acquisition begins with a 60-acre purchase along Mianus River Gorge in New York. Land Preservation Fund established.

Mianus River Gorge in New York.

1961

First Conservancy partnership with a public agency, the Bureau of Land Management, to co-manage an old-growth forest in California. First conservation easement, on six acres of salt marsh in Connecticut, donated to the Conservancy.

1965

First full-time president, Charles H.W. Foster, hired.

1967

First government co-op arranged, whereby the Conservancy purchased Mason Neck, in Virginia, with the intention of conveying it to the federal government.

1970

State Natural Heritage Network created—a biological inventory that introduces scientific rigor to land acquisition choices. Its sophisticated databases provide the most complete information about species and natural communities in the United States.

1973

First corporate donation of land to the Conservancy: 49,000 acres in the Great Dismal Swamp of Virginia, from Union Camp Corporation.

Great Dismal Swamp, Virginia.

1974

First international project: John D. Archbold donates 950 acres on the Caribbean island of Dominica to the Conservancy.

1980

The Conservancy's International Program launched to identify natural areas and conservation organizations in Latin America in need of technical and financial assistance.

1983

The Richard King Mellon Foundation donates $25 million to the Conservancy—the largest grant ever made by a private foundation for conservation purposes.

1983

The Conservancy becomes the first private entity in the American West to be granted "instream flow rights" when the state of Arizona legally recognizes the Conservancy's right to leave water in the San Pedro River rather than withdraw it for "beneficial use."

Republic of Palau.

1990

Office in the Republic of Palau opens, representing the Conservancy's first expansion beyond the Western Hemisphere.

1990

Gray Ranch, 502 square miles in southwest New Mexico, is purchased—the largest single private conservation acquisition in the United States.

1995

Conservation by Design adopted—a cutting-edge approach for setting conservation priorities and taking action.

1998

Partnership with Yunnan Provincial Government formalized, marking the Conservancy's first project in the People's Republic of China.

Yunnan Province, China.

1999

Membership surpasses 1 million.

2000

The Association for Biodiversity Information, later renamed NatureServe, is created when the Conservancy and the 85-center Natural Heritage Network formally separate.

2001

The Nature Conservancy turns 50.

Gray Ranch, New Mexico.

Offices of
The Nature Conservancy

U.S.-based Offices

Worldwide Office
4245 N. Fairfax Drive, Suite 100
Arlington, VA 22203-1606
(703) 841-5300

Alabama
2821-C Second Avenue S.
Birmingham, AL 35233
(205) 251-1155

Alaska
421 W. First Avenue, Suite 200
Anchorage, AK 99501
(907) 276-3133

Arizona
1510 E. Fort Lowell Road
Tucson, AZ 85719
(520) 622-3861

Arkansas
601 N. University Avenue
Little Rock, AR 72205
(501) 663-6699

California
201 Mission Street, 4th Floor
San Francisco, CA 94105
(415) 777-0487

Colorado
2424 Spruce Street
Boulder, CO 80302
(303) 444-2950

Connecticut
55 High Street
Middletown, CT 06457
(860) 344-0716

Delaware
Community Service Building
100 W. 10th Street, Suite 1107
Wilmington, DE 19801
(302) 654-4707

Florida
222 S. Westmonte Drive, Suite 300
Altamonte Springs, FL 32714
(407) 682-3664

Georgia
1330 W. Peachtree Street, Suite 410
Atlanta, GA 30309
(404) 873-6946

Hawaii
923 Nuuanu Avenue
Honolulu, HI 96817
(808) 537-4508

Idaho
P.O. Box 165
Sun Valley, ID 83353
(208) 726-3007

Illinois
8 S. Michigan Avenue, Suite 900
Chicago, IL 60603
(312) 580-2100

Indiana
1505 N. Delaware Street, Suite 200
Indianapolis, IN 46202
(317) 951-8818

Iowa
303 Locust Street, Suite 402
Des Moines, IA 50309
(515) 244-5044

Kansas
700 SW Jackson, Suite 804
Topeka, KS 66603
(785) 233-4400

Kentucky
642 W. Main Street
Lexington, KY 40508
(859) 259-9655

Louisiana
201 St. Charles Street
Baton Rouge, LA 70802
(225) 338-1040

Maine
Fort Andross
14 Maine Street, Suite 401
Brunswick, ME 04011
(207) 729-5181

Maryland
5410 Grosvenor Lane, Suite 100
Bethesda, MD 20814
(301) 897-8570

Massachusetts
205 Portland Street, Suite 400
Boston, MA 02114
(617) 227-7017

Michigan
101 E. Grand River
Lansing, MI 48906
(517) 316-0300

Minnesota
1101 West River Parkway, Suite 200
Minneapolis, MN 55415
(612) 331-0700

Mississippi
6400 Lakeover Road, Suite C
Jackson, MS 39213
(601) 713-3355

Missouri
2800 S. Brentwood Boulevard
St. Louis, MO 63144
(314) 968-1105

Montana
32 S. Ewing Street
Helena, MT 59601
(406) 443-0303

Nebraska
1019 Leavenworth Street, Suite 100
Omaha, NE 68102
(402) 342-0282

Nevada
One E. First Street, Suite 500
Reno, NV 89501
(775) 322-4990

New Hampshire
22 Bridge Street, 4th Floor
Concord, NH 03301
(603) 224-5853

New Jersey
200 Pottersville Road
Chester, NJ 07930
(908) 879-7262

New Mexico
212 E. Marcy Street, Suite 200
Santa Fe, NM 87501
(505) 988-3867

New York City
570 Seventh Avenue, Suite 601
New York, NY 10018
(212) 997-1880

New York State
415 River Street, 4th Floor
Troy, NY 12180
(518) 273-9408

North Carolina
One University Place, Suite 290
4705 University Drive
Durham, NC 27707
(919) 403-8558

North Dakota
1256 N. Parkview Drive
Bismarck, ND 58501
(701) 222-8464

Ohio
6375 Riverside Drive, Suite 50
Dublin, OH 43017
(614) 717-2770

Oklahoma
2727 E. 21st Street, Suite 102
Tulsa, OK 74114
(918) 585-1117

Oregon
821 SE 14th Avenue
Portland, OR 97214
(503) 230-1221

Pennsylvania
1100 E. Hector Street, Suite 470
Conshohocken, PA 19428
(610) 834 1323

Rhode Island
159 Waterman Street
Providence, RI 02906
(401) 331-7110

South Carolina
2231 Devine Street, Suite 100
Columbia, SC 29205
(803) 254-9049

South Dakota
c/o Great Plains Division
1101 West River Parkway, Suite 200
Minnesota, MN 55415
(612) 331-0700

Tennessee
2021 21st Avenue South, Suite C-400
Nashville, TN 37212
(615) 383-9909

Texas
711 Navarro, Suite 410
San Antonio, TX 78205
(210) 224-8774

Utah
559 E. South Temple
Salt Lake City, UT 84102
(801) 531-0999

Vermont
27 State Street
Montpelier, VT 05602
(802) 229-4425

Virginia
490 Westfield Road
Charlottesville, VA 22901
(434) 295-6106

Virgin Islands
52 Estate Little Princess
P.O. Box 1066
Christiansted, St. Croix, U.S.V.I. 00821
(340) 773-5575

Washington
217 Pine Street, Suite 1100
Seattle, WA 98101
(206) 343-4344

West Virginia
723 Kanawha Blvd. East, Suite 500
Charleston, WV 25301
(304) 345-4350

Wisconsin
633 W. Main Street
Madison, WI 53703
(608) 251-8140

Wyoming
258 Main Street, Suite 200
Lander, WY 82520
(307) 332-2971

International Offices

Worldwide Office
4245 N. Fairfax Drive, Suite 100
Arlington, VA 22203-1606
USA
(703) 841-5300

Australia
The Nature Conservancy
c/o Arup Engineering
Level 4, Mincom Central
192 Ann Street
Brisbane, Queensland 4000
Australia
61 7 3023 6000

Belize
62 Front Street
Punta Gorda, Toledo District
Belize, C.A.
(501) 722-2503

Brazil
SHIN Centro de Atividades 5
Conjunto J Bloco B Sala 301
Brasilia-DF
CEP 71503-505
(55 61) 468-4819

Canada
Canada/U.S. Partnership
1101 West River Parkway, Suite 200
Minneapolis, MN 55415
USA
(612) 331-0700

China
Xin Hua Office Tower, 20th Floor
#8 East Ren Min Road
Kinming, Yunnan 650051
People's Republic of China
(86-871) 318-2797

Costa Rica
Apartado 230-1225
San José, Costa Rica
(506) 220-2552

Dominican Republic
Plaza Universitaria, Local 1-B
Ave. Sarasota Esquina Winston Churchill
Santo Domingo, Dominican Republic
(809) 535-9238

Ecuador
Av. Juan González N35-26 y Juan Pablo
Sanz
Torres Vizcaya II, Piso 10
Quito, Ecuador
(593-2) 2248-588

Guatemala
12 Avenida 14-41, Zona 10
Colonia Oakland
Ciudad Guatemala, Guatemala 01010
(502) 367-0480

Honduras and Nicaragua
Colonia Florencia Norte
2da Calle, #2201
Tegucigalpa, Honduras
(504) 232-3298

Indonesia
Wisma Kemang, 3rd Floor
Jalan Kemang Selatan Raya No. 1
Jakarta 12560, Indonesia
(62-21) 781-7040

Jamaica
32 Lady Musgrave Road, Unit 5
Kingston 5, Jamaica
(876) 978-0766

Japan
2-5-1 Kita-Aoyama, Minato-ku
Tokyo 107-8077
Japan (81-3) 5414-2818

Mexico
711 Navarro, Suite 410
San Antonio, TX 78205
USA
(210) 224-8774

Micronesia
Federated States of Micronesia Office
P.O. Box 216
Kolonia, Pohnpei 96941
Federated States of Micronesia
(691) 320-4267

Palau
P.O. Box 1738
Koror, Palau 96940
(680) 488-2017

Panama
Ave. Samuel Lewis y Calle San Rita
Edificio Plaza Obarrio
1er. Piso Oficina No. 110
Ciudad de Panama, Panama
(507) 264-7883

Papua New Guinea
P.O. Box 2750
Boroko
Papua New Guinea
(675) 323-0699

Peru
1161 Av Miraflores
(antes Av. 28 de Julio)
Lima 18, Peru
(551) 446-1307

Solomon Islands
P.O. Box 759
Honiara, Solomon Islands
(677) 20940

South Pacific
P.O. Box 65-506
Mairangi Bay
Auckland, New Zealand
(649) 478-9632

Venezuela
Ave. 2 Lora, Urb. El Encanto
Oficentro El Encantro, PH 5
Merida 5101, Venezuela
(58-274) 263-2626

BOARD OF GOVERNORS
2002-2003

INDEX

Photographer Credits Cover lead: Richard Bickel; Cover (top left to right): Byron Jorjorian, Wendy Shattil/Bob Rozinski, Michael Melford; Cover spine: Milton Rand; Back cover (top left to right): Tom Blagden/Larry Ulrich Stock, Claus Meyer/Minden Pictures, Art Wolfe; Half-title page: George H. H. Huey; Title page: Byron Jorjorian; p 4: Katherine Lambert; p 6: Tom Bean; p 7: Ron Geatz/TNC; p 8: Will Heyman/TNC; p 9: Kike Arnal; p 13: (top to bottom): Raymond Gehman, Richard Bickel, Thomas Mangelsen/Minden Pictures, Chris R. Sharp/Photo Researchers, Douglas David Seifert; p 14: Raymond Gehman; p 15 and 16: Harold E. Malde; p 17: Phil Schermeister/Network Aspen; p 18: Richard Bickel; p 19: Tony Santana/U. S. Army Corps of Engineers; p 20 (left to right): Hardie Truesdale, Lynda Richardson; p 21: Frans Lanting/Minden Pictures; p 22: Thomas Mangelsen/Minden Pictures; p 23: Zhinong Xi/Wild China Films; p 24: Hermes Justiniano; p 25: Kevin Schafer/kevin-schafer.com; p 26: Chris R. Sharp/Photo Researchers; p 27 David T. Roberts/Photo Researchers; p 28 (left to right): Bill Keogh, John M. Randall/TNC; p 29: Phil Schermeister/Network Aspen; p 30: Douglas David Seifert; p 31: Doug Perrine/Seapics.com; p 32 (left to right): Kevin Schafer/Corbis, Nancy Sefton; p 33: Kevin Schafer/kevinschafer.com; p 38: Jim Brandenburg/Minden Pictures; p 39: Art Wolfe; p 40: George H. H. Huey; p 41: Mark Jones/Minden Pictures; p 42: Tom Till; p 43: Kevin Schafer/kevinschafer.com; p 46: Gerry Lang; p 47: Jeff Lepore; p 48: Frans Lanting/Minden Pictures; p 49: Art Wolfe; p 50-51: Thomas Mark Szelog; p 52: Larry Ulrich; p 53: Joe McDonald/Corbis; p 54: Hardie Truesdale; p 55: Mark Moffett/Minden Pictures; p 56 and 57: Jerry & Marcy Monkman; p 58: David Muench; p 59: Bob Krist; p 60 and 61: Hardie Truesdale; p 62 and 63: Elinor Osborn; p 64: Jeff Lepore; p 65: Raymond Gehman/Corbis; p 66: Michael Melford; p 67: Ed Reschke/Peter Arnold, Inc.; p 68: James P. Blair/Corbis; p 69: Royalty-Free/Corbis; p 70-71: Macduff Everton; p 72 and 73: Byron Jorjorian; p 74: Skip Brown; p 75: Jeff Lepore; p 78 and 79: Beth Young; p 80: Mike Fuhr/TNC; p 81: Doug Wilson/Corbis; p 82: Richard Bickel/Corbis; p 83: Jeff Lepore; p 84: Raymond Gehman; p 85: Peter Essick/Aurora; p 86 and 87: William Neill/Larry Ulrich Stock; p 88: David Muench/Corbis; p 89: Yva Momatiuk/John Eastcott/Minden Pictures; p 90 and 91: Beth Young; p 92: Elizabeth Zeschin; p 93: Wendy Shattil/Bob Rozinski; p 94 and 95: Tom Blagden/Larry Ulrich Stock; p 96 and 97: Byron Jorjorian; p 100: Tharran Hobson/TNC; p 101 and 102: Carol Freeman; p 103: Joel Sartore; p 104: Phil Schermeister/Network Aspen; p 105: Frank Oberle; p 106: Larry Ulrich; p 107: Tom & Pat Leeson; p 108: John Gregor; p 109 and 110: G. Alan Nelson; p 111: Frank Oberle; p 112: J. C. Leacock; p 113: Gerry Ellis/Minden Pictures; p 114: G. Alan Nelson; p 115: Paul Burton; p 118: Tim Fitzharris/Minden Pictures; p 119: Wendy Shattil/Bob Rozinski; p 120-121: Scott T. Smith; p 122 and 123: Jim Brandenburg/Minden Pictures; p 124: Frank Oberle; p 125: Jim Brandenburg/Minden Pictures; p 126: Phil Schermeister/Network Aspen; p 127: Layne Kennedy/Corbis; p 128: Roger Ressmeyer/Corbis; p 129: David Muench; p 130: George H. H. Huey; p 131· Wendy Shattil/Bob Rozinski; p 134: Richard T. Nowitz/National Geographic Image Collection; p 135: Scott T. Smith; p 136, 137 and 138: Joel Sartore; p 139: Harold E. Malde; p 140: Tom & Pat Leeson; p 141: Michael Wilhelm; p 142: Kevin R. Morris/Corbis; p 143: Keith Lazelle; p 144: Jack Dykinga; p 145: Will Van Overbeek; p 148: George H. H. Huey; p 149: George D. Lepp/Corbis; p 150: Mike Eaton/TNC; p 151: Wendy Shattil/Bob Rozinski;

Martha Hodgkins
editor

Nancy Gillis
project manager

Miya Su Rowe
art director

Melissa G. Ryan
director of photography

writers
Beth Duris
Sara Kaplaniak
Audrey Pritchard

contributing writers
Ron Geatz
Anne Gore
Jim Petterson

director, creative services
Kathleen Jamieson

designers
Danielle DeGarmo
Christopher Johnson

photo editors
Greta Arnold
Mark Godfrey

photo specialist
Pat Rolston

print production manager
Lynne Steltzer

maps
Paul Exner, XNR Productions

ecoregional maps
Leonardo Sotomayor

The Field Guide to The Nature
Conservancy *is a product of the
Marketing & Philanthropy Division.*

concept team
David Williamson, chair
Gideon Berger
Lynette Brooks
Beth Duris
Ron Geatz
Martha Hodgkins
Terry Richey
Charles Sheerin
Ylka van Bemmel